Sadie Starr

presents

Beading with Seed Beads, Gem Stones & Cabochons

Easy
Step by Step Instructions
so you
Can Create your Own
Unique, Hand-Crafted
Wearable Art

by

Sadie Starr

Great Niece of the Famed Belle Starr

Acknowledgments

Graphic Design Concept by Sadie Starr
Graphic Layout and Typesetting by William B. Brown Jr.
All Patterns are Sadie Starr Originals
Patterns Illustrated by Donna Ann Gordon
Printed by Complete Printing, Phoenix, Arizona

First Edition

Published by Shooting Starr Gallery Publications

Printed in the United States of America

Library of Congress Cataloging-in-Publication Data

Sadie Starr
    Beading with Seed Beads, Gem Stones & Cabochons

© 1993 by Sadie Starr

Acknowledgments

I would like to Dedicate this book to
MY MOTHER.

She recently passed away.

THANK YOU MOM
for the
Pride in Me and My Work.

AGAIN, VERY SPECIAL THANKS MOM,
THIS ONE IS FOR YOU.

Thanks also to my Family, especially my husband Glen for always LOVING and CARING.

To Ann & Keith, Bill & Fred for being there every Step of the Way.

THANKS,

Sadie

Hi,

My Name is Sadie Marie Starr,
My Married Name is Sadie Marie Vincent.

I am Cherokee and Chata Indian, born in Portland, Oregon and raised in Southern California. I spent a good part of my adult life in Northern California and then, about seven years ago moved to Arizona.

I had been designing and sewing clothes for many years when one day a friend of mine shared with me some basic stitches of Indian Beadwork.....I Was Hooked!!!

I went to the nearest Lapidary store and began buying inexpensive Cabochons and Stones. Immediately I started designing Earrings with glass seed beads, Austrian crystals and semi-precious gems.

Now you can create your own unique, hand-crafted wearable art: Earrings, Barrettes, Broaches, Buckles, Bracelets, Necklaces, Hat Bands, Beaded Crystals, Beaded Feathers, Beaded Purses and Much More.

I Hope that you enjoy my Designs and Techniques, and also enjoy creating your own "one of a kind" pieces.

If you are ever in Arizona, Please stop by the Shooting Starr Gallery in the small town of Camp Verde, a few hours south of the Grand Canyon and about one and a half hours north of Phoenix.

Remember... Take the time to Enjoy Life

- Sadie -

Table of Contents

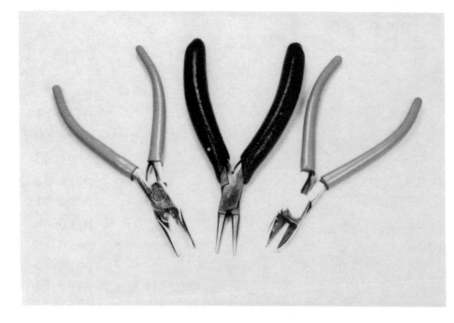

HAND TOOLS

Here are some hand tools that we will be using in the projects in the book. Buy the smallest sizes you can as they will be easier to work with. From the left, flat nose pliers, round nose pliers(center) diagonal cutters(right).

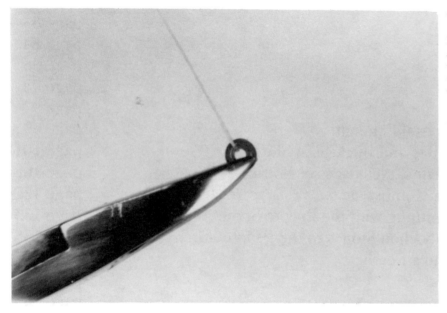

To snap off any bead that is either incorrect or unwanted, hold the thread with your left hand and use the small pair of diagonal cutters to snap it off. Hold the bead with the diagonal cutters and pull gently while cutting, keeping the cutters as far as possible from the thread. Wear glasses for safety.

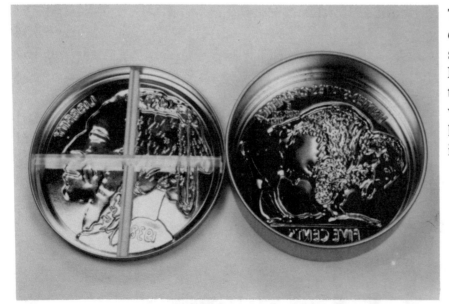

To make a bead tray, begin with a tin lid, or a small or large plate. Cut plastic straws to fit into the lid. Be creative. Here we have used a cross design. Glue the straws to the tin with GOO, cover with leather or suede. This will help to keep your beads separated while beading your projects.

Materials - Tools & Supplies

Here are some basic materials, tools and supplies that you will need to complete each project. For most of the projects in this book, size 11/0 seed beads will be used. Thread and needle size will vary depending on the stitch used.

Needles: The best beading needles are made in England. They come in a variety of sizes, from 10 to 15; 15 is the finest, 10 the largest. Beading needles are very fragile so keep extras on hand for replacements. They usually come in packages of 24.

Thread: White nymo thread is found in a variety of sizes: XXX, OO, O, A, B, C, D, and E. The smallest is XXX. The thread can be bought in: 73-110 yard bobbins, 200 yard spools, and in the case of A and B, and can also be purchased as 3 ounce cones.

The following chart will help you put the correct seed bead, thread and needle together.

Thread	Needle Size	Seed Bead Size
B	12 or 13	10/0,9/0. Size 11/0 only on recommended projects.
A	12 or 13	12/0, 11/0
O	12, 13 or 15	14/0, 13/0, 12/0, 11/0
OO	12, 13 or 15	14/0, 12/0, 11/0
XXX	15 or 16	22/0, 16/0, 14/0

Note: When you are having a hard time trying to sew back through any seed beads, stop and try a smaller needle. Always have a smaller needle on hand. Smaller thread may also be needed. Often, the techniques to be used in the project will determine the sizes of thread and bead. For example, the first project of this book is a Bugle Bead earring requiring a hidden knot. Size OO thread is used along with size 11/0 seed beads. The second project is another example, the Paua Stone earring. There are no visible knots to hide, but, strength is needed. For the Peyote Stitch Project, thread size O and seed bead size 11/0 are used.

White Candle: Most bead instruction books and or bead supply stores recommend bees wax. My experience has been that a white candle is best, it coats and protects without being sticky or yellowing.

Scissors: Embroidery scissors are the best to use. One pair of small and one pair of medium will be best and should be easy to find and sharp.

Seed Beads: We will be using 11/0 size glass seed beads in most of the projects in this book. The Japanese have a beautiful selection of 11/0 seed beads. They are uniform in size and have a wonderful color selection. They are usually sold in clear plastic tubes. I reccomend these to all of my students.

Czechoslovakian seed beads are not always as uniform as the Japanese but are of excellent quality, they are a little more difficult to work with. You will find them in hanks or bunches of 20 - 24 strings that are about 10 inches long. Czech or Czeko are abreviations used for Czechoslovakian later in the book.

COLOR SEED BEAD CHART

Opaque: A Solid non-transparent bead used in most traditional Indian beadwork.

Opaque Luster: A solid non-transparent bead with a pearlized, shiny finish.

Transparent: See-through Clear or See-through Colored.

Rainbow: Transparent or opaque with a shimmery surface, irridescent or multicolor finish. Also known as A-B finish.

Iris: Same as rainbow.

Lined: A transparent bead with a different color lining inside the inner hole of the bead.

Silver Lined: A transparent bead with a silver lining inside the inner hole of the bead.

Dyed: A bead that is usually opaque or silver lined. CAUTION - the dye is on the surface and many dyes will wear off or fade with time.

Metallics: Opaque with a metal-like finish. Colors such as the Japanese bronze hold up well.

Galvanized: Usually a white bead that has been coated with a metal-like finish. CAUTION - some of the color will wear off to white.

Pearl: Opaque bead with a pearlized finish on the surface of the bead.

Ceylon: A pearlized bead usually lined inside the hole with nice, soft, pastel colors. They are either transparent or opaque.

Cut Beads: Seed beads that come in many different sizes and colors. They are either transparent or opaque with facets cut on the surface. You will love the way that they glisten and shine in the light. NOTE - When buying seed beads always buy extra as dye lots vary.

Matte Beads: To either remove the shine from beads or to put on a matte finish use a small container of Velvet Etching Cream from the local stained glass store. Please follow the safety instructions carefully. Use a pair of rubber gloves to protect your skin. Carefully pour the cream into a small plastic container, approximately 1/2 full. Do a test of only 20 or so beads. Stir the beads into the cream with a wooden toothpick. Make sure that the beads are coated completely. Let the mixture stand overnight. Rinse in warm water, then spray with Lime-Away and let stand for one hour and then rinse again with water.

Bugle Beads: You will find them in almost as many colors as seed beads. A lot of the colors are made from the same kind of glass. They are tubular in shape. Bugle beads range in size from 1/8 inch to 1 1/4 inch (2.5mm - 40mm). Please note that we will abbreviate millimeters as mm. The following is a chart showing Czechoslovakian measurement, but it is always best to have a ruler handy to check the accuracy of stated lengths. NOTE: 1/8 inch = 1/8"

SIZE 1	1/8"	2 1/2mm
SIZE 2	3/16"	5mm
SIZE 3	1/4"	7mm
SIZE 4	3/8"	9mm
SIZE 5	1/2"	12mm

LONGER BUGLES are measured as millimeters, such as 15mm, 20mm, 25mm, 30mm, 35mm, 40mm. NOTE: Never use size 1 or 2 bugle beads with 10 seed beads in the top of a bugle bead earring. The bead is too big for that small a Bugle Bead.

Hand Tools: A small pair of flat nose pliers, small diagonal cutters, a medium or small pair of round nose pliers, a jewelers saw and size 3/0 blade, a mill file, leather awl, a ruler, a yard stick, rotary hole punch, small exacto knife-snap knife, and a loop turner. All of these tools won't be needed at once, so read the list of materials carefully for each project and buy each tool as needed.

Pellom: A felt-like material, also called interfacing and can be found at your local fabric store. Purchase one yard of medium weight, this will be enough for several projects. It is available in white or black. Ultra Suede may also be used as a substitute.

Glue: There are several types of glue that can be used: Goo - all purpose adhesive by Hobsco, Stix-All - by Elmers, Glue-Stix - by Elmers, 330 Glue (two part epoxy) - by Hughes Associates, clear finger nail polish, and any "super" glue gel, and JB Kwik by JB Weld.

Note Cards: 3x5 cards, you will need a pack of 100.

Materials for Backing: Thin Snake skin, thin Leather scraps, or thin Ultra Suede may be used. To avoid breaking too many needles be sure to test the material by sewing through it a few times first.

Cabochons: Any stone that is domed or has beveled edges and a flat backing. They come in a variety of shapes and sizes. Some bead stores carry cabochons made of glass, semi-precious or precious stones. For best results do not use damaged or poor quality stones. Your local jewelry or lapidary store are good sources. Cabochons are measured in millimeters(mm). Free Form Cabochons are stones that have not been formed, calibrated or measured. They are not uniform in shape and are not generally recommended for earrings unless you can find a pair are equal in size and shape. When pairing up earrings, a slightly shorter stone can be built up by turning it upside down and applying a thin coat of glue on the bottom. Let it dry thoroughly before matching it up with the other stone

Zip-Lock Bags: Great for bead storage, etc.

Findings: French earwires, surgical steel posts with pads are findings used for your earrings. Tiger tail is a plastic coated wire used for your cabochon necklace and treasure necklaces. Lobster claw and eyes are findings or clasps to be attached with crimp beads to the tiger tail. Pin backs for the brooch and barrette backs for barrettes are some of the other findings you will be using.

Feathers: There are many types of feathers that lend themselves to great beadwork. _It is important that you check with the local forest ranger or taxidermist before you bead a feather that you cannot keep!_ I recently was accorded a great honor by the Seminole Medicine Man and Chief. He asked me to bead their Eagle feather, and I of course agreed and used some of my very rare 14-0 cut beads. It was a great honor. A picture of the completed feather is shown in this book.

Crystals: Natural crystals come in a variety of colors, lengths, and diameters. Pick a crystal with the finished piece in mind. If you are beading earrings be sure to buy points that are 1 to 1 1/2 inches long. You want to have the same number of beads around each crystal so that the pattern you choose will come out correctly. Hand cut crystals are also available that are almost perfect to bead around. A good size is 6x20mm, about one inch long.

Crystals are thought to: stimulate brain function, amplify thought forms, dispel negativity; receive, activate, store, transmit and amplify energy. They are also thought to promote: alignment with the higher self, balance and emotional and mental clarity.

Larger, Beads: Beads used to add fullness to the bottom of your earrings. They are also used in the applique stitch. Diameters range from 4mm on up and are made of: precious or semi-precious stones, faceted glass, austrian cut crystal, fresh water pearls, molded glass, plated plastic and much more....The higher the quality, the higher the price.

Beading Tray: Be creative...take an old plate or shallow tray and glue a piece of suede, ultra suede or any suede-like material as a cover. This will help keep your beads from sliding around and mixing with other colors. Before you glue the fabric, cut up a drinking straw and glue to the plate, then glue the fabric. This will provide you with simple yet effective dividers.

Sterling Silver Supplies: The bear claw pendant requires 12 gauge half round sterling silver wire. There is usually a minimum order requirement at your local jewelery supplier, One foot will be enough for several bear claw pendants.

Chapter 1

- Purple Drop Earring -

MATERIALS & TOOLS NEEDED:

1 - White Candle.
1 - Pair of small, sharp scissors.
1 - Pair of small short, flat nose pliers.
1 - Pair of round nose pliers.
English Beading Needles, size 12
White Nymo Beading Thread, size OO
Glass Seed Beads, size 11/0, colors - silver, capri blue and bronze. 1- tube or 1- hank of each color needed. You will have extras that can be used on upcoming projects.
20 - Purple Bugle Beads-size, 15mm
2 - 6mm x 10mm Drops or
2 - 10mm glass beads of your choice.
8 - 4mm Plum Austrian Crystals
1 - Pair of Gold Plated French earwires.

NOTE: Please read all of the instructions for each project carefully, and more than once, particularly the materials and tools needed section. Also, review Important Notes. Your enjoyment of each project will be enhanced by taking this extra time.

TO BEGIN: Wax a two yard single strand of size OO beading thread. This is done by holding the candle in your left hand while pulling the thread across the candle. Once the thread has a thin coat of wax, thread the needle. A single strand of thread is used to make the PURPLE DROP EARRING.

You are now ready to start...

Also Please NOTE:

Bugle Beads, size 15mm, 12mm, 9mm & 7mm can be used for this earring when using size 11/0 Seed Beads.

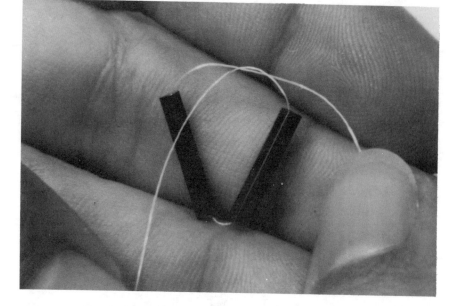

STEP 1

Measure the lengths of the seed beads and the bugle beads. This will keep the earring even and uniform.

Using a single strand of thread, begin sewing 2 - 15mm purple bugle beads together. Be sure to leave 8 to 10 inches of loose thread from the bugle beads.

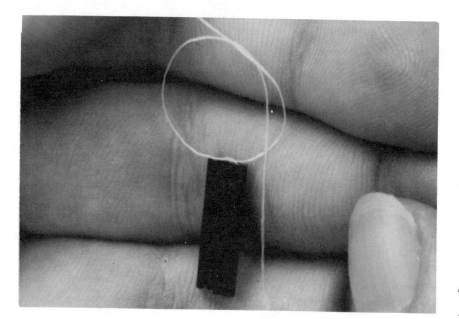

Step 2

Secure them by pulling the two bugle beads together with the thread and tying another loop to form a knot close to the top of the bugle beads.

Again - make sure that you are leaving 8-10 inches of loose thread.

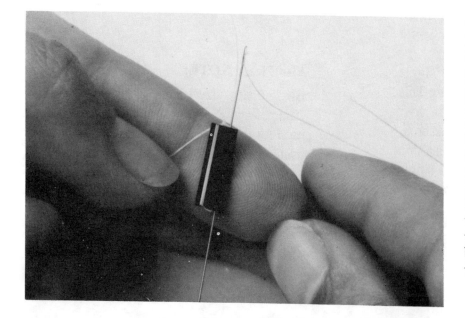

Step 3

Keeping the loose thread to the left, sew down through the second bugle bead to the right and pull the knot to the right side. NOTE:...If you are using (smaller) bugle beads or heavier thread for the earring, pull the knot down inside the second purple bugle bead to the right to hide it better. NOTE:...Another technique is eliminating the knot altogether by sewing back through the first two bugle beads twice to secure them together. If you plan to eliminate the knot, you will need to finish the earring by sewing both of the loose threads that are woven back through the beaded earring in steps 46-48 through the center silver seed bead to secure them both in place. Try all three ways and see which way is best for you.

Step 4

NOW, adding one more bugle bead, sew down through the second bugle bead to the right, keeping the loose thread to the left.....

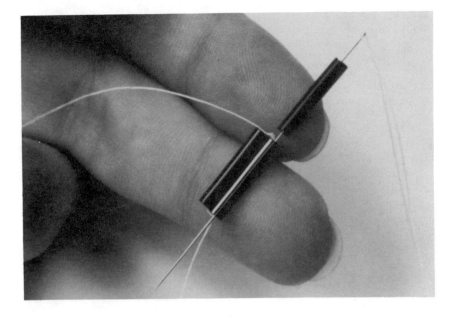

Step 5

After adding the third bugle bead, sew back up and through the same third bugle bead to the right.

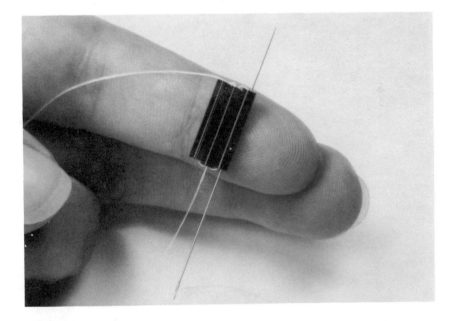

Step 6

Add another bugle bead and sew up through the third bugle bead to the left.

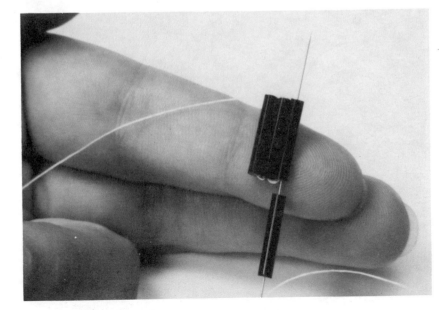

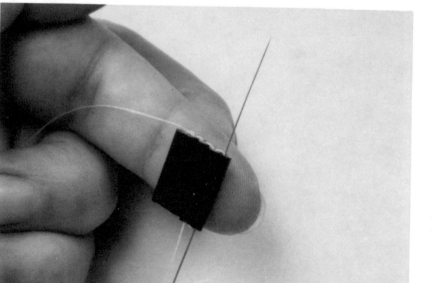

Step 7

Sew down through the fourth purple bugle bead keeping the eight inches of loose thread to the left.

Step 8

NOW, add on the fifth, purple bugle bead, sewing down through the fourth purple bugle bead to the right

Step 9

Sew back up through the fifth purple bugle bead. You will now have five bugle beads across to complete the top anchor row. Sew back through the fourth bugle bead to the right, and back through the fifth bugle bead. Pull the thread lightly to secure the end of this anchor row. Now turn the piece over so the eight inches of loose thread is to the top right side.

Step 10

Begin the first row of bronze, size 11 seed beads by adding one seed bead and coming from behind the bugle beads and sewing underneath the first loop of thread at the top of the bugle bead anchor row. Keep your eight inches of loose thread to the right.

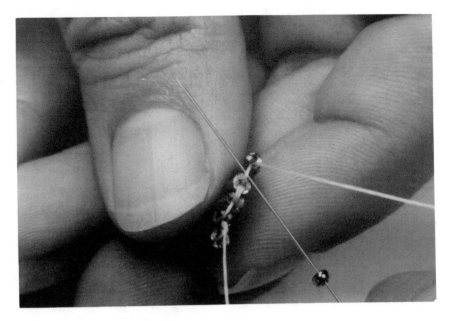

Step 11

Then, sew back up through the same seed bead. After the needle has gone through the seed bead, pull the thread gently to tighten the seed bead in place.

Step 12

Add the second bronze bead by sewing underneath the second loop of thread at the top of the bugle beads. AGAIN - keep your eight inches of loose thread to the right.

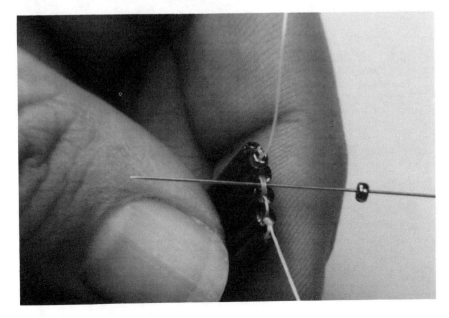

Step 13

Go back up through the same seed bead again and pull the thread gently to tighten it into place.

Step 14

Now you will add the third bronze seed bead. Sew underneath the third loop of thread at the top of the bugle beads.

Step 15

Go back up through the same seed bead to tighten it in place.

Step 16

One bronze seed bead will be the fourth and last seed bead in the first row. Sew underneath the fourth and last loop of thread at the top of your bugle beads.

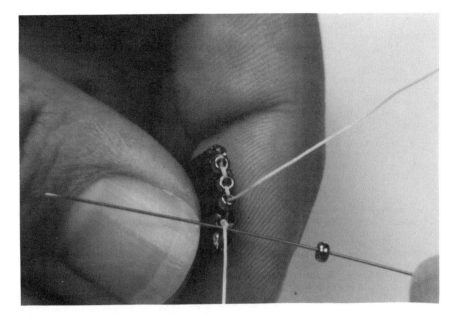

Step 17

Sew back up through the same seed bead, and gently pull the thread to pull the bead into place. Your first row is now complete. NOW turn the piece over so that the eight inches of loose thread is to the left.

Step 18

Start the second row of seed beads with a bronze seed bead. Sew underneath the first loop of threads that are between the first row of bronze seed beads.

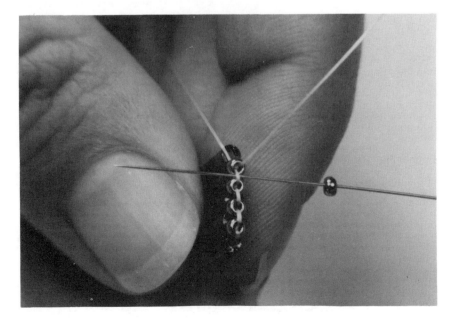

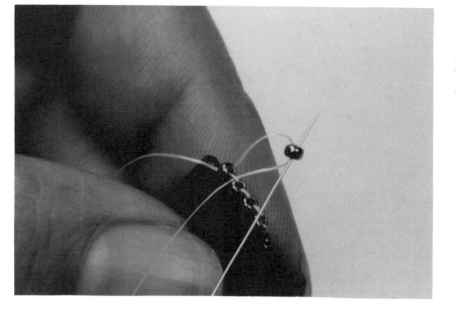

Step 19

Sew back up through the same seed bead and pull the thread gently, putting the bead into place.

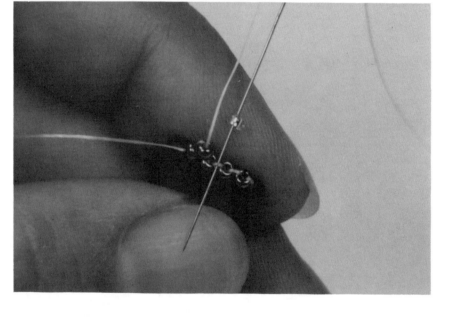

Step 20

The next seed bead is silver, sew underneath the second loop of thread that is between the seed beads.

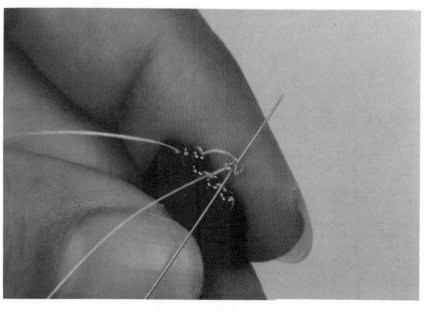

Step 21

Then, sew back up through the same seed bead and pull the thread, putting the seed bead into place. This silver bead will be called the center bead.

Step 22

Add one bronze seed bead and sew underneath the third loop of thread that sets between the seed beads.

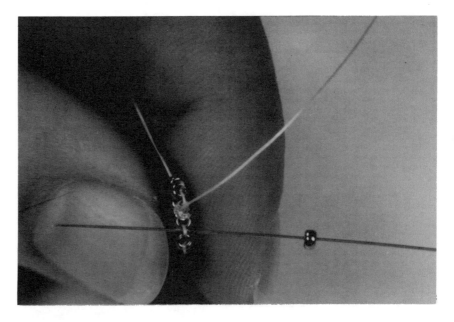

Step 23

Sew back up through the same seed bead and pull the thread putting the seed bead into place, your second row is now complete.

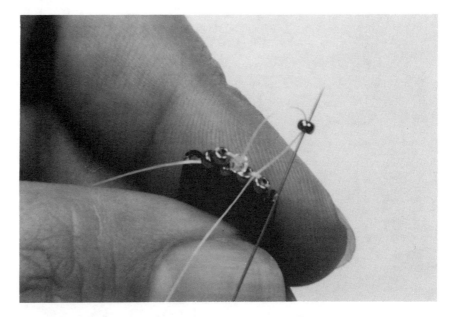

Step 24

Now, turn your piece over so the eight inches of loose thread is to the right. Add one bronze seed bead and sew underneath the first loop of thread to the left.

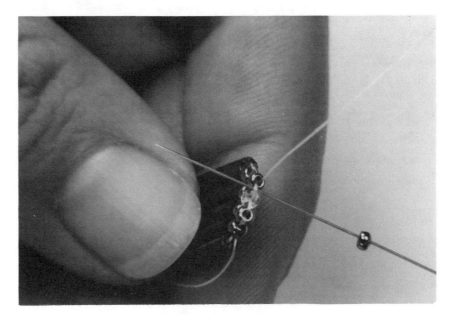

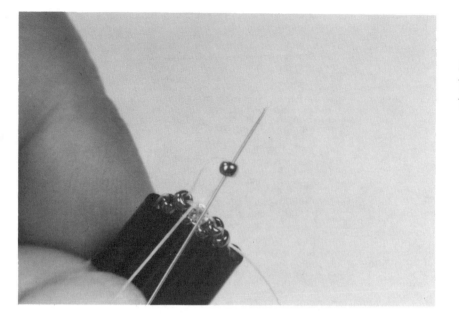

Sew back up through the same seed bead and pull the thread putting the bead into place.

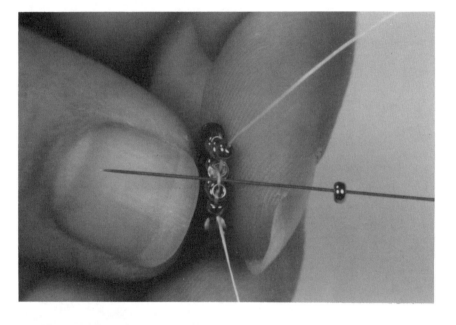

Step 26

The next and last seed bead in the third row is bronze. Sew underneath the second loop of thread in the third row.

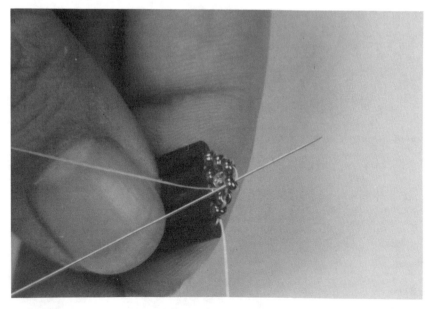

Step 27

Sew back up through the same seed bead and pull the thread putting the seed bead into place. The third row is now complete.

Step 28

Add four bronze seed beads for the top loop. Reverse the needle and sew through the first bronze seed bead in the third row to the left.

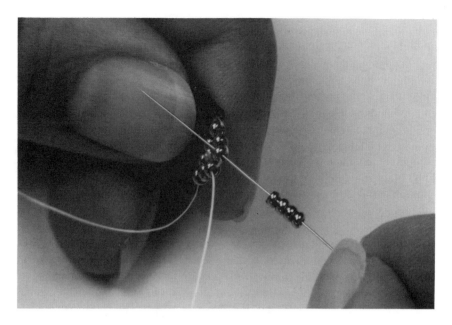

Step 29

Next, sew down through the center, silver, seed bead. This will form a loop. You will be attaching the French earwire to this loop at the end of this project.

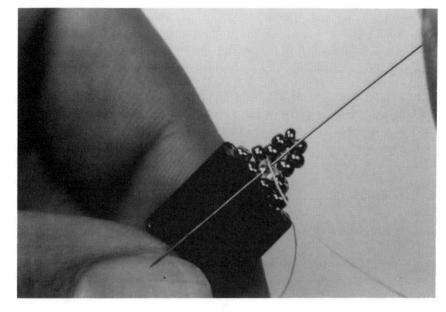

Step 30

Reverse the needle and sew back up through the bronze seed bead to the right in the second row of your seed beads.

Step 31

Sew back up through the next three bronze seed beads to the right. (The outside row of the loop.)

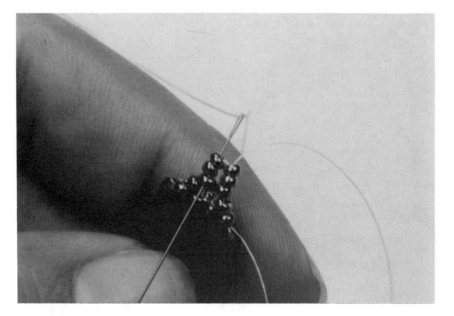

Step 32

Reverse the needle and sew down through the next three bronze seed beads to the left side of the loop.

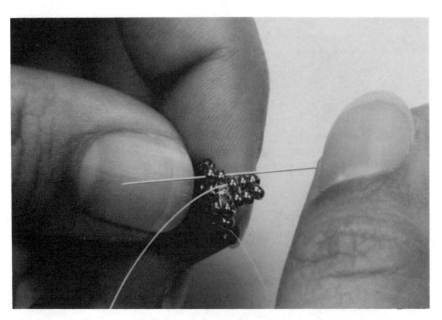

Step 33

Now, sew down through the last two bronze seed beads to the outside left.

Step 34

Sew down through the first purple bugle bead to the outside left.

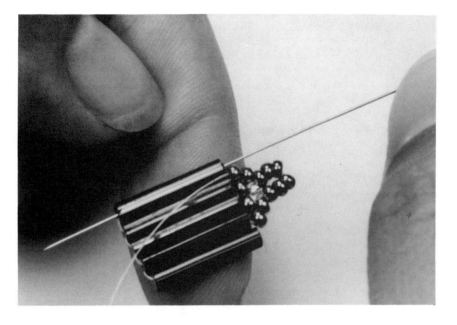

Step 35

The first row of fringe will be:
1- silver seed bead
1 - bronze seed bead
1 - blue seed bead
1 - purple bugle bead
1 - silver seed bead
1 - 4mm Plum Crystal
1 - blue seed bead
Drop the last blue seed bead and sew back up through the Plum Crystal and up through the first row of fringe until you are through the first purple bugle bead at the top of the first row.

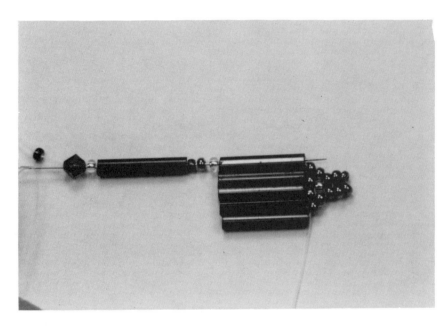

Step 36

Reverse the needle and sew over and down through the next purple bugle bead to the right. Your first row is now complete.

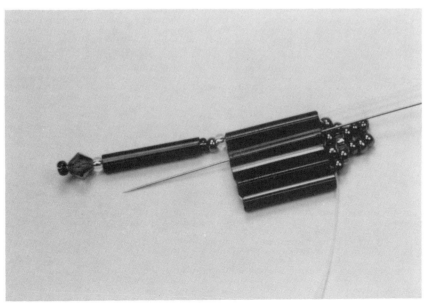

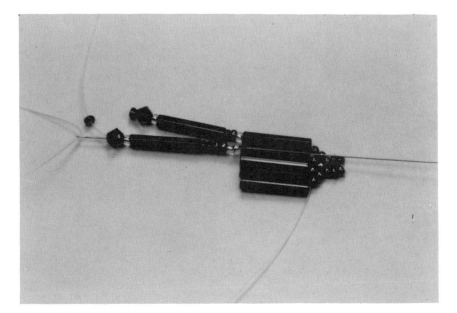

Row two.....
2 - silver seed beads
2 - bronze seed beads
2 - blue seed beads
1 - purple bugle bead
1 - silver seed bead
1 - Plum Crystal
1 - blue seed bead

Drop the last blue seed bead and sew up through the plum crystal and up through the second row of fringe until you are through the second purple bugle bead at the top of the row.

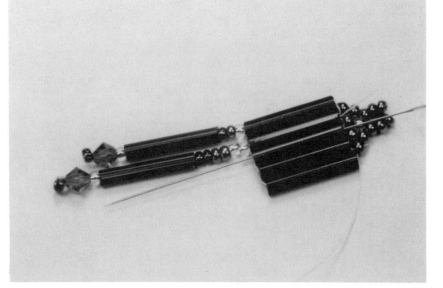

Reverse the needle and sew down through the third bugle bead to the right. Take note that each row of seed beads is increasing by three beads at a time until the center row is reached.

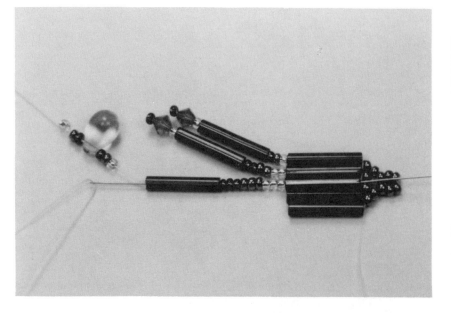

Row three.....
3 - silver seed beads
3 - bronze seed beads
3 - blue seed beads
1 - purple bugle bead
1 - silver seed bead
1 - bronze seed bead
1 - blue seed bead
1 - 6x10mm clear drop
1 - blue seed bead
1 - bronze seed bead
1 - silver seed bead

Sew back up through the purple bugle bead from the bottom of the fringe and up through the third purple bugle bead at the top.

Step 40

Now that the center row of fringe is now complete, reverse the needle and sew down through the fourth purple bugle bead to the right.
Row four will be.....
2 - silver seed beads
2 - bronze seed beads
2 - blue seed beads
1 - purple bugle bead
1 - silver seed bead
1 - 4mm Plum Crystal
1 - blue seed bead

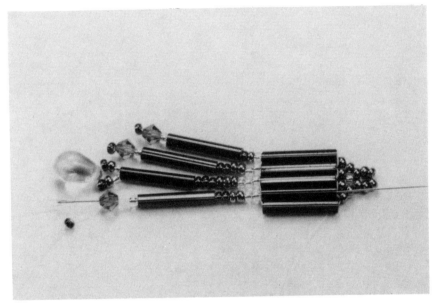

Step 41

Drop the last blue seed bead and sew back up through the plum crystal and up through the fourth row of fringe till you come out through the fourth purple bugle bead at the top of the earring.

Step 42

Reverse the needle and sew down throught the fifth purple bugle bead to the right.
Row five will be.....
1 - silver seed bead
1 - bronze seed bead
1 - blue seed bead
1 - purple bugle bead
1 - silver seed bead
1 - 4mm Plum Crystal
1 - blue seed bead

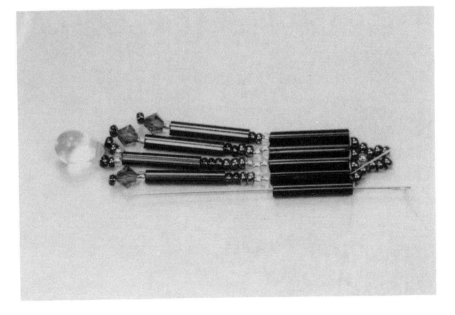

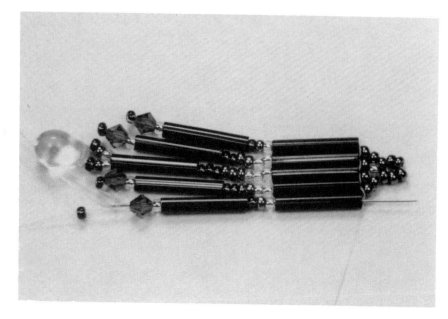

Step 43

This will be the fifth and last row of the fringe. Drop the last blue seed bead and sew up through the plum crystal and up through the fifth row of fringe until you come out through the fifth purple bugle bead at the top of the earring.

Step 44

Now that the fringe is complete sew up through the fourth bronze seed bead in the first row of bronze seed beads to the right at the top.

Step 45

Now, sew up through the third bronze seed bead in the second row to the right, and up through the next three bronze seed beads in the top loop. You will be sewing through a total of four seed beads in this step.

Step 46

Next, reverse your needle and sew down through the next three bronze seed beads to the left in the top loop and down through the center silver bead. Sew up through the next bronze seed bead to the right and up through the next three bronze seed beads on the top loop.

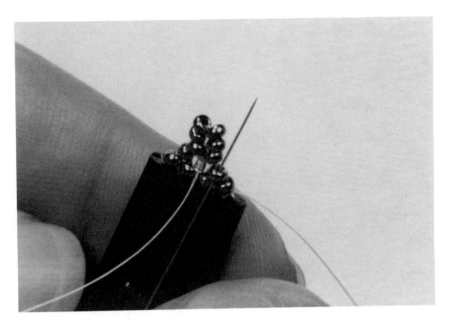

Step 47

Reverse the needle and sew down through the next outside five bronze seed beads to the left and down through your first row of fringe to the left, until you come out through the plum crystal.

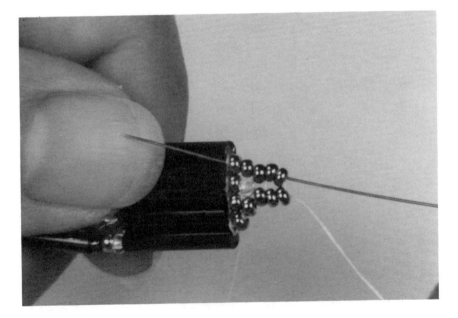

Step 48

With a small pair of sharp scissors, pull your thread while cutting. Stay close to the plum crystal. NOTE: Pulling the thread will allow the thread to travel up inside the purple bugle bead after the cut is made. Next, thread the eight inches of loose thread onto the needle, refer back to and repeat steps 44, 45 & 47. Do not sew through the center silver bead in this step. Only sew through the top loop and again down through the first row of fringe and come out through the plum crystal. Now, cut the thread as we have done previously.

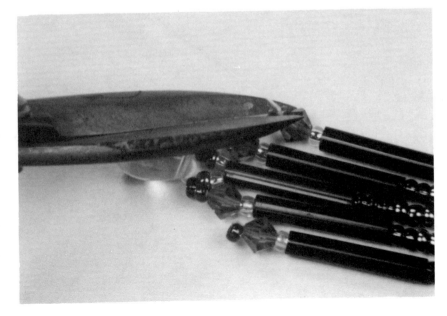

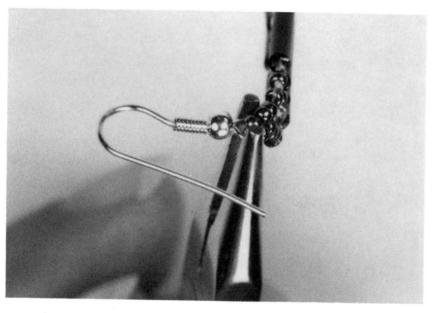

Step 49

Next, attach your earring to a French earwire or a clip-on finding. Open the French earwire by pulling straight back with a pair of round nose pliers. Try not to twist the loop you are pulling on, it could break.

Step 50

Close the loop with a pair of flat-nose pliers by pressing slowly. BE CAREFUL NOT TO BREAK THE SEED BEADS AT THE TOP OF THE EARRING.

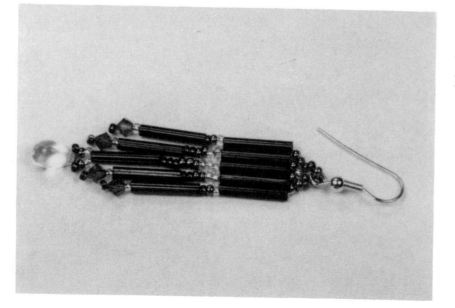

Step 51

Your first earring is now complete! Make another to match and enjoy them.

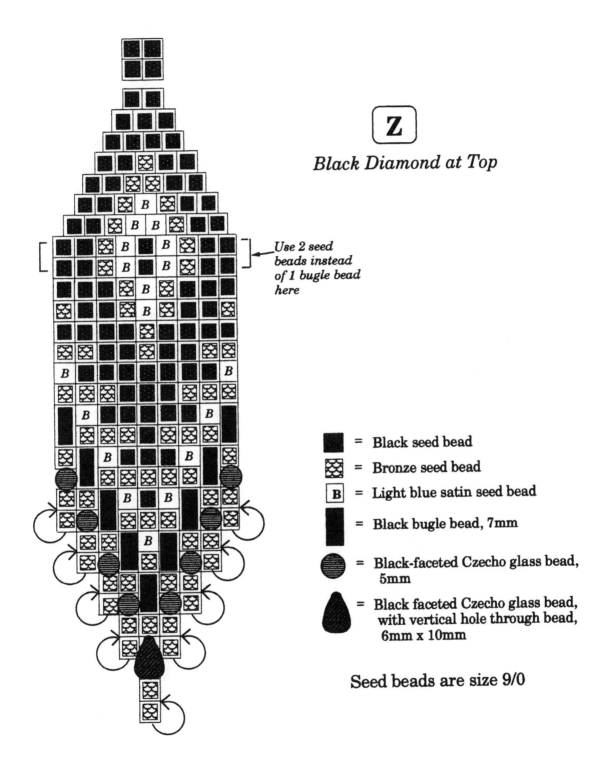

Use 2 seed
beads instead
of 1 bugle bead
here

Z

Black Diamond at Top

■ = Black seed bead

▨ = Bronze seed bead

B = Light blue satin seed bead

▮ = Black bugle bead, 7mm

⬭ = Black-faceted Czecho glass bead,
5mm

🔻 = Black faceted Czecho glass bead,
with vertical hole through bead,
6mm x 10mm

Seed beads are size 9/0

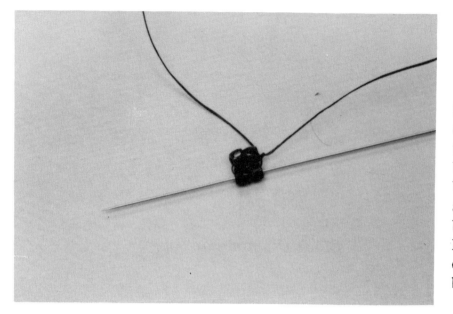

- The Triangle Earring -

Step 1

Has the same steps as the bugle bead earring(Purple Drop Earring) except that you use two seed beads for every bugle bead used in the first project.
Use a single strand of waxed thread and begin by sewing four black seed beads together. Make sure that you leave 8-10 inches of loose thread. Sew down through the set of two black seed beads to the right.

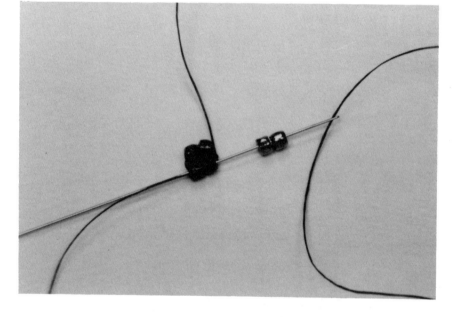

Step 2

Keep the loose thread to the left and add two bronze seed beads and sew down through the second set of two black seed beads to the left.

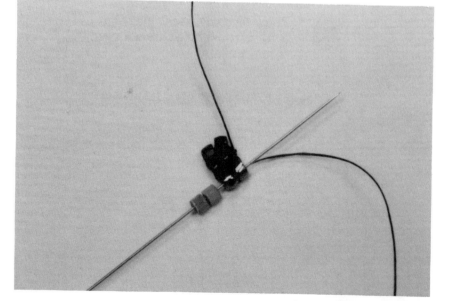

Step 3

Add two light blue seed beads and sew up through the third set of seed beads to the left.

Step 4

The next five sets of two seed beads at a time will be:

2 - black seed beads
2 - light blue seed beads
2 - bronze seed beads
2 - black seed beads
2 - black seed beads

Add on two seed beads at a time until you have nine rows of seed beads in sets of two. This will complete the anchor row.

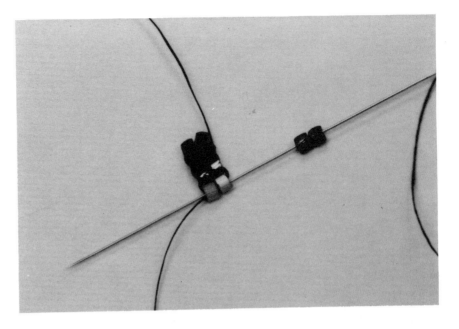

Step 5

Check the pattern on page 31. Turn the piece over and add one black seed bead. Come from behind and sew underneath the first loop of thread at the top of the first anchor row. Keep the eight inches of loose thread to the right and sew back up through the same seed bead. For the rest of this row and the rows to come, add only one seed bead at a time.

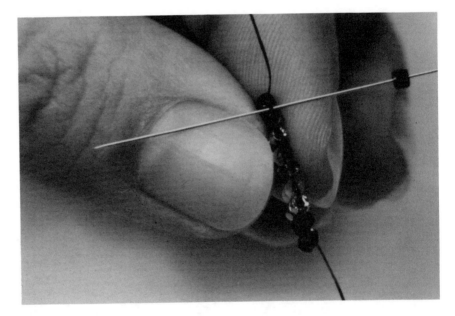

Step 6

Add the first row of fringe and sew back up through the two black seed beads of the anchor row. Remember, the two seed beads you added each time in the anchor row will be considered one bugle bead as in the bugle bead earring instructions.

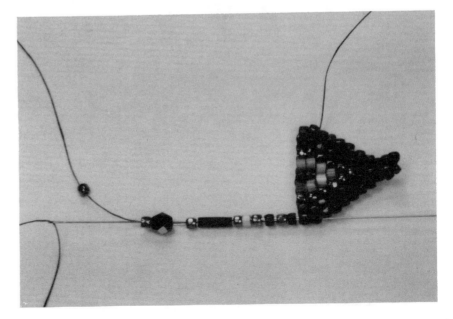

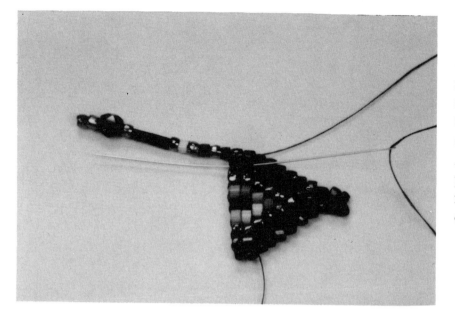

Sew down through the next two anchor row seed beads to the right. Add the second row of fringe and go back up through the same anchor you just came out of.

Again the steps are the same as in the previous project, except for the anchor row which has two seed beads instead of one Bugle Bead.

Your earring is now completed as the earrings in the picture. The one on the left is called a side ways earring. This has the same steps as the project you have just completed.
See Pattern CC.

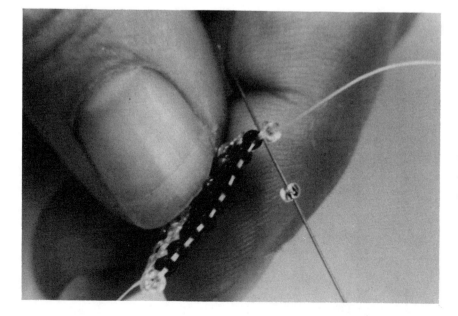

To make a diamond shape triangle earring with or without loops, turn the top part of the beaded triangle beaded piece over, and add the bottom half by starting from the first loop of threads on the left. Weave back up through the earring to end it, or add fringe by weaving through the bottom part of the beaded triangle. See Pattern UU

- Porcupine Quills -

Some bead stores may carry porcupine quills. They are very fragile and should be handled with great care. They can be used in beaded earrings and/or applique work in place of bugle beads. Try to pick only the thickest ones. In this picture we are comparing an average size quill to a 20mm bugle bead.

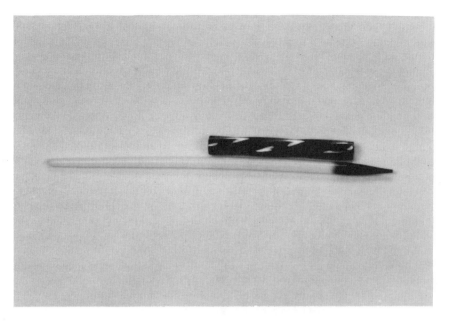

Only cut one quill at a time. Use a bugle bead to measure the correct length. Cut the hard black tip off with a sharp pair of scissors. Do not cut on a slant. Leave approximately 2mm of the black end. Turn the quill and the bugle bead over and cut the opposite end off.

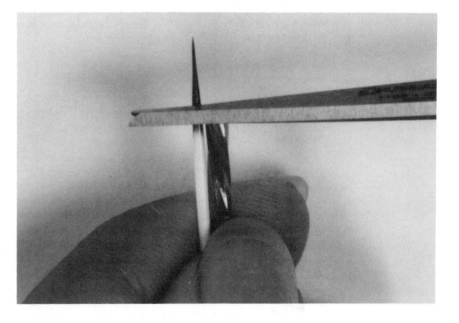

Keep the fringe part of the beadwork as loose as possible when using quills in beaded earrings. Always use a straight beading needle when sewing through quills.

To repair earrings that are too tight, snap one seed bead off in the center row. If the earring is still too tight, snap off one more on either side of the center row. Try to keep the pattern as uniform as possible when snapping off beads.

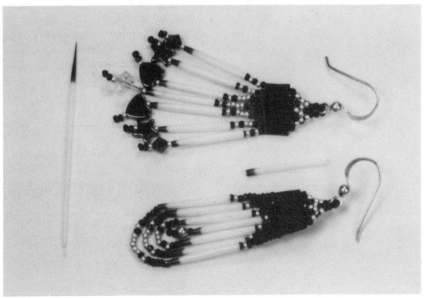

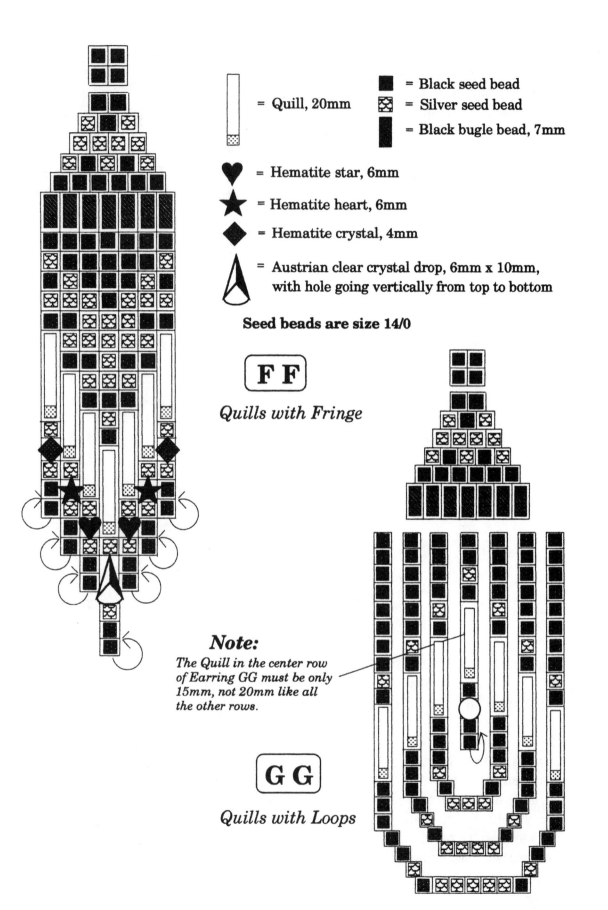

= Quill, 20mm

◼ = Black seed bead
▦ = Silver seed bead
▮ = Black bugle bead, 7mm

♥ = Hematite star, 6mm

★ = Hematite heart, 6mm

◆ = Hematite crystal, 4mm

= Austrian clear crystal drop, 6mm x 10mm,
with hole going vertically from top to bottom

Seed beads are size 14/0

F F

Quills with Fringe

Note:
*The Quill in the center row
of Earring GG must be only
15mm, not 20mm like all
the other rows.*

G G

Quills with Loops

Chapter 2

- *Paua Stone Earring with a Post* -

MATERIALS & TOOLS NEEDED:

English Beading Needles, size 12
Nymo Beading Thread, size B. Do Not Wax, already coated.
Seed Beads, size 11/0, bronze, light blue or aqua and plum.
2 - 13mm x 18mm Paua Stones
Cabochons of matching colors and sizes.
1 - Small pair of sharp scissors
1 - Small pair of flat nose pliers
1 - 3 x 5 White note card
1 - 3 x 5 Piece of white medium weight pellom.
1 - Tube of glue (GOO, by Hobsco)
or (STIX-ALL by Elmers)
1 - 3 x 5 Piece of thin, black snake skin, black leather or
ultra-suede for the backing.
2 - 10mm Surgical steel pads with posts.
2 - Comfort backs (Large plastic disks that attach to the back
of the posts).

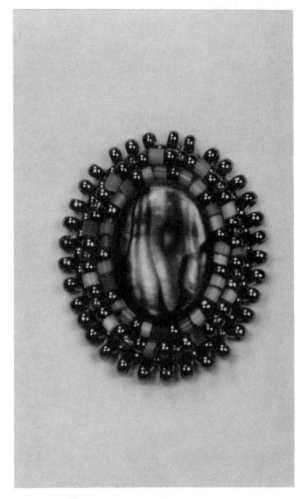

Step 1

To Begin - glue each stone separately to a 2 x 2 inch piece of medium weight pellom. Make sure the stones are centered. Let dry for two hours. Then, select a two yard single strand of thread, thread the needle and tie a knot on the longest end.

NOTE: Please read all of the instructions for the project carefully, and more than once, particularly the materials and tools needed section. Your enjoyment of the project will be enhanced by taking this extra time.
We have made a point to call for more than will be needed of note card, snake skin and pellom in case an error is made in cutting these materials.

TIP: *How to blend seed beads of different sizes and shapes together. Seed beads are not always uniform in size and you may have to remove some of the steps in order to have the pattern fit. If in doubt...take it out! or just use one solid color all the way around the stone. Don't give up, this pattern will work even if the stone size is different. The pattern is based on the first row of beads, just make sure you have two light blue seed beads and one bronze seed bead every step of the way, all of the way around the first row of the stone.*

Step 2

Now that you have glued the stone to the Pellom and let it dry for two hours, place a drop of glue on the center in the back of the Pellom, in back of the glued stone. Place it on the top of the 2 x 2 inch note card. Let it dry for an hour. Always place note card or paper on the back of the Pellom. It will help the beadwork lay flat and stay in place.

Step 3

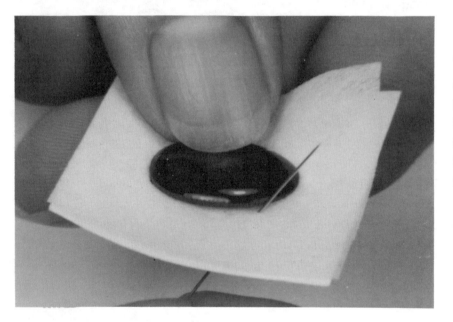

Using the needle and a two yard single strand of thread with a knot on one end, come from behind the piece, sew up through the note card and the Pellom, staying very close to the stone. Pull the needle through until the knot has touched the back of the piece.

Step 4

Your first three seed beads will be: two light blue seed beads and one bronze seed bead. Pick them up in this order on the needle.

Step 5

Once the beads are on the thread and close to the stone, measure three beads wide, push the seed beads back with your right thumb to place them close to the thread that has come from the back of the piece.

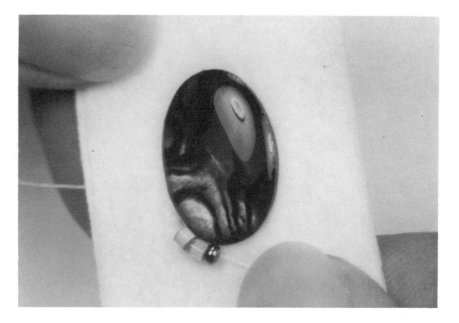

Step 6

Hold the three seed beads down with your left thumb while you are sewing the needle through the Pellom and note card, right at the exact end of the three seed beads. This stitch will always help in any applique project. You can determine exactly where you want the seed beads to lay.

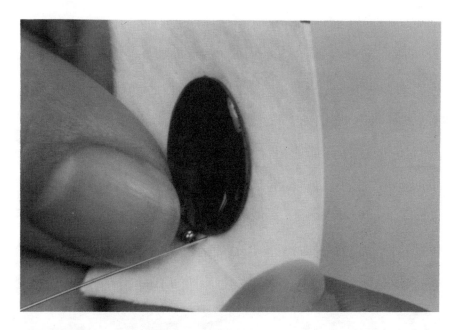

Step 7

Coming back up through the beadwork, sew up and through the first stitch. Pull the thread and make sure the three seed beads are laying flat and close to the stone. If in doubt, take it out.....

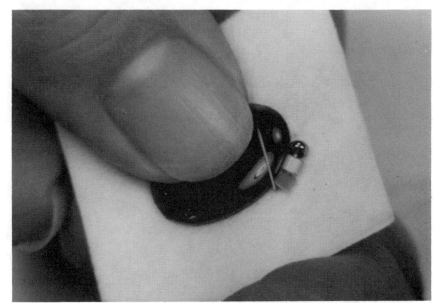

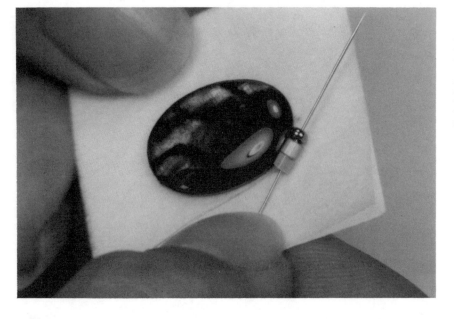

Step 8

Now, sew through the same three seed beads, pull the thread through, then, push the three seed beads back with your right thumb, adjusting the three seed beads in place.

Step 9

In this step, add two light blue seed beads and one bronze seed bead, in that order. Place them close to the beads already sewed on.

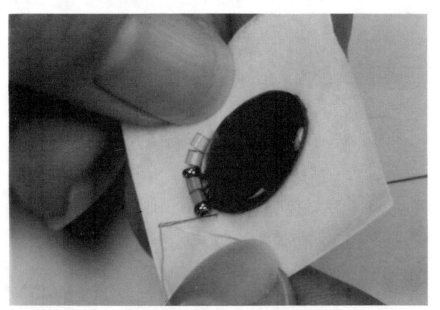

Step 10

Staying close to the stone, again, hold the three seed beads in place with your left thumb while sewing the needle through the Pellom and the note card, right at the exact end of the three seed beads you have just added.

Step 11

Staying close to the stone, come through from the back of the beadwork. Sew up through the inside of the first row, approximately four seed beads back

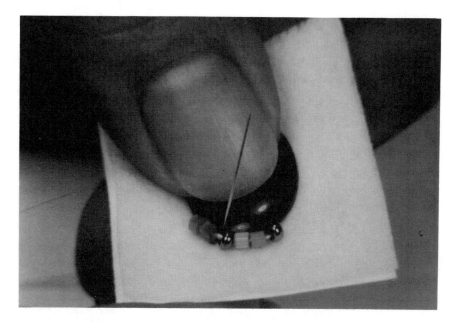

Step 12

Sew through the four seed beads and then add the next three seed beads, two light blue and one bronze seed bead. Repeat the same pattern with steps 9, 10, 11 and 12, until you have gone all around the stone. See Pattern (A).

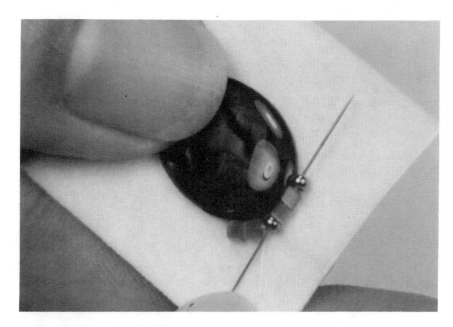

Step 13

Make sure that the bead pattern fits. If not, a few of the steps may have to be removed, or, add a thicker bead, or, a thinner seed bead to make sure that the pattern is correct. It should be: Light blue, light blue, and bronze, all the way around the stone. Beads are like people, they are not perfect, so be patient. Remember, when in doubt, take it out.....

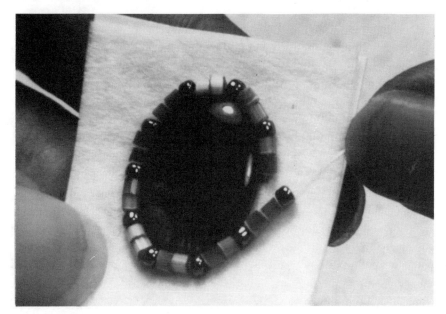

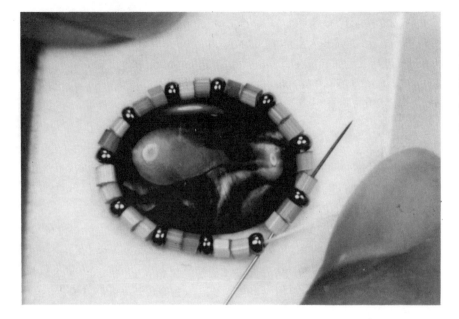

Step 14

After you have made sure that the pattern does fit, begin by sewing through the first four seed beads in the first row, pull the thread to connect up the first row.

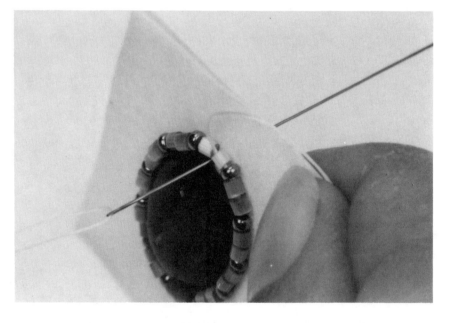

Step 15

Stitch down through the Pellom and the note card while staying close to the stone, right at the end of the last seed bead you have gone through.

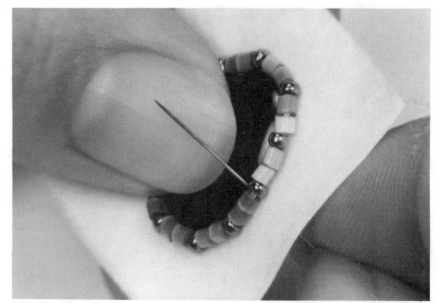

Step 16

Staying close to the stone, come back about eight seed beads and sew up through the note card and the Pellom.

Step 17

Sew through the next six seed beads. If the first row of seed beads around the stone is very loose, keep sewing through the whole row until you have returned to this step again. Then, pull the thread lightly to tighten this first row of seed beads.

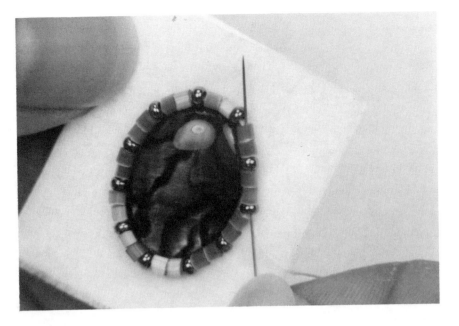

Step 18

Staying close to the stone, sew down through the Pellom and the note card right at the exact end of the last seed bead you have gone through. The first row is now complete.

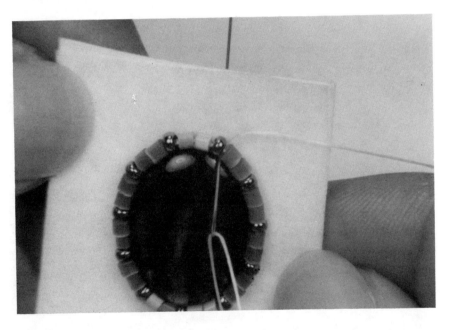

Step 19

Now for the second row of seed beads. Measure approximately one seed bead away from the first row. Sew up through the note card and the Pellom.
The first three seed beads will be: light blue, bronze and plum. Make sure that the plum seed bead in the second row is always opposite the bronze seed bead in the first row.

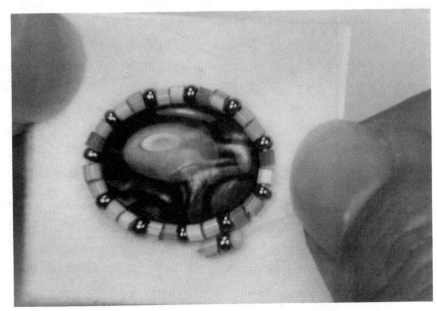

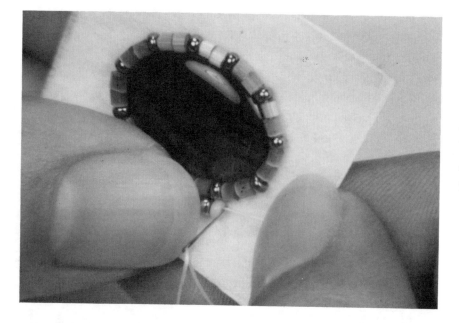

Step 20

Next, stay close to the first row of seed beads. Hold the three seed beads in place with your left thumb while sewing down through the Pellom and note card to the exact end of the three seed beads you have just added. Pull lightly on the thread. Adjust the seed beads into place.

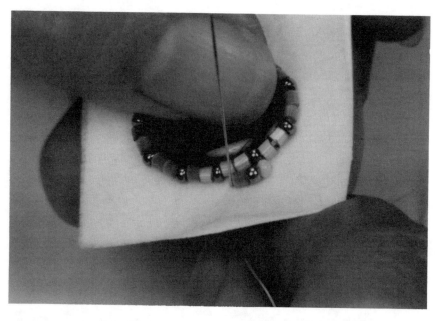

Step 21

Sew up through the note card and Pellom, through the first stitch. Make sure the seed beads are laying flat and close to the first row of seed beads.

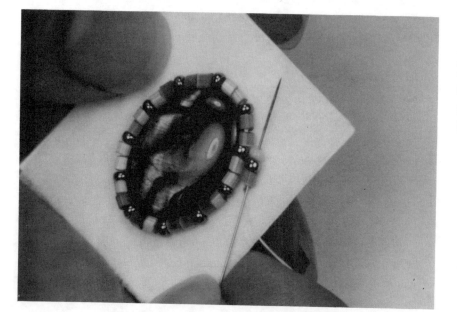

Step 22

Sew through the same three seed beads. Pull lightly on the thread and, with the right thumb push back against the plum seed bead adjusting the three seed beads into place.

Step 23

The next three seed beads will be: bronze, light blue and bronze. Make sure the light blue seed bead you have just put on is opposite and centered between the two light blue seed beads in the first row. This will result in the Starr pattern.

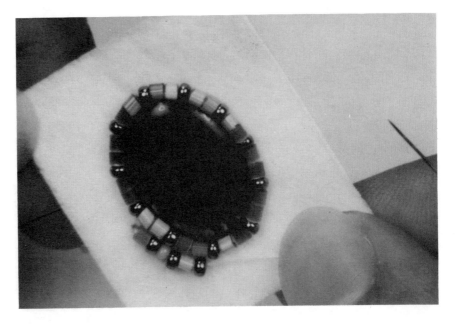

Step 24

Again, measure approximately one bead away from the first row. Sew down through the Pellom and note card while holding the last three seed beads in place with your left thumb. Pull the thread through, adjusting the seed beads into place.

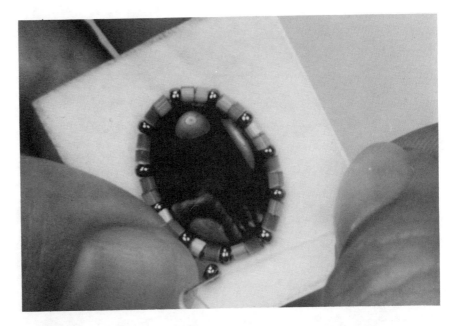

Step 25

Count back four seed beads and sew up through the note card and Pellom in between the first and second row of seed beads.

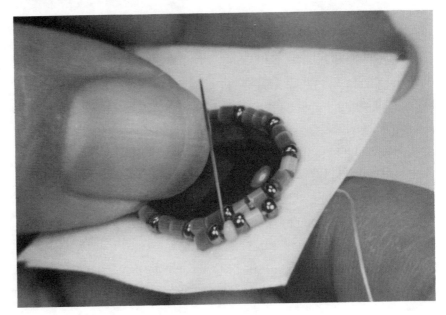

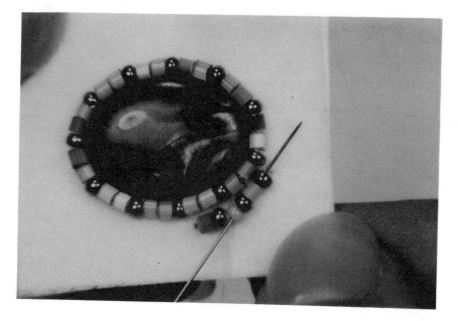

Sew through the four seed beads. Pull lightly on the thread and, with your right thumb, push back against the last bronze seed bead while adjusting the four seed beads into place.

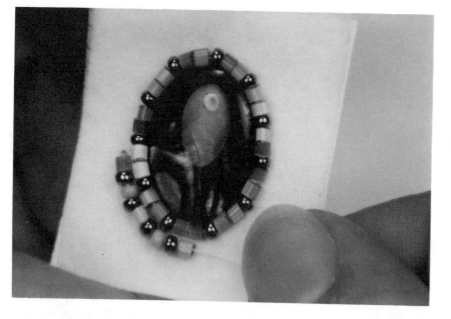

Step 27

The next three seed beads will be: plum, bronze, and light blue. Again, make sure that the light blue seed bead in this step is opposite and centered between the two light blue seed beads in the first row.

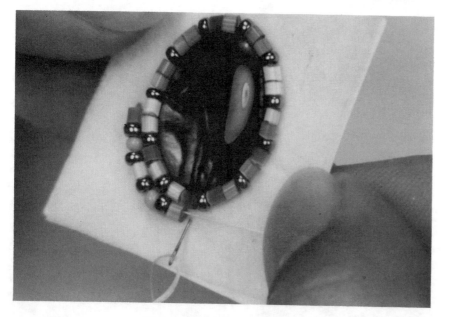

Step 28

Stay close to the first row of seed beads and hold the last light blue seed bead down with your left thumb while sewing down through the Pellom and the note card at the exact end of the last three seed beads you have just put on.

Step 29

Come back four seed beads and sew up through the note card and Pellom in between the first and second rows of seed beads. Now, sew through the same four seed beads and add the next step.

Step 30

The next three seed beads will be: bronze, plum, and bronze. To make sure that the pattern is correct; as you add each light blue seed bead in the second row, note that it should be opposite and centered between the two light blue seed beads in the first row. See the pattern at the right.

Ⓟ = Plum (or light purple) seed bead

◉ = Light blue (or aqua satin) seed bead

◯ = Bronze seed bead

Seed beads are size 11/0

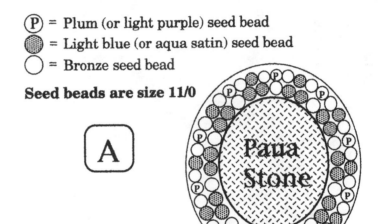

Step 31

After you have made sure that the pattern does fit, sew through the first four seed beads in the second row. Then pull the thread lightly to connect the second row together.

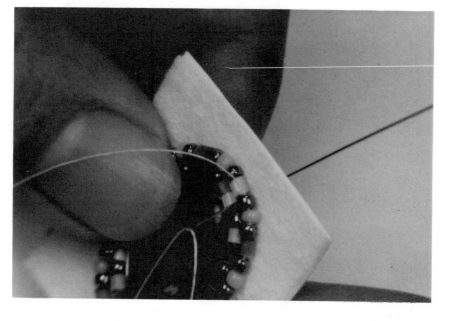

Step 32

Now you will sew through the Pellom and note card in between the first and second rows of seed beads, right at the end of the four seed beads you have just gone through.

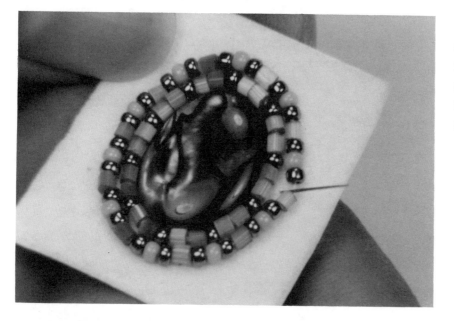

Step 33

Count back about seven seed beads from the step you have just gone through and sew up through the note card and the Pellom in between the first and second rows.

Step 34

Now, sew through the same seven seed beads.

Step 35

Using a small pair of scissors, cut around the bead work as close as you can. Be careful not to cut any of the threads in the back.

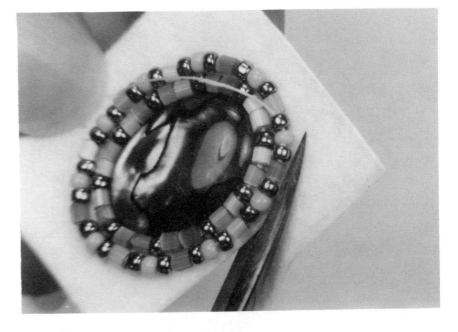

Step 36

For this oval earring, cut a rectangular shaped piece of snake skin, thin leather or ultra suede that is slightly larger than the bead work. Fold it in half and place a pencil mark on the center inside back of the snake skin, 1/4 inch down from the top. Pierce a small hole at the pencil dot with a large enough sewing needle or #3 soft sculpture needle to insert a post. NOTE: Never use an ink pen to mark a spot.

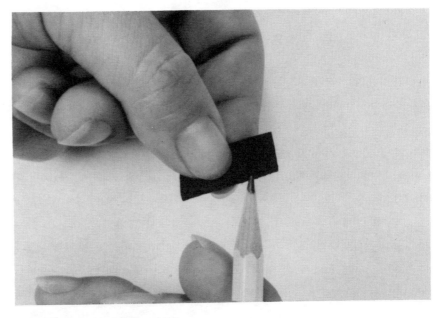

Step 37

Place a very small amount of glue around the hole on the back side of the snake skin you plan to insert the post through. Insert the post into the back of the snake skin and make sure you are leaving at least 2mm of space from the top of the post pad to the top of the snake skin.

Step 38

Next, Place a thin layer of glue on the back of the bead work and press the two pieces together with the post at the top.

Step 39

Let dry for two hours. Keep the loose thread away from the scissors and cut around the beadwork very closely. Make sure that you don't cut into the bead work.

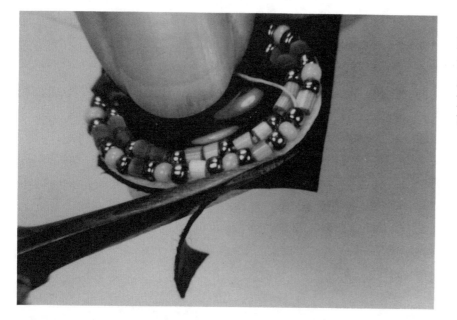

Step 40

To begin the outside trim, stitch down underneath the second row of seed beads and come out between the Pellom and snake skin. Be sure that the needle is between these two materials, before starting the outside trim or edge stitch.

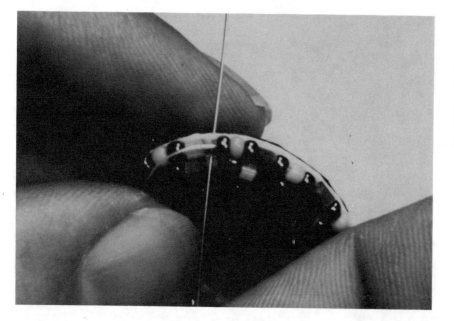

Step 41

This begins the first step of the outside trim. Start with three bronze seed beads. Measure about one seed bead over from the thread and sew down through the Pellom, note card and the backing approximately 2mm deep. NOTE: Be careful not to catch the thread in the second row of seed beads.

If you have a hard time pulling the needle through, use a pair of short, flat nose pliers. Hold the needle about 1/2 inch down from the point of the needle and pull gently.

Step 42

Come over and sew up through the third seed bead and pull gently. The third seed bead is the last bronze seed bead to the right in step one of the outside trim.(Step 41)

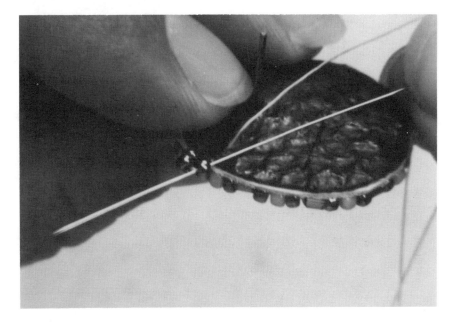

Step 43

Next add two bronze seed beads. Measure approximately one seed bead over and sew down through the Pellom, note card and backing, approximately 2mm deep.

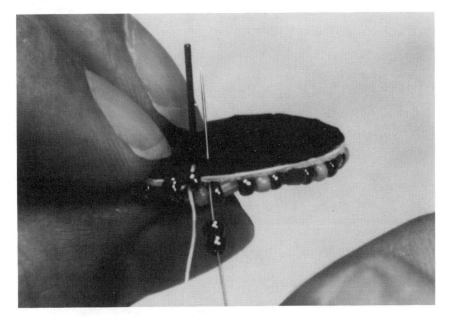

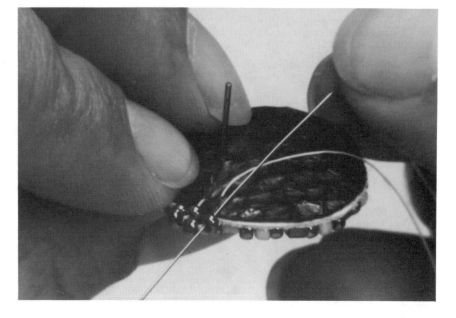

Sew back up through the second bronze seed bead. This is the last one you put on. Repeat the last two steps until you are all the way around the earring. Only add two bronze seed beads at a time.

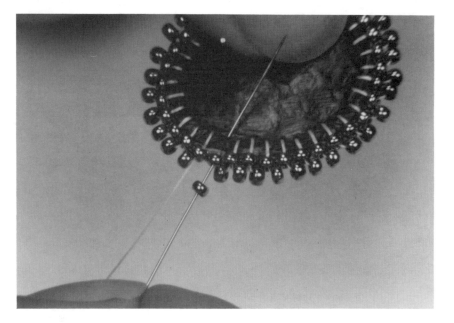

Step 45

Once you are all the way around and have come to the first bronze seed bead in the inside trim, add one bronze seed bead and sew through the first bronze seed bead in the inside row of trim and then through the Pellom, note card and backing approximately 2mm deep.

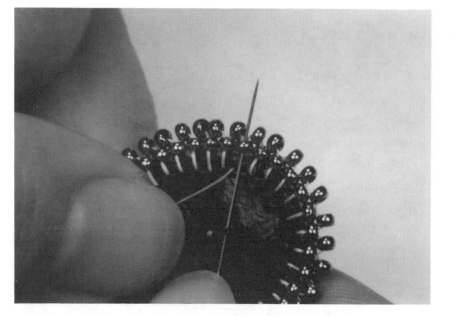

Step 46

Now, sew back through the same first bronze seed bead in the inside trim. NOTE: Pull lightly every time you add seed beads, but, be careful not to tear the snake skin backing.

Step 47

Sew through the next outside bronze seed bead to the right.

Step 48

Now, sew through the next inside bronze seed bead to the right, in the outside trim.

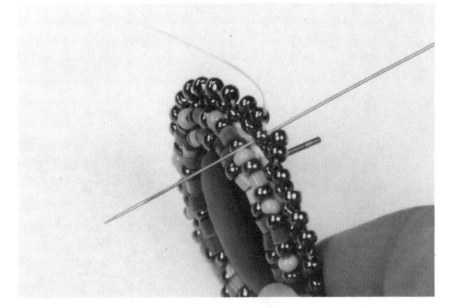

Step 49

Sew underneath the bead work. Only sew through the Pellom and notecard. Do not sew through the snake skin backing. As you sew up through the Pellom and the note card, sew towards the top left of the earring.

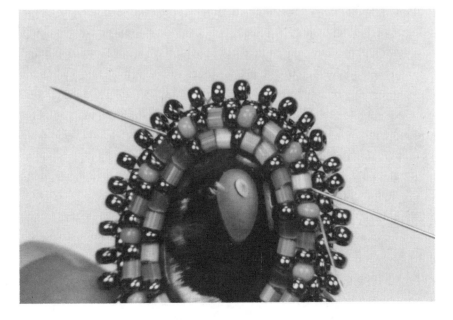

With the single strand of thread, tie a loop knot underneath the bead work and pull it as close as you can to hide the knot underneath.

Step 51

Now, sew underneath the bead work to the right side. Lay the earring down on a table, pull on the thread lightly while you cut the thread very close to the bead work. Attach the Con Fort back to your earring post. Your earring is now complete. Make another earring to match and enjoy.

NOTE: If you make an earring with a smaller stone, use a smaller post and pad (5mm Pad with Post).

Step 52

ADDING ON A TOP LOOP:

You must start at the beginning of the Paua Stone Earring by not adding on the surgical steel pad with post. This step will be for a French earwire and other attachable earring findings.

Step 53

Use a 1/2 yard of thread to add on the top loop. Sew the single strand underneath the beadwork. Sew only through the Pellom and the note card starting from the right side and sew underneath to the left.

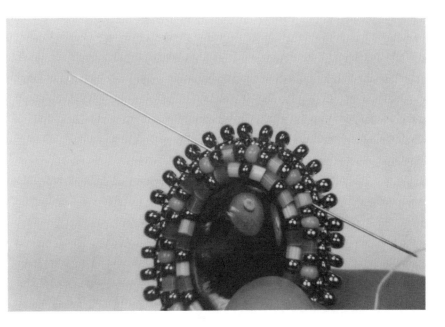

Step 54

Sew or weave underneath the bead work until you have come out near the top of the earring. Take your needle and measure to find the top center of the earring.

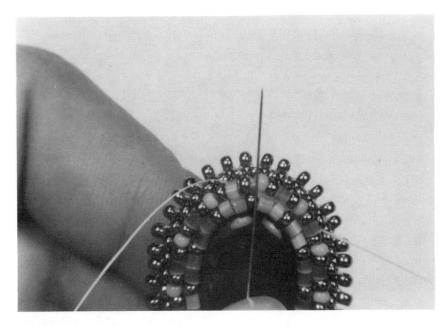

Step 55

Sew up through the next inside seed bead of the outside row of trim to the left. NOTE: Be careful not to catch the threads in the second row of bead work.

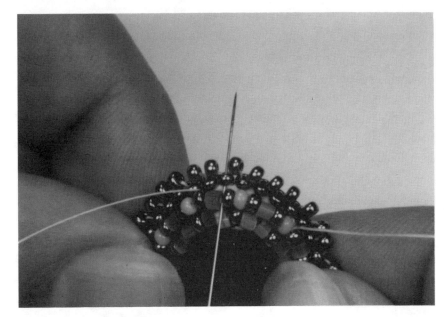

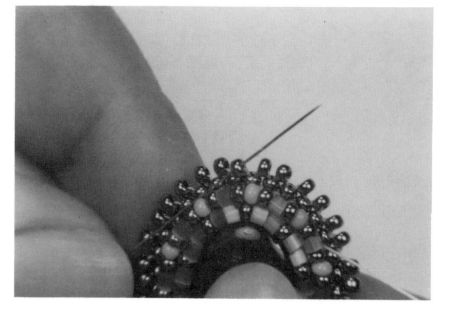

Sew through the next outside bronze seed bead to the right. You are now ready to add the top loop.

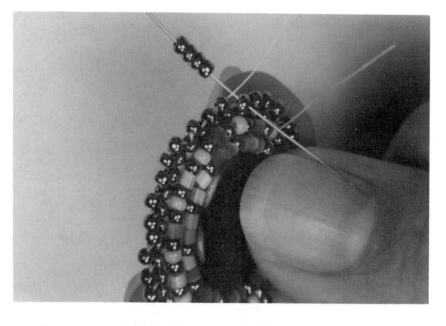

Step 57
Add four bronze seed beads and come over and sew through the next bronze seed bead in the outside row of trim, to the right. Pull the thread lightly to form the loop of two bronze seed beads on the right and two bronze seed beads on the left.

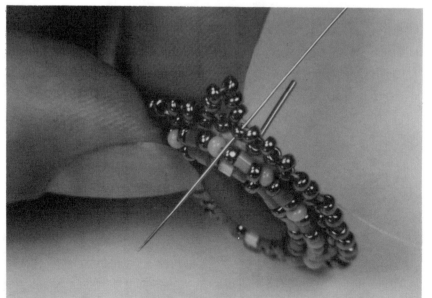

Step 58
NOTE: Please disregard the post in this earring as we are using the previous earring as an example.

Now, sew down through the next inside bronze seed bead in the outside row.

Step 59
The loop is now complete. In order for it to be a strong loop, sew back through the whole loop by repeating the last six steps without adding any seed beads.

Step 60
Once you have gone through the whole loop, tie a loop knot and pull it close and underneath the bead work to hide it. If you have another loose thread, weave it back underneath the beadwork a few times and cut the thread.

Step 61
Now, sew underneath the bead work to the right side. Lay the earring down on a table and pull on the thread lightly while you cut the thread very close to the beadwork. The earring is now complete and ready to add a French ear wire or any other finding of your choice.

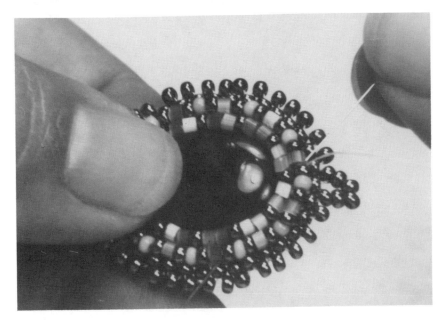

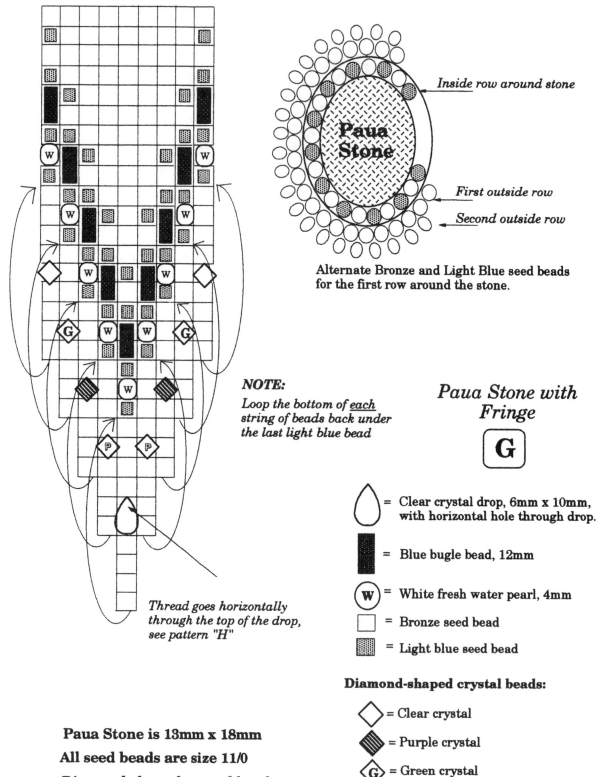

Inside row around stone

First outside row

Second outside row

Alternate Bronze and Light Blue seed beads for the first row around the stone.

NOTE:
Loop the bottom of each string of beads back under the last light blue bead

Thread goes horizontally through the top of the drop, see pattern "H"

Paua Stone with Fringe

$\boxed{\textbf{G}}$

= Clear crystal drop, 6mm x 10mm, with horizontal hole through drop.

= Blue bugle bead, 12mm

Ⓦ = White fresh water pearl, 4mm

☐ = Bronze seed bead

▨ = Light blue seed bead

Diamond-shaped crystal beads:

◇ = Clear crystal

◆ = Purple crystal

◈G = Green crystal

◇P = Pink crystal

Paua Stone is 13mm x 18mm

All seed beads are size 11/0

Diamond-shaped crystal beads are size 4mm

Step 62

ADDING ON FRINGE:
We are working with a different Paua Stone earring than before, however these adding on fringe steps will work for the earring that we have just made or this one which has only one row of seed beads around the Paua stone plus the outside trim.

NOTE: This earring is Pattern G on Page 58.

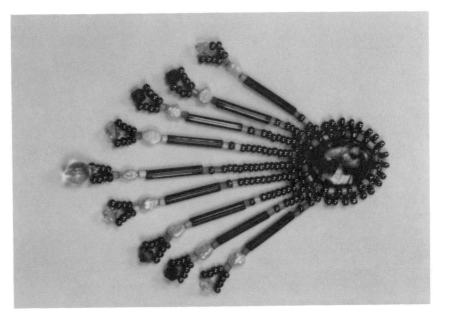

Step 63

Make sure you have enough thread to complete the fringe by starting with at least one yard of thread. With your needle, find the center of the bottom of the earring. Include the center and count five spaces over to the left.

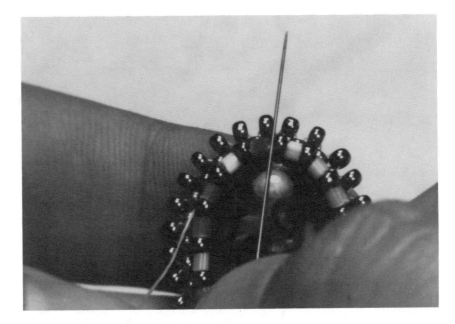

Step 64

After counting five spaces over, sew through the next inside bronze seed bead in the outside row of trim to the left.

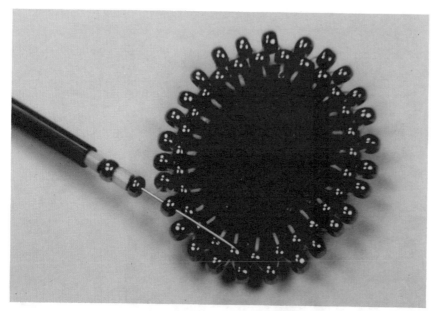

Step 65

Since we are using Sharp Beads on the end of this fringe, wax the remaining single strand of thread now, before adding on the fringe.

Now, sew through the next outside bronze seed bead in the outside row of trim to the right. The first row of fringe will be.....

Step 66

1 - bronze seed bead
1 - light blue seed bead
1 - bronze seed bead
1 - light blue seed bead
1 - 12 mm Capri Blue Bugle bead
1 - light blue seed bead
1 - 4 mm fresh water pearl
1 - light blue seed bead
4 - bronze seed beads
1 - 4 mm clear crystal
4 - bronze seed beads

Sew back up through the last light blue seed bead and up through the first row of fringe.

Step 67

Once you are through the fringe, sew through the next bronze seed bead in the outside row of trim to the right or left.

NOTE: Right or left will depend on the side of the earring you are working from, for this position the step will be to the right.

Step 68

The second row of fringe will be.....

4 - bronze seed beads
1 - light blue seed bead
1 - bronze seed bead
1 - light blue seed bead
1 - 12 mm Capri Blue Bugle bead
1 - light blue seed bead
1 - 4 mm fresh water pearl
1 - light blue seed bead
4 - bronze seed beads
1 - 4 mm green crystal
4 - bronze seed beads

Sew back up through the last blue seed bead and up through the second row of fringe and up through the next bronze seed bead in the outside row of trim to the right.

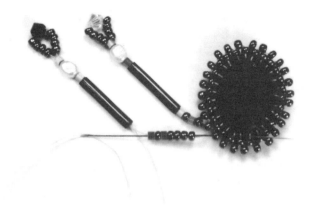

Step 69

This fringe pattern is letter G in the patterns. It will be nine rows wide. Continue to add each row of fringe and sew up the next bronze seed bead in the outside row of trim to the right. After the nine rows are completed, sew through the next inside bronze seed bead in the inside trim.

Step 70

Sew underneath the bead work, only through the Pellom and note card towards the right side of the earring. Check the pattern now. This will be the only chance you will have to take the fringe out to correct any errors that have been made.

Step 71
Tie a loop knot underneath the bead work and pull it as close as you can to hide the knot underneath

Step 72
Next, sew underneath the bead work. Sew only through the Pellom and note card towards the left side of the earring. Lay the earring down on a table and pull on the thread lightly while you cut the thread very close to the bead work. The earring is now complete. Attach the Con Fort back to the earring post.

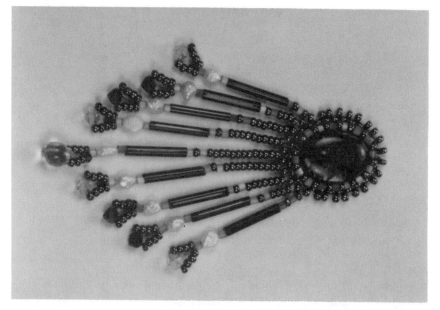

Step 73
Make another earring to match and enjoy.
If you want to shorten the earring, repeat the pattern and eliminate the 12 mm Capri Bugle beads in each row. This will yield a shorter and fuller earring.

Chapter 3

- Paua Stone Necklace -

MATERIALS & TOOLS NEEDED

English Beading Needles, size 12

Nymo Beading Thread, size B

Seed beads, size 11/0. Colors - bronze, light blue or aqua, plum, gold, green, and dark blue.

1 - Paua Stone, size - 22 mm x30 mm

8 - Clear 4 mm Austrian Crystals

8 - Pink 4 mm Austrian Crystals

8 - Purple 4 mm Austrian Crystals

8 - Green 4 mm Austrian Crystals

1 - 6 mm Pink or Clear Crystal Star

24 - 4 mm Fresh Water Pearls

17 - 12 mm Blue Bugle Beads

17 - 6 mm Gold Rice Beads

21 - 5 mm Bronze Nailhead Beads

17 - 2 or 3 mm Light blue Glass Beads

1 - 6 mm x 10 mm Clear Crystal Drop

1 - 3 x 5 note card

1 - 3 x 5 inch piece of medium weight Pellom

1 - tube of glue (GOO or STIX-ALL)

1 - 3 x 5 piece of Black Snake skin, thin leather or thin ultra suede

1 - 30 foot roll of .012" diameter Tiger Tail Jewelery wire

2 - Gold Plated Crimps

1 - 6 mm Gold Plated Lobster Claw

1 - medium Gold Plated Eye

1 - Small pair of short, flat nose pliers

1 - Small pair of sharp scissors

1 - pair of diagonal cutters

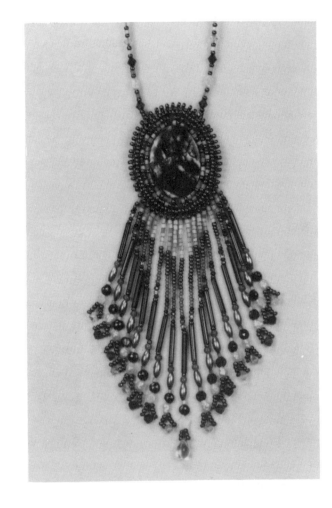

Step 1

To begin your Paua Stone Necklace, glue the one Paua Stone, size 22 mm x 30 mm to a 2" X 3" piece of medium weight Pellom. Make sure that the stone is centered. Let dry for two hours. Thread the needle, tie a knot at the end of the longest thread and begin.....

NOTE: Please read all of the instructions for the project carefully, and more than once, particularly the materials and tools needed section. Your enjoyment of the project will be enhanced by taking this extra time.
We have made a point to call for more than will be needed of note card, snake skin and pellom in case an error is made in cutting these materials.

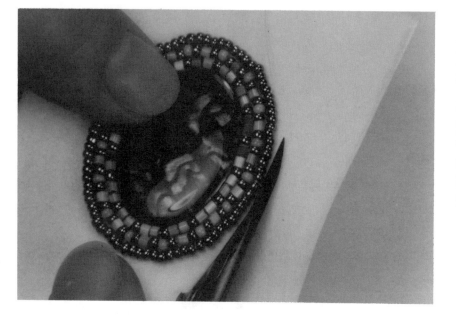

PAUA STONE NECKLACE
pattern -B-
This first step of the Paua stone necklace will be the same pattern as the paua stone earring that we have just completed. Repeat Pattern - A - around the stone and add one more row of all bronze seed beads for the third row. See Pattern -B-

**Step 3**

Cut around the bead work. Be careful not to cut the threads in the back. The threads in the back of the bead work should be about 2 mm away from the edge that you have just cut.

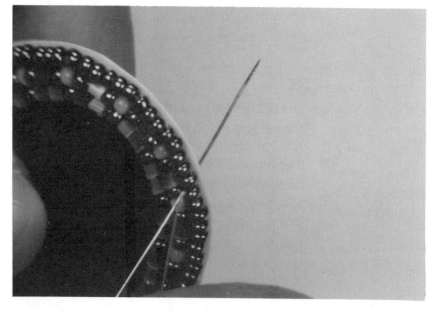

**Step 4**

Now you will sew down through the Pellom and note card in between the second and third rows of seed beads right at the exact end of the last bronze seed bead you have just gone through.

Step 5

Lay a 32 inch piece of tiger tail down on the back of the bead work. This will show how the tiger tail is to lay. Lay it carefully around the back of the beaded piece as if to almost fold it into a circle. NOTE: Do not bend the tiger tail.

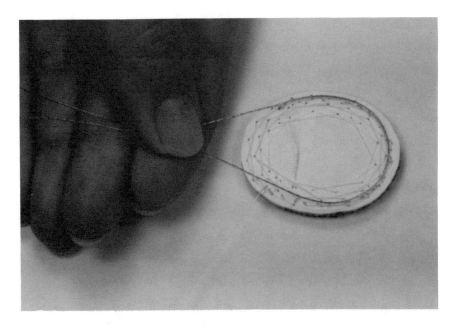

Step 6

We will first begin at the top of the necklace, with the 32 inch piece of tiger tail in place. Sew over the tiger tail down through the second and third row of seed beads. Only sew through the Pellom and note card. Hold the tiger tail in place while stitching around the stone.

Step 7

Come over about 2 mm and sew down through the second and third rows of seed beads. As you come out through the back of the bead work, try to stay close to the tiger tail.

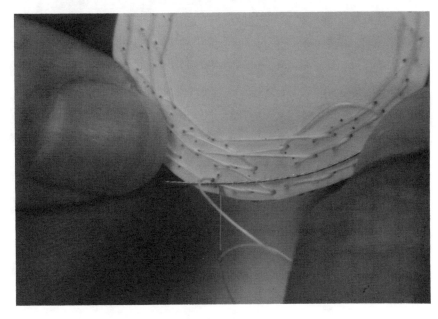

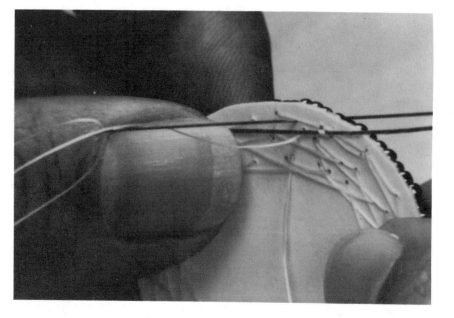

Step 8

Now, come over the tiger tail and sew down through the note card and the Pellom, and out through the front of the bead work between the second and third rows of seed beads.

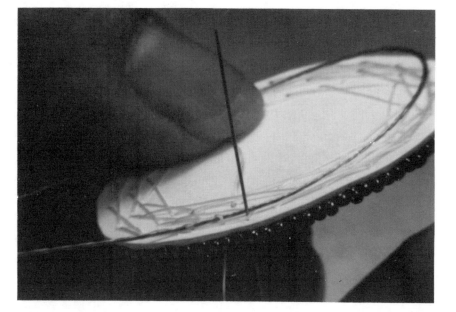

Step 9

Always hold the tiger tail in place while sewing around the stone. Stitch over the tiger tail and down through the note card and pellom. Repeat this stitch until you are two inches away from the tiger tail from where you started.

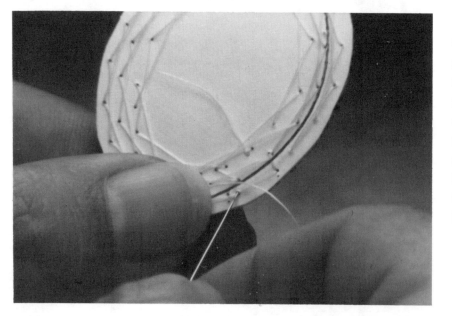

Step 10

Once you are around the stone and approximately two inches away from the tiger tail you have first stitched down, you will now be again at the top of the necklace. Make sure that the tiger tail is even. Try to imagine this as a necklace and how even it will be. The two tiger tail wires should be horizontal, across from each other, and will be the necklace chain.

Step 11

Now that you are all the way around the necklace, tie a knot twice to insure the knot will not come apart. Keep the knot close to the back of the bead work. Cut the thread 1/4 inch away from the knot.

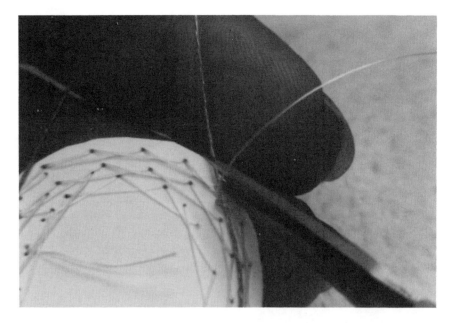

Step 12

ADDING ON THREAD

Cut two yards of thread and tie a knot at the end of one of the single strands. Sew through the back of the bead work, sewing through the note card and the Pellom. Come out through the front of the bead work, in between the second and third rows of seed beads.

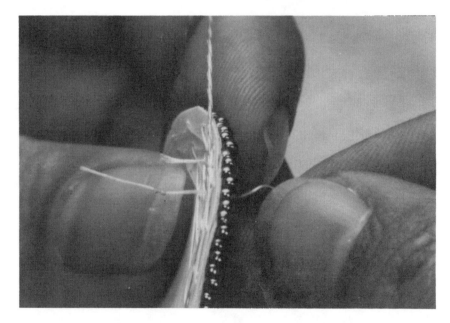

Step 13

Place a thin layer of GOO on the note card in the back of the bead work. Then, carefully place the beadwork onto the backing. Let it dry for two hours. Now, cut around the bead work, only cutting off the excess backing. Then sew the same trim stitch around the the outside edge that we have done previously in the Paua Stone earring. Then, add the fringe, it's Pattern B.

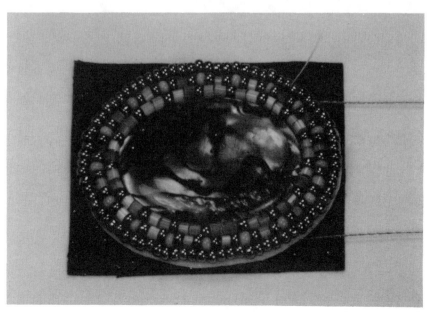

Step 14
Once the fringe is completed, you can add the chain pattern onto the tiger tail, see Pattern -B-.

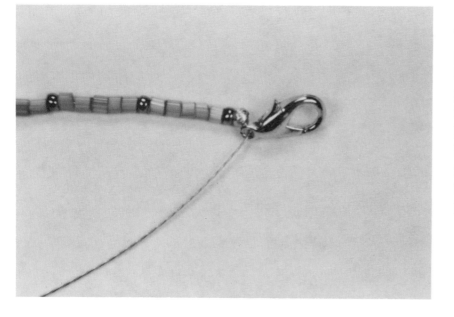

Step 15
The last bead on each chain will be one gold plated crimp bead. Now, insert the tiger tail through the 6 mm gold plated lobster claw and back down through the gold plated crimp bead and back through approximately 10 seed beads in the chain. Use a pair of short, flat nose pliers to pull the wire and bring the chain of beads up close to the lobster claw.

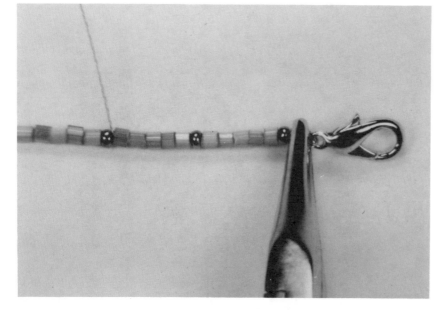

Step 16
Try not to leave any large gaps between the beads that will allow the tiger tail to show through. Next with a pair of short, flat nose pliers, carefully press the crimp bead until it is flat. Be very careful not to break any beads. Cut off the excess tiger tail with the diagonal cutters.

Step 17

Repeat the last two steps for the opposite chain of the necklace, except change the finding to an eye.

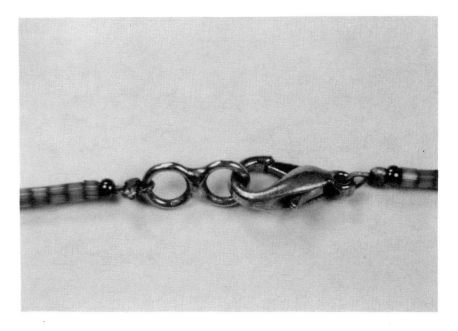

Step 18

Your necklace is now complete. For larger stones, use a heavier gauge of tiger tail or double the .012" diameter tiger tail I have recommended. Do not use heavier gauge tiger tail if you are going to double it, it will be too thick to go back through the beads where the findings are to be attached. Two crimp beads are also needed to attach findings when using larger stones.

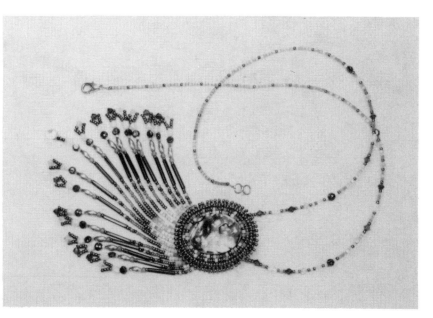

Step 19

This collection is complimented with the Paua Stone or the Paua colors, I call them garden colors. I have sold this collection as individual pieces and also in sets. The Paua Stone may be used with different cabochons such as: turquoise, amethyst, jade, lapis, or malichite. Try the stones of your choice and enjoy.....

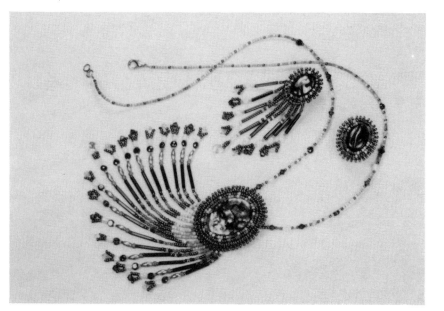

NAVAJO ROSETTE NECKLACE

The medallion part of this necklace is called a rosette. The chain is strung with glass seed beads and cedar beads or to the Navajo Indian, Ghost beads. These beads are said to ward off evil; spirits.

Begin this necklace chain with size B thread or invisable nylon thread. Use the same steps as, adding on a top loop. Come out from the bead work through an outside trim bead. First, add a single strand of chain, then weave back through the rosette. Sew back through the same outside trim bead and to the right. Add one seed bead in between the outside trim bead you just came through. Then sew through the outside trim bead to the right.

NOTE. The seed beads in the outside trim stitch of this Navajo necklace may look incorrect. The seed beads on the inside row are very far apart. The seed beads on the outside trim fall to the inside of the trim. This is how some Indian artists choose to sew the outside row in the necklace. I prefer the inside trim row of seed beads to touch one another.

Second Loop.
Add the same pattern of the first chain until you have about six inches of beads to connect the second row to the first. Sew through a cedar bead or any 5 mm x 6mm bead of your choice. Sew through the first chain until you come out the other side. Come out of the chain six inches before you come to the rosette and add the second row on the opposite side just as the first step of adding the second loop. Sew back through the chain two to three times to secure. End the necklace as you would the Paua Stone, by tying a knot and weaving underneath the beaded rosette.

Chapter 4
-Barrettes & Brooches-

Step 1

To keep larger pieces, (Barrettes, Brooches, Hat Bands, or any other large piece of applique bead work) in place while beading, use a glue stick and glue the Pellom and the note card together.

Always start larger pieces by drawing a straight line down the center of the Pellom to help keep the bead work even.

Step 2

Start the bead work in the center and work out to the right side, adding three to four seed beads at a time. Tie a knot and cut the thread. Start again from the left side, working your way to the left, making sure that the bead work is straight. Next cut away all excess Pellom by starting in the sharp corners of your work and cutting around the piece in sections.....

Step 3

Always start the outside trim stitch of large projects with at least two yards of thread so you don't run out of thread. Do the next three steps with a piece of note card or even a piece of paper. This will be the paper pattern. Here we will cut a rectangular piece slightly larger than the bead work. Lay the bead work down onto the paper and trace around it with a pencil. Never use an ink pen.

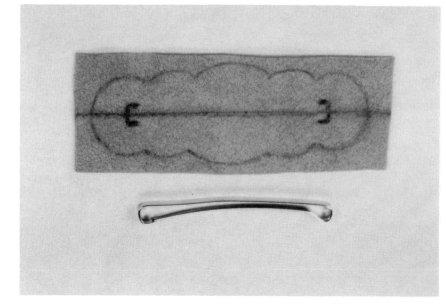

Draw a straight horizontal line across the center of the paper barrette tracing. Next lay the barrette down onto the horizontal line and measure from the end of the finding to the edge of the tracing. Trace guide lines at each end so the finding can be inserted in the proper place. Cut a piece of ultra-suede the same size as the pattern. Use an Exacto knife, also referred to as a snap knife. Make cuts into the paper and ultra-suede slightly smaller than the guidelines at the end of each edge in the finding tracing. NOTE: Only make cuts where the metal finding will be inserted.

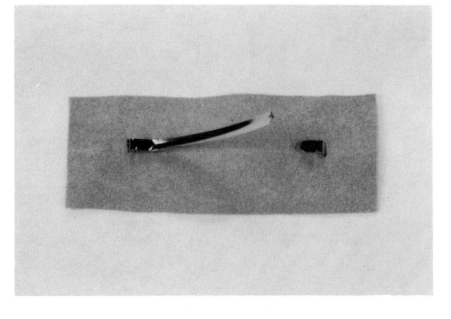

Step 5
Insert the finding through the two small cuts. Make sure that the ultra-suede backing lays flat with the finding.

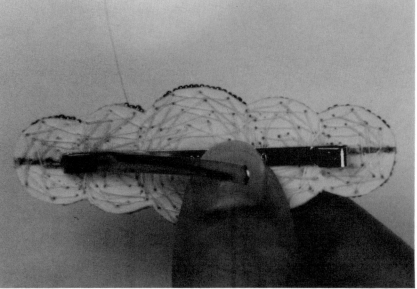

Step 6
Lightly trace guidelines on the back of the bead work. You want the barrette to set in the center of the bead work. Next glue the finding to the back of the bead work by placing a very thin layer of STIX-ALL or GOO on the top, flat part of the barrette finding. Let dry two hours. Now, place a thin layer of glue on to the back of the bead work and on the back of the barrette finding. Place the two pieces of bead work and ultra-suede backing together, and let dry for three to four hours.

Step 7

Trim off the excess ultra-suede backing as close to the bead work as possible. Make sure not to cut the thread in the back.

The outside trim stitch will start the same as the Paua Stone earring (Chapter 2) except for the sharp corners in the barrette, add only one seed bead instead of the usual two, do this only once and only in the center of the sharp corner. Next, return to the regular step of two seed beads at a time. NOTE: Adding only one seed bead at a time in the outside trim is called the Easy Outside Trim stitch. Finish the outside trim the same as the Paua Stone earring.

If you would like to add fringe and run out of thread, see the chapter on Large Hat Bands to learn how to add thread. NOTE: Some artists will sew the barrette finding onto the outside of the ultra-suede backing. I feel that it looks so much nicer under the backing. The choice is yours. The barrette is now complete.

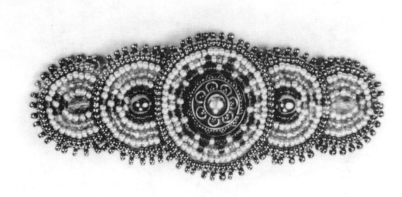

For larger and more complex barrette findings, you will need to take them apart. Again, only make cuts where the metal will be inserted. Always make the cuts slightly smaller than measured.

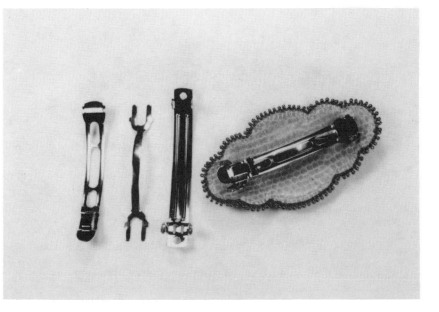

MORE COMPLEX BARRETTE

Step 1

For this barrette clip, the findings have been removed. On the end that the clip will be snap closed, only make cuts along the side where the metal protrudes. See the top pencil. Carefully slip the cuts through and inbetween the center two pieces of metal that fold over each other in the center. See the bottom pencil.

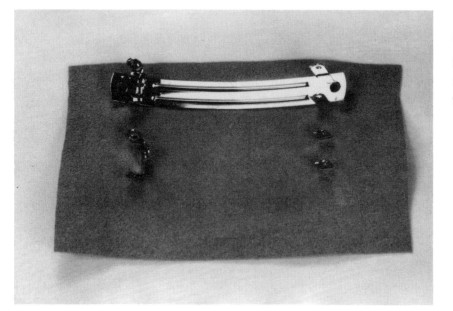

Step 2

The opposite side of this finding is much easier to insert through. As you can see, there is no metal folded over in the center.

Step 3

Here is a technique for adding 4 mm crystals to the barrette or any other applique stitch. Sew the 4 mm crystals down three at a time. Once all of the crystals are in place, come back through the Pellom and add one row of six to eight, size 14 seed beads between each 4 mm crystal. Sew back through each row to secure the beads. This technique will help fill in unwanted gaps in your bead work. Always add one row of seed beads for the next step when using this technique.

Chapter 5
- Bolo Ties -

Step 1

Also called "The Southwest Tie". Place the backing on without making any cuts for findings. Add the outside trim stitch. If you want to add trim, do it next.

Step 2

Buy a Bolo Finding that locks. The cheaper type slides and will not stay in place. Find the center of the bolo finding and the center of the back of the bead work. Use Super Glue Gel and place a 1/2 inch circle of glue on the back of the finding. Carefully place the finding onto the center back of the beaded piece. Let dry for one hour. Place the Bolo Cord through the finding and add two Bolo Tips by gluing one to each end of the cord.

Step 3

Once the piece is dry, if there is a hole at the inside bottom of the bolo tie, you may sew through from the front of the bead work. Using two threads, sew back through to the front of the bead work. Repeat this step four to six times. End this step in the front of the bead work to hide the knot underneath the rows of seed beads.

Chapter 6
- Belt Buckles -

Step 1

Use GOO Glue. The stone in the center of this buckle is a petrified wood cabochon. Because the stone is set very high, 4 mm round glass beads are used around the stone first. Size 10 beads are used to finish the rows. Press the buckle finding down onto a piece of note card to make an impression of the peg part of the buckle. The peg is the blunt protruding nail that is to the right, in the back of the buckle finding. For oval buckles use oval stones, for square buckles, use square stones.

Step 2

Punch a small hole with a hole punch at this point. Place the finding through the hole. With both thumbs, press against each side of the steel buckle loop finding at the opposite end to make another impression. Place a pencil dot at each end. Punch small holes at the pencil dot, then, draw a straight line connecting the two holes. Cut along this line with an Exacto knife, making an opening for the buckle loop finding to be inserted through. This is the paper pattern to place down on the backing.

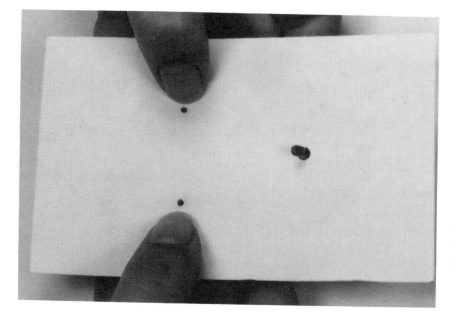

Step 3

Once the buckle is glued, stitch the opening back together with size B thread or heavier. The easy outside trim stitch is another stitch that can be used for the outside trim part of this project. See Large Hat Bands, Chapter 8 for the instructions for this stitch. The Buckle is now complete.

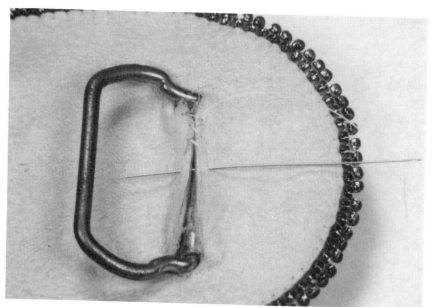

Chapter 7

- *Small Hat Bands* -

Step 1

CONCHOS & BEAD WORK. Turn over and fill in the back with Goo glue until the concho is almost level. Let dry 24 hours. Now, add enough glue to make it completely level. This concho size is 3/4 inch.

Step 2

Turn concho over and place it down onto the Pellom and note card. If you are planning to make a hat band, you will need at least a 3 x 5 inch piece of note card and Pellom. If a longer piece is required, a piece of typewriter paper is OK. Any paper close to the thickness of the note card is OK.

Step 3

Here is an easy way to make sure that the piece is straight. Lay a two foot piece of tiger tail across the middle of the piece. Make sure that you have an even amount of tiger tail on each side. Sew the tiger tail down to the back of the hat band with the same steps used in the Paua Stone Necklace except that you will be sewing straight across the piece instead of around it. Skip all of the places where all of the conchos or stones have been glued. The needle won't go through.

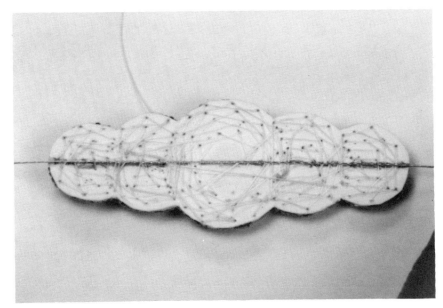

Step 4
We have used ultra-suede for the backing. Once you have completed sewing down the tiger tail, place a thin layer of glue over the back of the bead work and place it down onto the ultra-suede. Cut off the excess ultra-suede and add the outside trim, the same stitch as the earring, necklace and barrette.

Step 5
The colors in this hat band are the Paua Stone colors. Next, add the beads of your choice onto the tiger tail. Use five size 11 bronze seed beads first. You may use Austrian crystals, hemitite stars, Czechoslovakian cut bronze glass beads that are 4 mm, 5 mm or no larger than 6 mm for the hat band chain.

Step 6
Measure the beads around a hat and leave about four inches of space for the findings in the back. Use two crimp beads at the end of each beaded chain. Attach each tiger tail chain to a three inch length of sterling silver chain. This link type of chain is called 4.7 mm short and long.

Step 7

Attach one 3 x 9.3 mm sterling silver lobster claw about one inch from the end of one silver chain, using flat nose and round nose pliers and one 4 mm sterling silver jump ring. Close the jump ring as even and as close together as you can. Place a tiny drop of Super Glue gel on the cut-line of the jump ring you have just closed. This will be an extra safety measure. Glue all jump rings in this way.

Step 8

Hook the lobster claw to the opposite chain. Try to leave almost the same length of chain on each side to add the dangles. Here I have attached two, 1/2 inch long natural crystal points with two, 4 mm jump rings. 1/4 inch silver plated bell tips are Super glued to cover the top of the 1/2 inch crystal points. Small silver charms or other small momentoes can also be added to hang as a dangle.

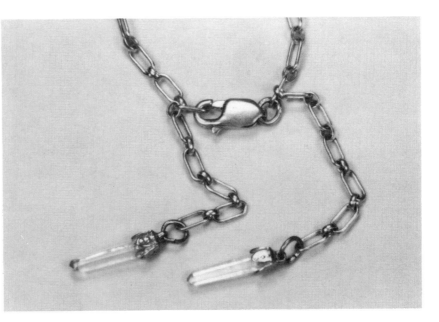

Step 9

Take an idea from your hat band and make earrings to match.

The price of this Hat Band or any other bead work that you create should be based on the value of the materials you have used plus a reasonable hourly wage.....$5 to $10???... You should decide what your time is worth.
Hat Band - $200.00
Heart Earring - $90.00

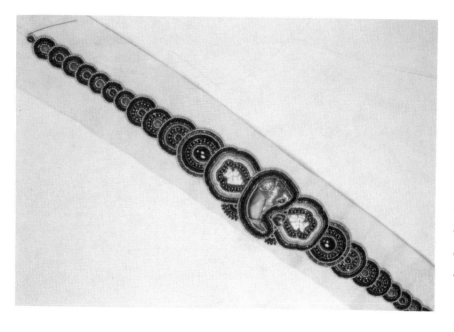

Chapter 8
-Large Hat Bands-

Step 1

Glue a strip of paper onto the back of the Pellom with a thin layer of glue. Let dry overnight. Always start the hat band by sewing or gluing the center-piece first. Use GOO or STIX-ALL. When using cabochons, only glue them where they can lay flat. The front, center is usually always a safe place for a stone that will not be sewn down.

Step 2

From the center of the hat band, sew to the right, adding one row at a time. Here we are showing you how to sew around a 4 mm hemitite bead, adding three to four seed beads at a time. Once each row is completed, go back up through the paper and Pellom at the beginning of each row where you have added the first seed bead. Now sew the needle through the whole row of seed beads. This will take a few steps to sew through the whole row. When you have come out of the seed beads at the end of each row, sew down through Pellom and paper at the exact end of the last seed bead. Pull on the thread lightly to tighten the row.

Step 3

When the bead work is completed, add on thread to tack down seed beads that are sticking up. Sew up through the bead work and in between the row that needs this step.

Step 4

Sew over the row where the two seed beads need to be tightened. The thread should slip between the two seed beads. Pull the thread lightly. Tie a knot in the back of the bead work to hold this step in place.

Step 5

Refer back to Conchos & Beadwork (Chapter 6) for this step. Measure the bead work around the hat band as you are adding each row of bead work. For the last row, we will add a sterling silver, 1/2 inch, concho earring post. Measure from the post in back to the edge of this concho. Place a pencil mark on the center-line of the Pellom. Poke a hole with a large sewing needle, or soft sculpture needle at the pencil mark. Push the concho through the hole. The concho should be as close to the bead work as possible. Add one row of silver seed beads around the concho.

Step 6

To make a pattern for the leather ties, measure and cut out two strips of paper, 1/2 inches x eight inches. Cut the leather strips out from this pattern and place a pencil mark at one end of the strip. Center the dot 1/4 inch from the edge. Poke a small hole with a large sewing needle or soft sculpture needle to place the post through the leather.

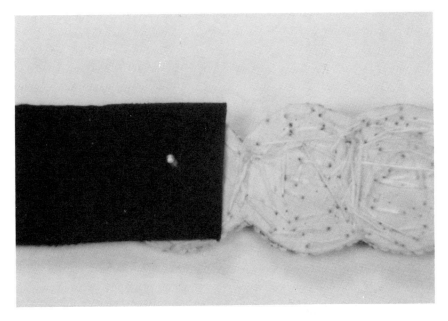

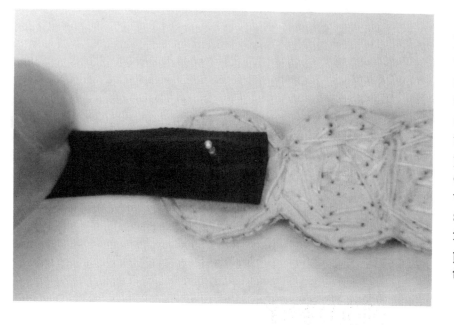

Next fold the leather over so that the two outside edges of the strip meet in the center. Press each side down so they will lay flat in the center and touch each other. Press down all the way to the end of the strip. With a tooth pick, place a thin line of glue down the inside center of the strip. Press the strip all the way down again. The folded leather strip should meet in the middle and lay flat. With the flat nose pliers, bend the post over and flat, towards the center of the bead work.

Step 8

Turn the piece over and adjust the leather strip to center it with the concho.

Step 9

Lay the hat band down onto a long strip of leather. You want to have about 1/2 inch of excess leather all the way around the bead work. Trim both edges so that the long strip of leather backing will end at the edge of each concho. Put a thin layer of STIX-ALL glue only over the back of the bead work. Place the bead work down onto the suede side of the leather. Press gently again to make sure that the leather backing is right to the edge of the concho.

Step 10

EASY OUTSIDE TRIM STITCH:
Adding on the bottom outside trim. Sew the outside trim stitch in the bottom row of the hat band by only adding one seed bead at a time. Do this stitch only on the bottom half. For the top half, sew the outside trim stitch the same as in the Paua Stone earring. The reason for only one seed bead at a time on the bottom half is to help the hat band lay nice and clean against the hat.

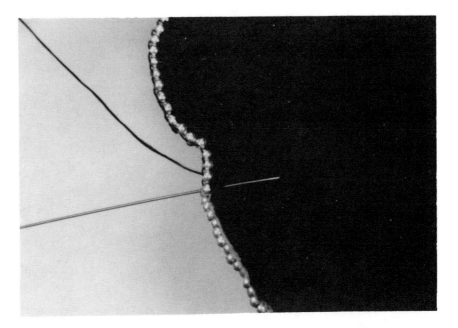

Step 11

Once you are close to running out of thread and there is about six to eight inches left, add the last seed bead and sew through and between the snakeskin and the Pellom. Come up through the Pellom two to three rows of seed beads and up through the Pellom and bead work. Once you are through the Pellom and bead work, tie a knot to secure the thread. Sew through the Pellom a few times, sewing away from the knot. Pull on and cut the excess thread as close as possible to the bead work.

Step 12

HOW TO ADD ON MORE THREAD:
Start with a two yard single strand of thread with a knot on one end. Sew through and between any two rows of bead work at least 1/2 inch from the outside trim stitch and through the one seed bead before the last seed bead you have added. Sew through the next seed bead to the right as if you were adding on this bead. Now you may continue adding on the outside trim.

Step 13

Once you come to the end of the bottom row of the hat band(after you add the last seed bead for this bottom row) sew through the leather until you come out through leather in the strip. Come out about 2 mm from the top center of the strip. Stitch the leather strip together as we have shown in the beaded belt buckle. The thread should not show through the front of the strip. The strip can also be sewn with a sewing machine. Buy a loop turner that includes instructions. Only use the loop turner for the strips just before attaching them to the conchos.

Step 14

Place the hat band on the hat to see where it will need to be connected together. Stitch the two strips together at this point. One or two stitches will hold it. Cover this spot with a small piece of leather about 1/2 inch wide. 1/2 wide Peyote bead work can also be added over the band. Here we have attached the two strips together by placing a silver concho over the two strips. The concho will need to have two small strips of copper or other soft metal soldered to it and bent over with a pair of flat nose pliers. Always lay the strips on top of each other in a crisscross manner.

Step 15

Next, use Super Glue gel or GOO to glue a sterling silver miniature bolo tip to the end of each strip. Peyote stitch can also be used on the end of the strip. Your hat band is now complete.

Chapter 9
-The Lizard Stick Pin-

Step 1 Applique Stitch

With a pencil, trace over any drawing onto tracing paper or a thin piece of Pellom. Place the drawing on a piece of Pellom or ultra-suede and note card backing. For texture, I have glued a 5 mm x 15 mm black onyx cabochon so the lizard's back will set up. Bead right over the stone and sew through each row of seed beads twice. This will secure the beads in place. Make sure that the beads lay flat and tight against the object. Less expensive objects can be used, but it is neat to be able to say that he has a real gem for his tummy.

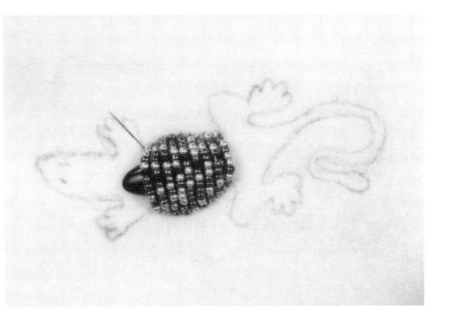

Step 2

Cut off the excess Pellom when the bead work is done. Make a pencil dot in the back of the lizard where the stick pin can be safely placed. Leave enough space on each side of the stick pin pad for the outside trim stitch to fit. We will use a snake skin for the backing. Trace around the lizard bead work with a pencil. Poke a hole at the pencil dot in the snake skin tracing and insert pin back through the hole. Remove the pin back and, then, glue the stick pin to the back of the bead work and let dry for two hours.

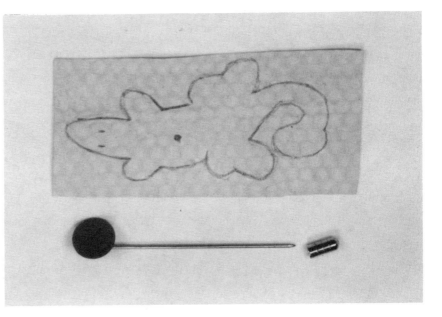

Step 3

Next, place a thin layer of glue on the back of the beaded lizard and put the snake skin backing and bead work together. For a clean look, use the easy outside trim stitch, adding only one seed bead at a time all the way around. See Large Hat Bands for this stitch. NOTE: Always wipe off excess glue on the backing. The lizard is now complete.

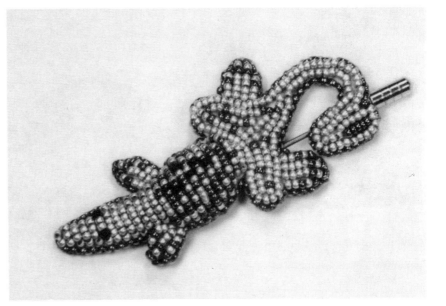

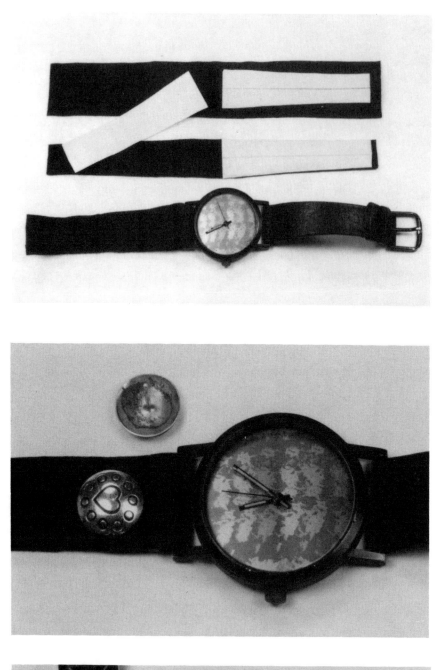

Chapter 10
- Beaded Watch Bands -

Step 1

First, the pin holding the watch band in place will have to be removed, it's also called a spring bar. A smart husband or your local jeweler will remove it for you. Trace four paper patterns using the side of the band that has no buckle. Draw a line down the center of each paper pattern. Fold a strip of ultra-suede in half and cut a strip slightly larger than the pattern and twice as long. Glue the two wide ends of the patterns facing each other about 3 mm apart down onto the ultra-suede strip, use a glue stick.

Step 2

Place the spring bar back onto the watch. Trim the strip and insert it through the bar. Make sure it fits evenly. If you plan to use a concho, be sure to fill the back with glue. Refer back to conchos & beadwork.

Step 3

A concho earring post can be used by placing the post through the top layer of ultra-suede. With a flat nose pair of pliers, bend the post back towards the opposite direction of the watch face. Be sure the post back lays flat.

Step 4

This strip can be glued down to a larger strip of Pellom. This will make the piece easier to hold while beading. To measure the beaded band to fit correctly, use tape or small straight pins to temporarily put the band around your wrist. For this watch band, I will use a treasure watch clasp. Other clasps may be used, try to use one that opens easily.

Step 5

Hearts and gem stone beads, or other objects with holes drilled through them may be used. Objects that can be sewn down are the safest to use. I do not recommend cabochons for this project.

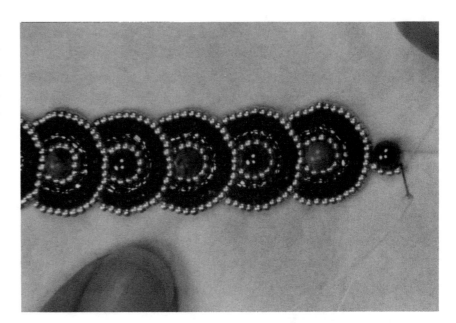

Step 6

Once the band is the correct size, insert it through the clasp. Again, be sure that it fits before you do any trimming. Trim off excess ultra-suede and also trim the end of the band. Leave about 1/2 inch of the band. Fold the two ends together facing each other so they do not show in the back of the watch. Trim off the excess ultra-suede. Glue the watch band strips and stitch the band ends together at the fold and add the outside trim. Do not sew an outside trim stitch around the clasp.

Chapter 11
- The Easy Whip Stitch -

Step 1

Begin by tracing around a sterling silver 3/4 inch concho onto a thin piece of snake skin or thin piece of leather. Cut out the piece by following the pencil line. Next, cut this circle in half. Use GOO and glue each half to the back of each concho. Let dry three hours. A button or cabochon may be used for this project.

NOTE: You will need to cut three snake skin circles for this project.

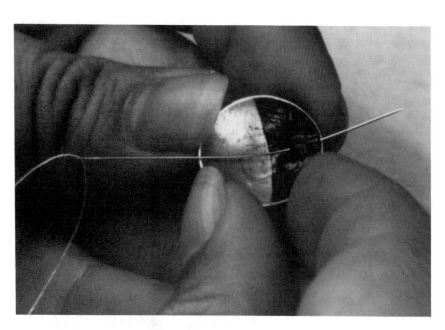

Step 2

This stitch is great for larger discs, also to eliminate the outside trim for a clean smooth look. Tie a knot at the end of a single strand of thread approximately one yard long. Sew down through the center of the circle about 1/8 inch from the edge. Add the center row of beads for the first row. See Pattern Y on the next page.

Step 3

Once the first row has been added, sew back up through this first row and up through the snake skin, 2 to 3 mm to secure the first row of beads.

= **Hand-stamped Sterling Silver concho, 3/4 inch**

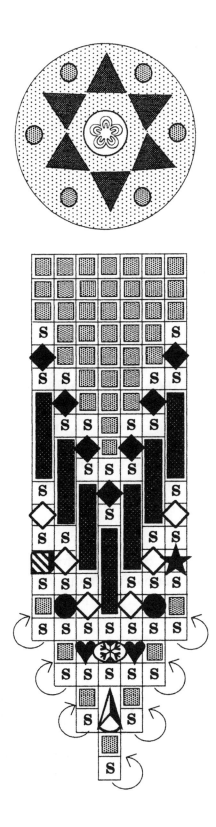

$\boxed{\text{Y}}$

Silver Concho with Treasure Fringe

▦	= Black matte seed bead, 14/0
S	= Silver seed bead, 14/0
◆	= Grey Austrian crystal, 4mm
◇	= Aurora Borealis cut glass, 5mm
♥	= Black onyx heart, 6mm
★	= Hematite star, 6mm
●	= Czecho nailhead, 5mm
✳	= Bali spacer bead, 6mm
◩	= Square Hematite bead, 4mm
▮	= Black matte bugle bead, 20mm
△	= Austrian crystal drop, 6mm x 10mm, with vertical hole through drop

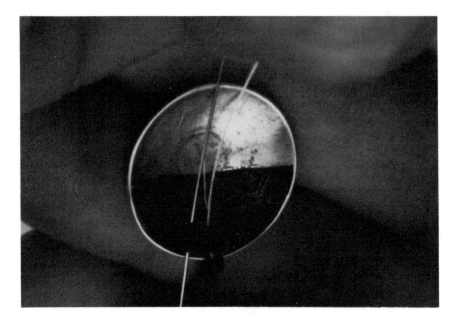

Step 4

Reverse the needle and come over 2 mm to the left, and sew down through the snake skin. Hold the snake skin in place, each time you sew and pull the needle through.

Step 5

Add four more rows until you have five rows across from the center of the concho to the left. Once you have sewn back up through the snake skin after adding five rows, tie a knot at the top of the row to secure all five rows. Now, sew over to the center row of the concho, reverse the needle and sew down through the snake skin, 2mm over to the right, from the center row of the concho. Add four more rows until you have a total of nine rows. Tie a knot at the top of the last row and cut the thread.

Step 6

To add the backing, use one of the snake skin circles. Pierce a hole 1/4 inch down from the top, center of the circle. Place a drop of glue on the hole before inserting the post. Put a thin layer of glue on the back of the concho and press the backing into place. Trim any excess backing that is showing through the front, around the top of the concho. Your earring is now complete.

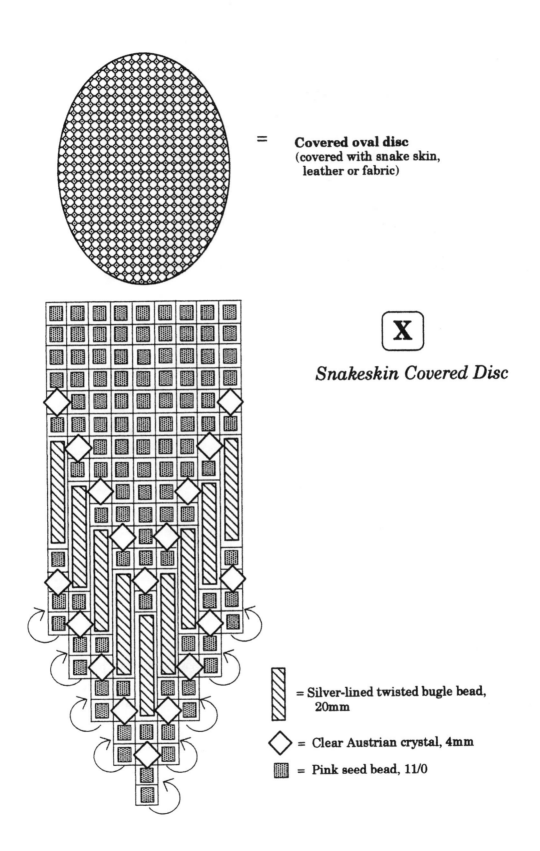

= **Covered oval disc**
(covered with snake skin,
leather or fabric)

$$\boxed{\textbf{X}}$$

Snakeskin Covered Disc

= Silver-lined twisted bugle bead,
20mm

= Clear Austrian crystal, 4mm

= Pink seed bead, 11/0

Chapter 12

- Covering Objects -

Step 1

Cover an object with snake skin, leather or fabric with a metal cover-quick ear clip. Start by cutting off the tabs that are on the outside edge of the back of the clip with a pair of diagonal cutters.

Step 2

Using the front part of the cover-quick ear clip, trace and cut around this domed disc about 3 mm larger than the disc, with a pencil. Wet the edges with water. With your fingers pressing lightly, fold the extra 3 mm over the back of the disc.

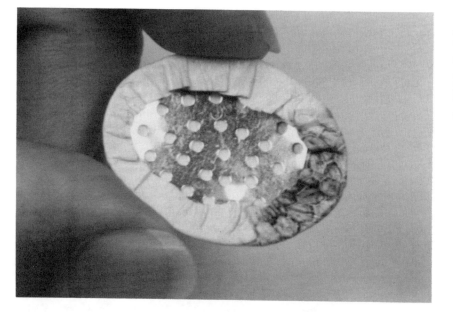

Step 3

Now, press the 3mm of snake skin over and against the back of the disc with your right thumb and fold the edges to lay flat and smooth over the disc. Let dry two hours.

Step 4

With a single strand of thread with a knot at one end, start by sewing down through the snake skin in the center, underneath the folded edge.

Step 5

Add the first row of beads, see pattern X. Sew back up through the same hole in the first, center row of beads.
NOTE: This will be the longest row of beads in this earring. Put at least 12 seed beads on to start the pattern for an earring that is to be nine rows across.

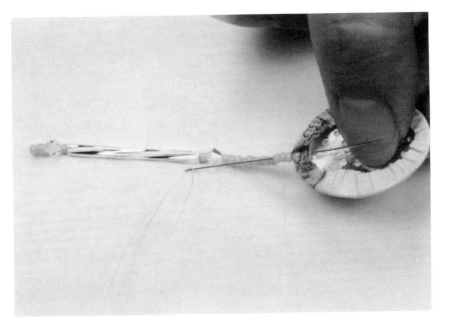

Step 6

Sewing to the right, come over approximately 2 mm and sew down through the snake skin. You will be reducing this pattern by two seed beads each row

Step 7

Add the second row and sew back up through the same hole. Repeat the last two steps until you have five rows to the right. Tie a loop knot underneath the fold to secure the five rows. Next come back to the center row and sew down through the snake skin 2 mm to the left of the center row. Add the next four rows of beads sewing only to the left of the center row until you have a total of nine rows across. Tie another loop knot underneath the fold to end the last row.

Step 8

Using STIX-ALL glue, add a thin layer of glue to the back of the beaded disc, only on the 3mm folded edges of snake skin. Place the back of the clip onto the back of the beaded disc and let dry for three hours.

Step 9

Your earring is now complete.

When a stone is set very high, you can build it up with a second row of bead work.

Glue the stone onto the Pellom and bead a single row around the stone. Add another row on top of the first row by using the same steps and sewing to the inside of the first row, down through the Pellom. Stay close to the stone at each step.

When making a heart earring, use a 5 mm post pad. Once the bead work is complete, trace around the heart and cut out the heart shape tracing. This will be the pattern to find the correct place for the post to be inserted. For a sideways earring, you want the post to be to the right or left corner, depending on which earring you are making. For a left sideways earring the post will set to the top right and vice versa.

For an earring where the heart sets straight up in the normal heart position, the post will be at the top center as the Paua stone earring. That is the straight up position. You will also have to trace a pattern to find the right place to insert the post.

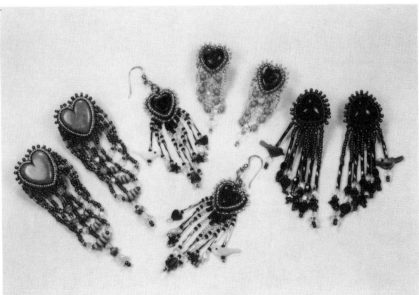

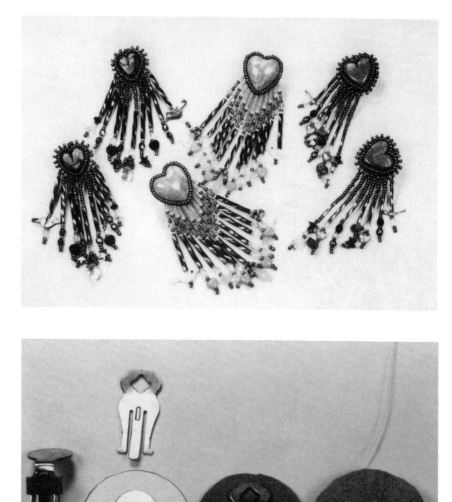

If you want to eliminate the outside trim when beading one row around the stone refer to the easy whip stitch to complete this earring. Add on the fringe by beading down from the note card and Pellom backing

Hearts can also be done with the same technique of only beading one row around the stone and eliminating the outside trim. See the center pair of heart earrings in this picture.

CLIP-ON EARRINGS

Make a paper pattern to plan exactly where you need the clip-on to be placed. The clip back part of this finding has been removed to make it possible to make smaller cuts. Squeeze the clip back carefully at the spot where it is connected to the pad. Mark small dots on each side of the metal finding at the bottom of the pad. Draw a straight line across from one dot to the other. This will be the spot to cut. Always make cuts slightly smaller than measured. Place the clip back on to the pad when the earring is complete.

BROACHES & FINDINGS

Cut a paper pattern for your broach. A base metal pin back finding will be needed slightly smaller than the bead work. Make cuts slightly smaller than the smallest side of the pin back finding so that you can weave the large lock side of the pin back through the front right side first, as you will see in this diagram. Do not glue the pin back to the back of the bead work first. You will need to draw guidelines on the back of the beadwork to put this finding in the correct place. Glue the pin back to the backing first. Let dry for one hour, then, glue the finding and backing to the back of the bead work.

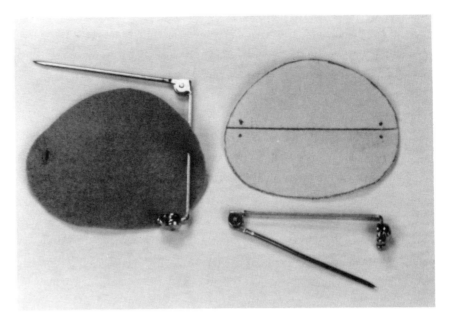

HAIR TIES

Hair ties can be made with either a concho or a beaded rosette. Thin leather or ultra-suede can be used for the backing. Punch small holes in the backing with a hole punch to insert the leather or elastic tie through. Glue the tie first to the back of the concho or bead work by placing a small amount of JB Weld Quick onto the center fo the backing. Let dry. Insert the tie or plastic through the punched holes and use GOO to glue the backing to the bead work or concho. For mini elastic ties, see hair tie on the right side. You must cut a small straight cut to insert the plastic through.

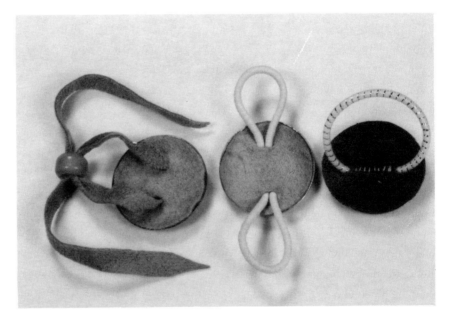

SMALL ROSETTES

Start small rosettes by sewing down 4 mm to 5 mm beads first. You can also glue down small cabochons. Always use one solid color of seed beads for the first row around the small bead or cabochon. The third earring from the left is a mountain scene. You will need to begin this earring by drawing a guideline across the center of the Pellom.

CONVERTIBLES

This porcelain rose with a post, glued on the back with 330 glue is fun to try. Attach different triangle earrings to the back without gluing them to the post. That will make this project two earrings instead of one. Antique buttons may also be used. NOTE: The bugle bead earring is not very pleasing for this project.

THE WEAVE

This stitch can only be used with an earring that is wide enough at the bottom to count 14 rows across. You will be adding on the pattern from every other row. Carefully fold the beads where you need to sew through the thread. B thread is heavy enough to use. Two threads can also be used for the weave. For two threads use size O. Try it both ways to see which is easiest for you.

The weave earring to the left is beaded with size 14 seed beads and 3 mm black Austrian crystals. When adding rows of seed beads above the stone, you need to make a pattern of the earring to find the correct place for the post to be inserted. The earring on the right is beaded with size 11 sead beads and 5 mm cut glass. The weave is the same, even though the seed bead size is different.

UNTWISTING TWISTED BEADING THREAD

Beading thread will tend to twist and tangle. Here we show a helpful hint to easily un-twist it. When thread begins to knot or twist while beading, hold the beaded piece by the end of thread where the needle is. Let the beaded piece spin in mid air until it stops. If the piece is too large to hold in mid air, hold it and let the whole strand of thread spin and untangle.

ADDING SEED BEADS BETWEEN 4MM & 5MM BEADS

Here we are using 14/0 seed beads. Come out through the note card and Pellom as close to the 4mm or 5mm bead as possible. Sew over and in between the beads using 7 to eight seed beads. This will hide any gaps the large beads can make. After this step is complete, then, one row of size 14/0 seed beads should be added all the way around this row of beads.

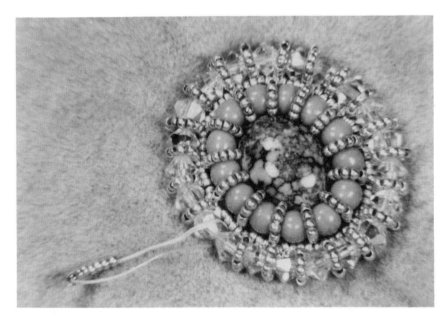

ATTACHING A CONE CLASP

Use silk cord, size four, to string 4 to 5mm beads. To attach a cone, wire wrap a small loop of 22 gauge sterling silver wire approximately three inches long. Insert the thread through the silver loop and tie the thread as close to the loop as possible. Paint a very small amount of Henrietta's glue onto the knot. Cut the thread 1 to 2mm away from the knot. Pull the silver wire through a small cone and wire wrap the remaining wire to a hook and eye. Refer to wire wrapping conchos.

NOTE: You will use one cone on each side of the necklace chain, attach the hook to one and the eye to the other cone.

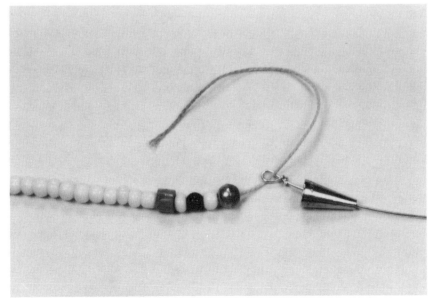

INDIAN CORN EARRINGS

Cut the top part of a tooth pick, one inch long. Cut a piece of ultra-suede to measure 1/2 inch X 1 1/4 inch. Use 1 1/2 inch of 22 gauge wire to make a loop for the French wire to be attached. See combining silver smithing with Peyote stitch to make the loop. Glue the tooth pick and wire on to the ultra-suede at one end and roll them up until they are completely covered by the ultra-suede. Glue the open end closed and revue the steps of beading around a feather. Once you are at the bottom of the corn cob, sew up through the last row you have added, pulling the thread to draw it close together to a point. Cut out a corn husk with ultra-suede, about 1 inch x 1/4 inch wide. Trim the ends to a point and make a small slit in the center to insert through loop.

BUGLE BEAD CONVERTIBLES

Here is a unique technique to add on a sterling silver 1/2 inch concho with a post on the back, to a bugle bead earring. Place the post through an opening in the earring in between the first and second row of the seed beads at the top of the earring. Bend the post up towards the top to lay flat. The post must be attached to the center of the concho for this step to work properly. Make a pattern from the concho to cut two ultra-suede backings. Glue the ultra-suede backing onto the back of the concho to hide the post and seed beads.

This step can also be used for an earring on a post. Just remember not to bend the post over. Place it through the seed beads and cover it with the ultra-suede backing. NOTE: Use a long post for this project.

WIRE WRAPPING A CRYSTAL PENDANT

Start by cutting two - eight inch pieces of 22 gauge half hard Sterling Silver wire. Lay one silver wire on each side of the crystal. You want the crystal to be in the center with an equal amount of silver wire on each side. Use flat nose pliers. Twist the two wires together two to three turns. Use your finger to press the twisted wire up towards the top and flat against the crystal

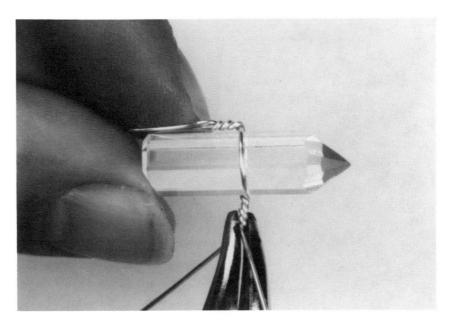

Step 2

Once the two twisted sides are flat against the crystal, cross one wire from each side across the front of the pendant. Do this in the front of the crystal and also the back. Next, twist the two wires that will now meet on each side. Also, press them flat against the top of the crystal. Press the four wires towards the top center above the crystal and wrap one set of two wires around the other set. Do this wrap three to four wraps. Then, cut off the remaining wire from the wire you just wrapped. Use the round nose pliers to make a top loop and wrap it three or four times.

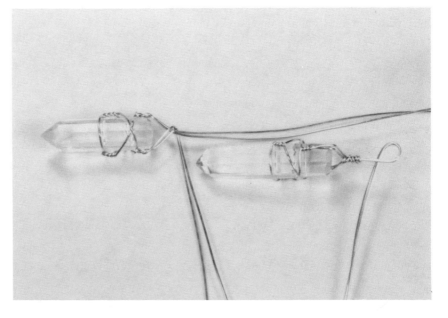

Step 3

Use a pair of flat nose pliers and gently take a hold of the wire in front of the crystal and twist it to the right. Do this also on each side of the crossed wire that is right above the twist. This will tighten the wire and secure the crystal in place. The wire wrap is now complete. NOTE: A 10mm crystal bead may be placed on the wire at the top before the top loop is made. The choice is yours. ENJOY...

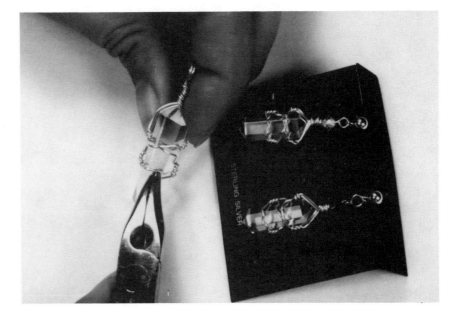

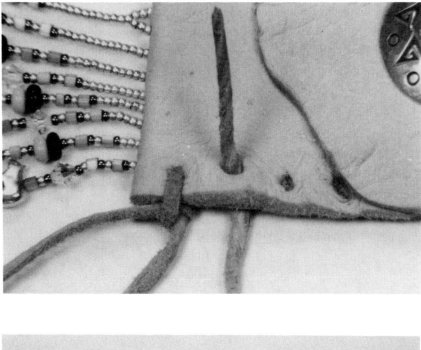

LEATHER LACED BAGS

Use a small pair of leather shears to cut a 2 1/2 inch by 8 inch piece of thin leather. Also cut 2 thin 20 inch strips for the neck strap. Fold the bag in place to have a 5 inch flap over the front. Add the beaded fringe now by sewing out through the bottom of the bag using the easy whip stitch. Use a hole punch to punch small holes approximately 1/4 inch apart up the side of the bag. Do not punch holes in the flap. Tie 1 neck strip to the bottom of the side of the bag. Leave approximately 1 1/2 inch of loose leather strip to hang from the bag. Take the long opposite end of the strip and come from behind the bag. insert it through the next hole up to the right. Repeat this last step till you come to the top.

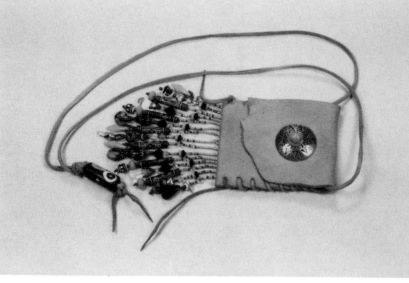

Tie the ends of the 2 strips together to complete this special bag. A large bead can be added to the end. Tie a knot after the large bead to secure it in place. Crystals, herbs, or hand carved miniature animals can be placed inside the bag to ward off evil spirits, or to bring good luck. The choice is yours.

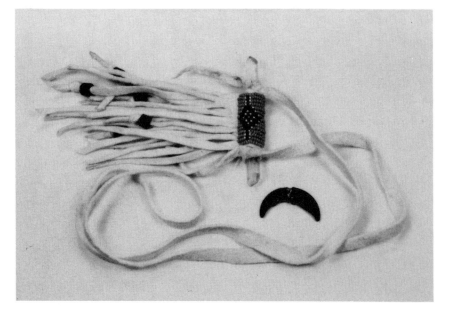

CRYSTAL AND MEDICINE BEAR CLAW PENDANTS

The top end of 2 crystal points or 2 bear claws, can be glued together with 330 Glue horizontally and covered with long strips of brain tanned buck skin leather. Old trade beads can be added to the fringe. This buck skin leather is usually white in color and velvety soft. It is tanned in a traditional Indian way. Ceremonial indian bags, clothing and other adornments are made from this soft leather hide.

BRAIDED BUCK-SKIN BAG

(Braided, buck-skin bag.) Beadwork can be done right onto a buck-skin circle, but, most leather hides are much too tough to sew through with a beading needle. It is best to start the beadwork on ultra swede or Pellom. This rosette is 12 rows of beadwork plus the out side row of trim, and fringe.

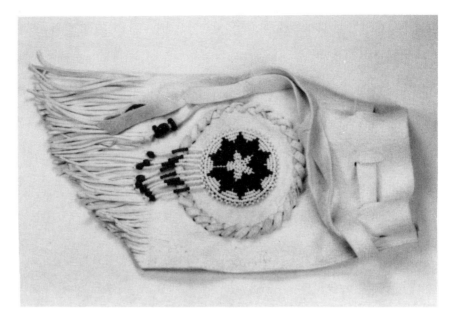

Step 2

Place a pencil dot in the center of the circle and glue the note card or paper on the back and begin the beadwork at the pencil dot. Be sure to put a thin leather or ultra swede backing on the beaded rosette before stitching it down. When beadwork is completed use a small pair of leather shears and cut a perfect circle approximately 3 1/2 inches wide, or at least 1/2 inch larger then the beadwork. This measurement will work for 12 rows of beadwork.

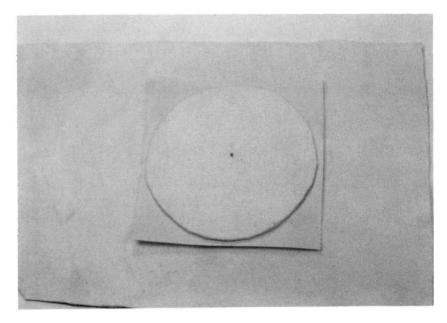

Step 3

Some household sewing machines can be used to sew thin garment leather, but you will need to buy a leather needle for your machine. Heavier thread is also needed. Use the paper pattern to cut out the 2 pieces of thin buck-skin or thin leather for this bag, which will be 6 inches by 11 inches. Next, use a yard stick to measure and cut 1 strip of leather for the strap, 1 yard long and 1/4 inch wide.

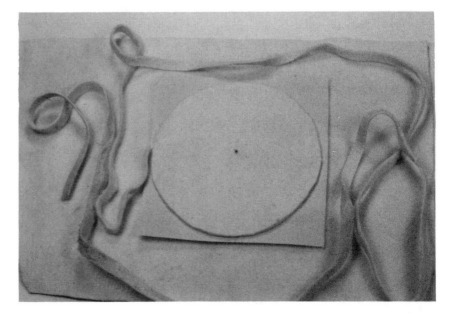

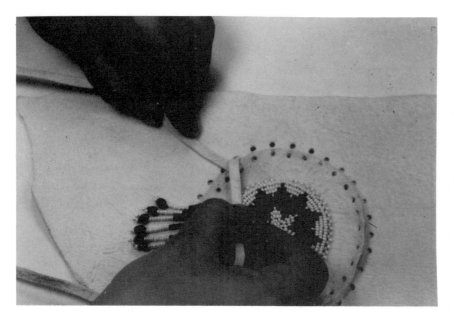

Step 4

Once the bead work is complete, glue, then stitch the bead work down onto the leather circle you have cut out for the top of the beaded bag. Glue the bead work and circle down on to the center of the bag. Make pencil dots to punch holes around the edge of the leather circle about 1/4 inch apart. Next, punch holes that will match up with the previous holes onto the outside of the leather circle. come from behind the bag and insert the one yard leather strip up through any of the holes that are beside each other. Pull the two strips together to measure the length on each side to be the same.

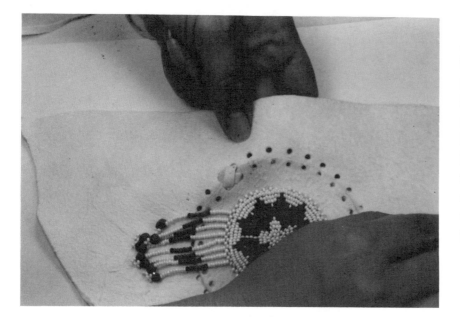

Step 5

A leather awl can be used to insert through the holes to keep them round. Once you are through the front side of the bag, cross the two strips, laying them over each other. Insert each strip into the next two holes down. Pull on each strip lightly to lay them flat in place. Trim the end of each leather strip to a point. This will help you to insert each end through each hole much easier.

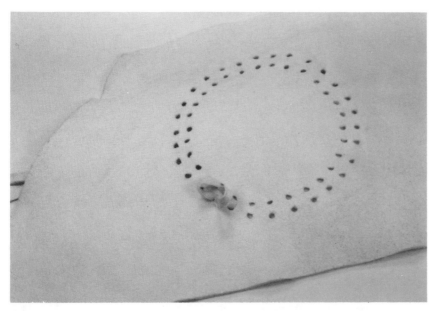

Step 6

Once the strips are inserted through to the back of the bag, cross the 2 strips and place them back through the same 2 holes you have just came out of. Pull on the strips lightly to lay them flat and in place. You will be repeating the same 2 previous steps until you are all the way around the circle.

NOTE: this technique can be used on many different projects, smaller or larger. The braid will protect the beadwork and also add a nice look to any finished piece

Step 7

Once you are back through the front side of the bag, cross the 2 strips, laying them over each other, and insert each strip into the next 2 holes down. Pull on the strips lightly to lay them flat in place.

Step 8

Once your through the back of the bag, again cross the 2 strips and place them through the same 2 holes you have just came out of. Pull on the strips lightly to lay them flat in place.

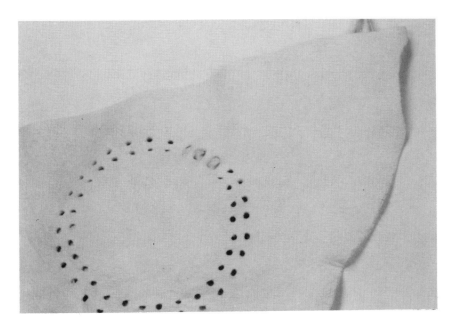

Step 9

Repeat the same two previous steps until you are all the way around the circle. Insert each strip back through the same 2 holes where you began, in the back side of the bag. Sew the 2 strips together while laying them as flat as you can. Place this front part of the bag down onto the back part. Place a small dot of GOO glue on the inside of the bag at each of the 4 corners where you will sew it together. This will hold the bag in place while you are sewing.

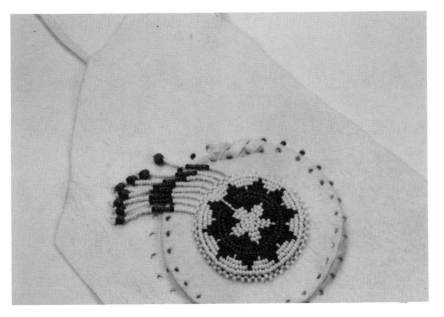

You will need a leather needle for your sewing machine to sew the bag together, sewing very slowly always practice sewing each bag with a piece of leather scrap first. Once the bag is sewn, trim the sides as close to the stitches as possible. Next, with a ruler place pencil dots approximately 1 1/4 inches apart, with a hole punch. Punch a hole at each pencil dot. Cut the slits for your bag. Cut towards the top, the opposite direction of the beadwork.

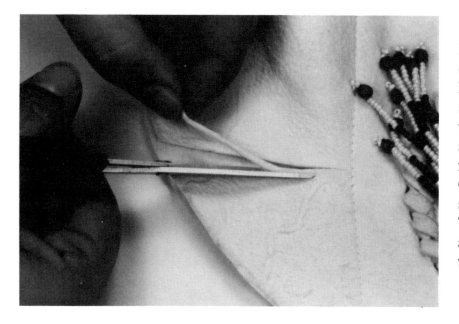

Step 11

If you planned for fringe, start in the center and cut thin strips. Once you have 1 inch of the strip started, hold the strip with your left hand and pull lightly while cutting. Always cut your fringe starting in the center, and to the right for a twisted affect on your fringe. Once all the fringe is cut, wipe each strip with a small amount of water. Twist the strip and hold the twist for approximately 1 minute. Pull lightly on the twisted strip and let go.

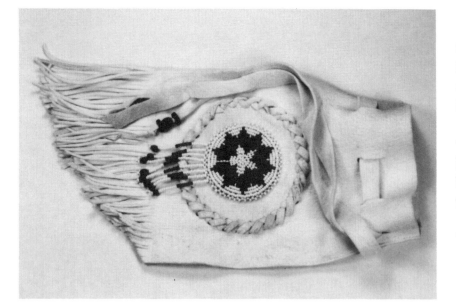

Step 12

Cut a strap, 1/2 inch by 32 inches. Place it through the slits, weaving both ends of the strap through to one side of the bag.

PLEASE NOTE: Try to always use thin leather or brain tanned buck skin for making bags. For smaller bags you will need to place the slits for the strap closer together.

Your bag is now complete.

BEADED PURSES AND BAGS

The bag on the right is an old beaded bag I bought years ago. It was beaded front and back and damaged on the sides. I took the bag apart and restored one beaded side back to the original style. The other beaded side I took and made a beaded purse. I braided around the beadwork with the same techniques I showed you in the Braided Buck-Skin Bag. To make the braid set higher, I placed a bolo tie cord underneath the braid. A piece of leather strip sewn into a tube can also be used. Use a loop turner to make the tubing.

For applique patterns place a paper drawing on the material you plan to bead onto, and bead right over it. With this hummingbird rosette I plan to make a white leather purse for my mother-in-law. I used size 16 seed beads for the birds face and size 14 cuts for the remaining steps. The background are those rare antique aluminum beads from France but she's worth it. The 4mm beads on the last row are amazonite, a yummy, greasy, transparent light green.

SNAKE SKIN HATBANDS

Use small snakes for hatbands. This hatband is 35 inches long after being cleaned and cured. Buy your snakeskin already tanned unless you have already learned how to do so. Trim the white outside belly first. Make a pattern by wetting and folding the snakeskin on the edges only, so the full part of the front snake pattern lays to the center. If you are making a rattlesnake hatband, you want the rattles to lay over the opposite end of the band 2 to 5 inches. Once the band is dry make a thin leather or felt pattern to insert into the band and another to cover for the snake backing.

Beaded White
Buckskin Shirt

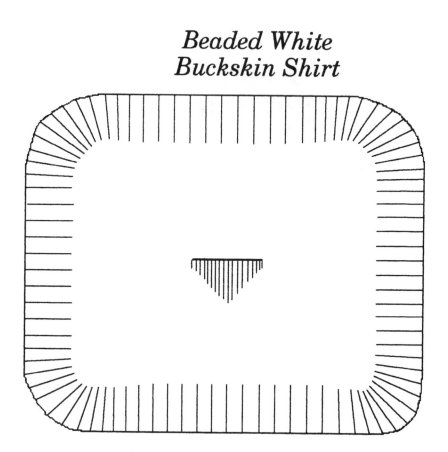

Fold leather hide in half. With a small pair of leather shears or an Exacto knife, cut neckline opening 10 inches across the fold in the center. Cut fringe on only one side of opening. Then cut fringe around the outside edge. Cut the fringe strips as straight as possible.

Add the beads last.

Fold in half length-wise. Tie two strips together underneath each arm to make sleeves.

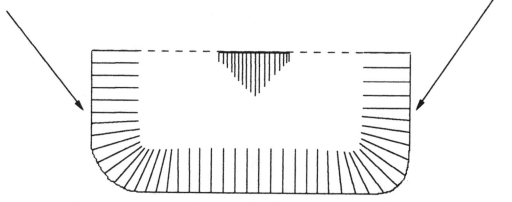

BEADED BUCKSKIN SHIRT WITH FRINGE

This shirt can be made without a sewing machine. This small hide is very soft from the special technique of the way it is brain tanned. It is white unless it is smoked, which will turn the hide yellow and give it a nice smoked flavor. It is so soft, a beading needle just simply glides right through it. It is very expensive and ranges from $10-$20 a square foot.

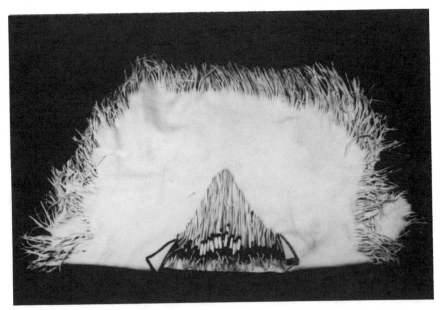

This hide measures 32 inches wide and 40 inches long. Fold the hide till the 2 longest ends meet. Use a small pair of leather shears or an Exacto knife to cut a neck line opening 10 inches across the fold in the center. Cut the outside fringe of the shirt about 3 to 4 inches long by cutting with the natural shape of the hide. To cut a v-neck fringe, use a ruler to place a pencil dot 6 inches down the center of the neck opening Draw a triangle pencil line from the dot back up to each side of the neck opening. Cut a straight line, 6 inches long, down the center to the pencil dot.

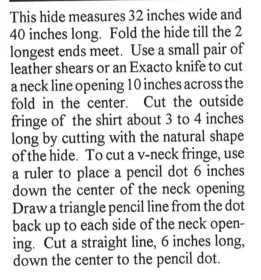

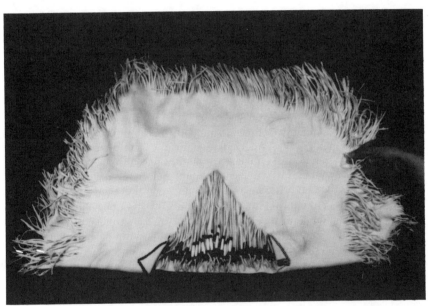

Cut your fringe from this center. Cut to the right. Work your way to the top by following the triangle pencil line, until you are approximately 2 inches from the top. This 2 inches will be folded over to the front to make a small collar. This will be tacked down by sewing on 5 seed beads at a time, at a slant, all the way up to the top of the fold. Cut to the left to complete the opposite side of the triangle neck fringe. Try the shirt on and tie 2 strips of leather underneath the arm of the fringe to make a sleeve. Add 5 to 10 mm beads with large holes to the neck fringe by tying a knot at the end of each fringe. This can be worn with or without a cotton turtleneck shirt underneath depending on the season.

Page 107

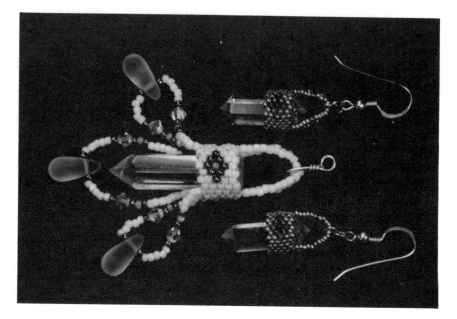

CHAPTER 14

- PEYOTE STITCH PENDANTS, NECKLACES, AND BOTTLES -

MATERIALS & TOOLS NEEDED:
English Beading Needles, size 13
White Nymo Beading Thread size 0
Seed beads, size 11/0,
Colors: white, bronze, turquoise.
1 - Crystal Point, approximately 9mm by 34mm for the Pendant, or
2 - Crystals approximately 6mm by 20mm for earrings.
1 - Tube of STIX-ALL glue.
1 - Pair of short, flat nose pliers.
1 - Pair of small round nose pliers
1 - Small pair of diagonal cutters
4 - Inches of Sterling Silver, 22 gauge half hard wire or
4 - 4mm Sterling Silver Jump Rings for crystal earring or pendant with or without drops.
1 - 20 inch Sterling Silver Necklace Chain for crystal pendant.
2 - Sterling Silver French Earwires.

CRYSTALS AND PEYOTE STITCH

Remember a crystal is a special gem that is grown naturally all over the world. It will stimulate brain functions, amplify thought forms, dispel negativity, receives, activates, stores, transmits, and amplifies energy. You will be in exact alignment with the Higher Self, with emotional, mental clarity and balance for love, life and happiness............HERES A PIECE OF THE ROCK......................
I mean earth...* * * * * *

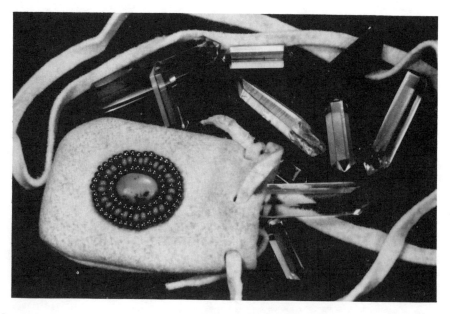

For every crystal you will use a different number of beads, but it will always be an even amount such as 10,12,14,16,18,20 and so on. Odd numbers, such as 11,13,15,17 will not work. Make sure the number of beads you start with are always an even number. Include the first bead you tie the knot to in your count. This crystal is approximately 9mm X 34mm and will be 22 beads around.

Step 1

For your peyote stitch project you want to start with approximately two yards of size O thread and one white seed bead size 11/0. Tie the thread together near the end and leave about ten inches of loose thread at the end of your bead.

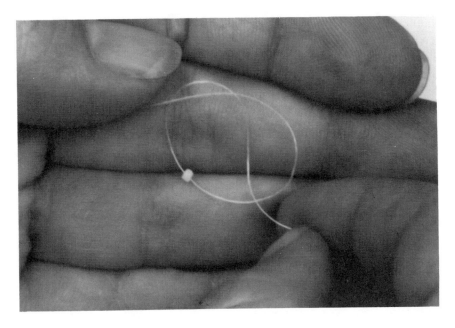

Step 2

Tie the thread together again, that will form your knot. You want it to be tight and very close to your first seed bead. Leave the same ten inches of loose thread from the bead until the end of the thread.

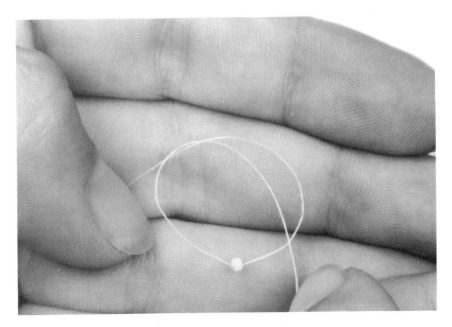

Step 3

For every crystal you will use a different amount of beads, but it will always be an even amount such as 10,12,14,16,18,20 and so on. 11,13,15,17 will not work. Include the first bead you tie the knot to in your count. This crystal is approximately 9mm X 34mm and will be 22 beads around. We will start with 22 beads and place them around the top to make sure they fit.

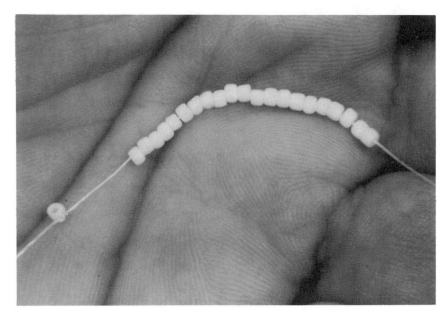

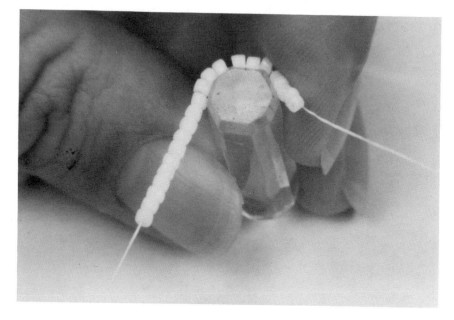

Step 4

With the 1 seed bead you tied a knot to plus the 21 seed beads you added on, you now have 22 seed beads to start with. Place them around the top of the crystal to make sure they fit closely. Do not leave a gap between the first seed bead and the last seed bead. Once you find the right amount of seed beads to wrap around the crystal, *make sure the count is always an even number.*

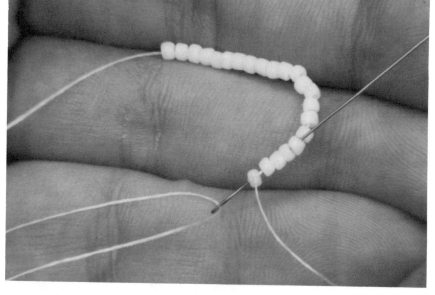

Step 5

Now take the loop of seed beads off the crystal and sew through the very first seed bead you have tied the loop knot to and then sew the next 4 seed beads. Finish the loop by sewing through the rest of the seed beads, forming a circle.

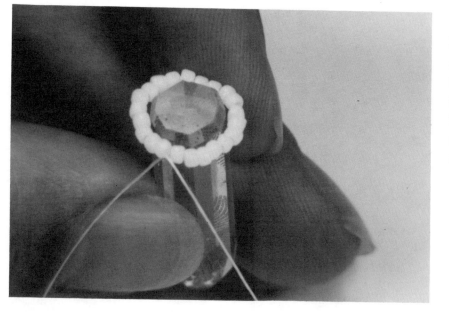

Step 6

Pull the circle together by pulling the thread lightly. The last seed bead you should sew through will be the first seed bead you have tied the loop knot to. Now, place the seed beads back around the top of the crystal. The first row is now complete.

Step 7

For the first step in the second row, you want to hold the 10 inches of loose thread down with your left thumb, to keep it out of the way. Add 1 white seed bead and skip a seed bead in the first row, and sew through the next white seed bead in the first row.

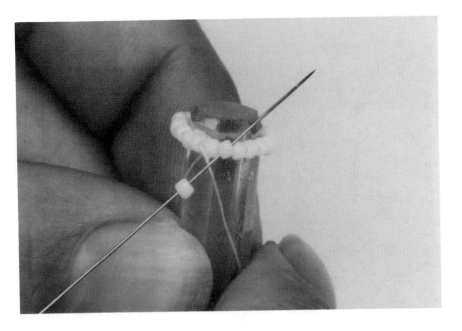

Step 8

Pull the thread to put the first white seed bead into place. This second row will have a total of 11 seed beads all the way around the crystal.

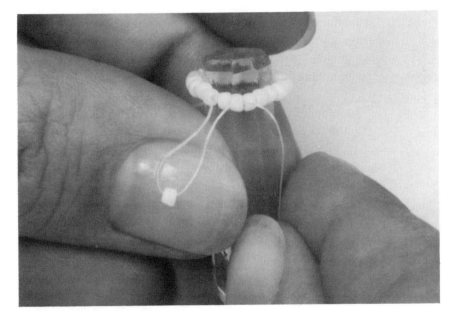

Step 9

Next add one white seed bead. Skip a bead and sew through the next white seed bead in the first row. Now add one white seed bead each time you skip a bead and go through every other white seed bead in the first row. The white seed beads you will add for the second should always lay underneath the white seed beads you are skipping in the first row. Follow this step until you are all the way around the second row, until you come to the last seed bead in the first row.

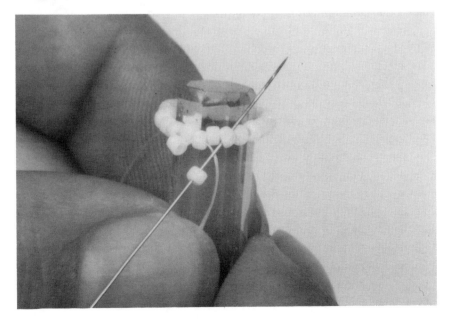

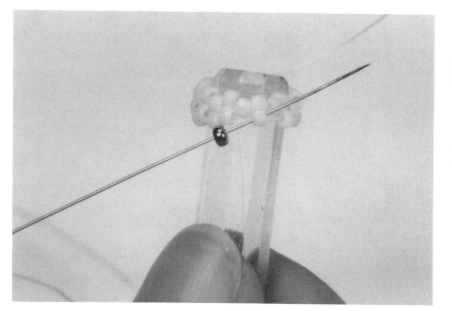

When you come to the last seed bead in the first row add 1 white seed bead, skip a bead and sew the last white seed bead in the first row and the first white seed bead in the second row. The second row is now complete. For the third row repeat the same steps as the second row. Add 1 white seed bead, skip a bead and so on until you are approximately 1/2 the way around the crystal.

Step 11

This will be the center of the crystal. Now add 1 bronze seed bead which will be the center diamond pattern. Continue to add 1 white seed bead. Skip a bead and so on till you are all the way around the crystal till you come to the first white seed bead in the second row.

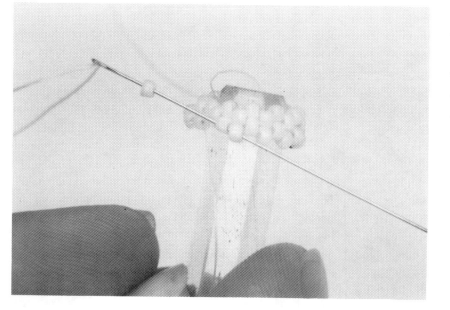

Step 12

Now add 1 white seed bead, skip a bead and sew through the first white seed bead in the second row and the first white seed bead in the third row. Your third row is now complete.

Step 13

For the fourth row , add one white seed bead. Skip a bead and so on till you are all the way round the crystal till you come to the first bronze seed bead, which is in the center diamond pattern. Add 1 bronze seed bead before you sew through the first center bronze seed bead.

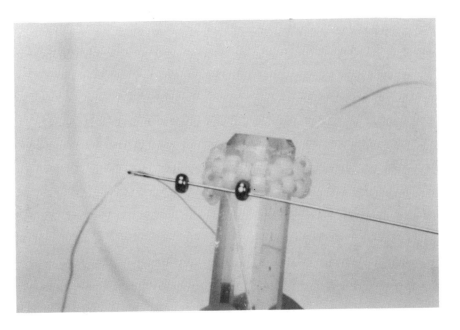

Step 14

Once you are through the center bronze seed bead, add 1 bronze seed bead. Skip a bead and sew through the next white seed bead in the third row. Continue to add 1 white seed bead. Skip a bead and so on until you are all the way around the crystal, until you come to the first white seed bead in the third row.

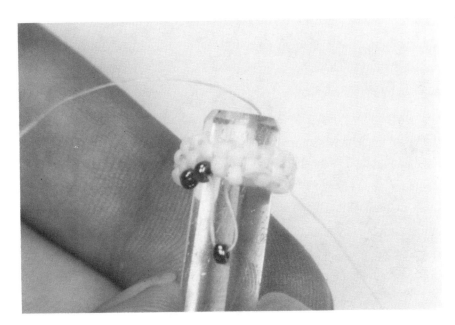

Step 15

Next add 1 white seed bead, skip a bead and sew through the first white seed bead in the third row and the first white seed bead in the fourth row. Your fourth row is now complete.

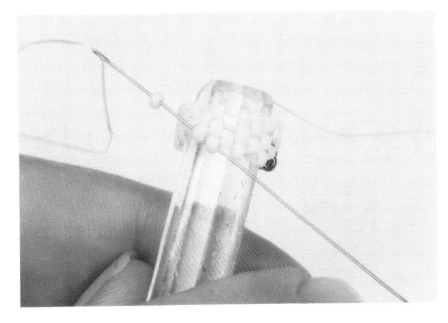

The fifth row will be, continue to add 1 white seed bead. Skip a bead and so on until you come to the bronze seed bead, the first bronze seed bead of the diamond pattern. Add 1 bronze seed bead before you sew through the first bronze seed bead in the diamond pattern.

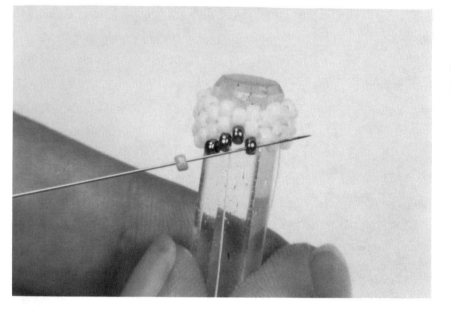

Step 17

Next add 1 turquoise seed bead, which is the center of the diamond pattern. Sew through the next bronze seed bead.

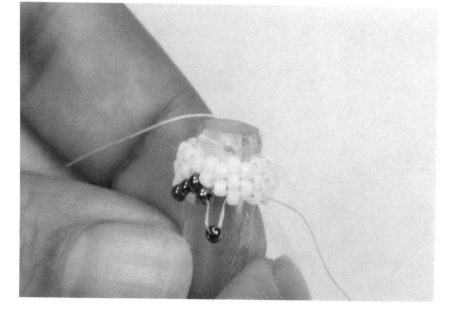

Step 18

Now add 1 bronze seed bead, skip a bead and sew through the next white seed bead. Make sure you always skip a seed bead before sewing through each step... Next continue to add 1 white seed bead. Skip a bead and so on till you are all the way around the crystal till you come to the first white seed bead in the fourth row.

Step 19

Add one white seed bead, skip a bead and sew through the first white seed bead in the fourth row and the first white seed bead in the fifth row. Your fifth row is now complete. For the sixth row continue to add one white seed bead. Skip a bead and so on till you are all the way around the crystal and you come to the bronze seed bead, the first bronze seed bead of the diamond pattern.

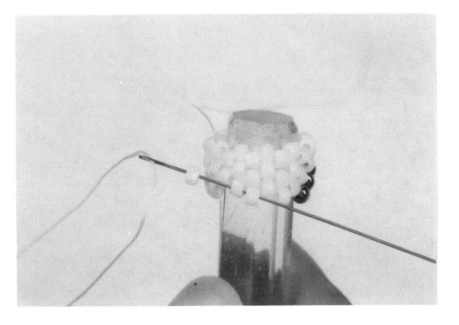

Step 20

Add one white seed bead. Skip a bead and sew through the bronze seed bead then skip a bead, add one bronze seed bead, skip a bead and sew through the turquoise seed bead which is the center of the diamond pattern.

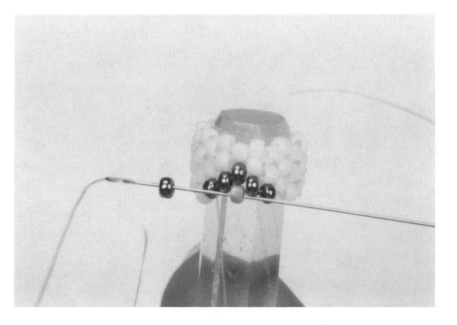

Step 21

Add one bronze seed bead, skip a bead and sew through the next bronze seed bead in the diamond pattern. Next, continue to add one white seed bead. Skip a bead and so on until you are all the way around the crystal and you come to the first white seed bead in the fifth row.

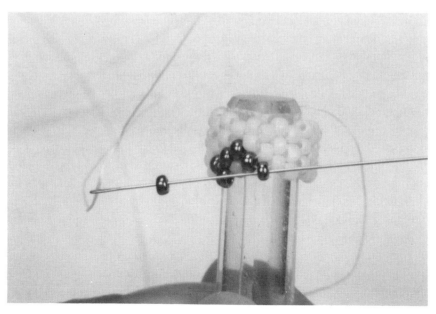

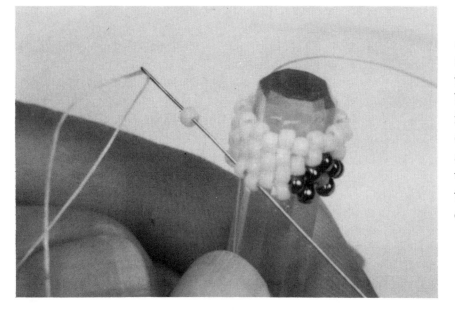

Add one white seed bead. Skip a bead and sew through the first white bead in the fifth row and the first white seed bead in the sixth row. Your sixth row is now complete. For the seventh row, continue to add 1 white seed bead. Skip a bead and so on until you are all the way around the crystal, and you come to the first bronze seed bead of the diamond pattern.

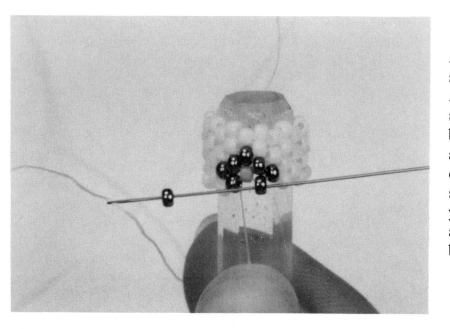

Step 23

Add 1 white seed bead, skip a bead and sew through the bronze seed bead. Add 1 bronze seed bead, skip a bead and sew through the next bronze seed bead. The bronze bead you have just added should be under the turquoise center bead. Continue to add 1 white seed bead. Skip a bead and so on until you are all the way around the crystal, and you come to the first white seed bead in the sixth row.

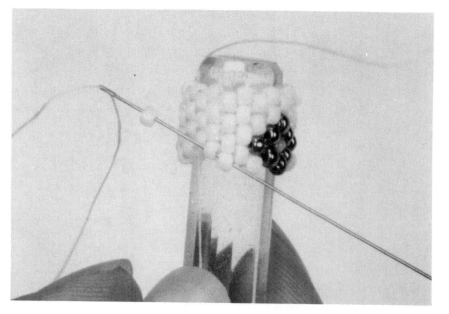

Step 24

Add 1 white seed bead, skip a bead and sew through the first white seed bead in the sixth row and the first white seed bead in the seventh row. The seventh row is now complete.

Step 25

For the eighth row, continue to add 1 white seed bead. Skip a bead and so on until you come to the last center bronze seed bead. Add 1 white seed bead, skip a bead before the center bronze seed bead. Then, sew through the center bronze seed bead. Continue to add 1 white seed bead. Skip a bead and so on until you are all the way around the crystal, and you come to the first white seed bead in the seventh row.

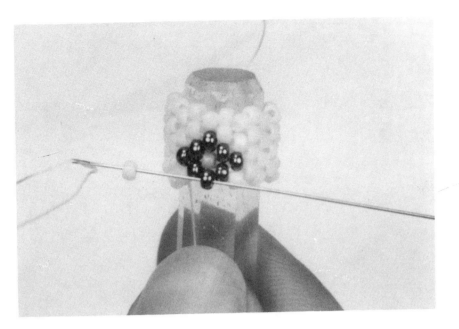

Step 26

Add 1 white seed bead, skip a bead. and sew through the first white seed bead in the seventh row and the first white seed bead in the eighth row. The eighth row is now complete.

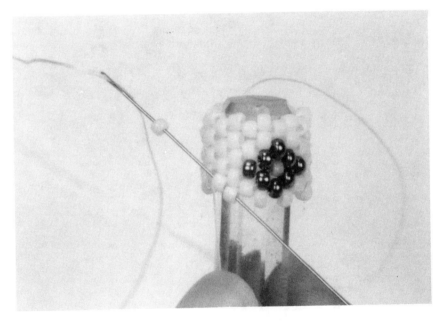

Step 27

For the ninth row, continue to add 1 white seed bead. Skip a bead and so on until you are all the way around the crystal and you come to the first white seed bead in the eighth row, and the first white seed bead in the ninth row.

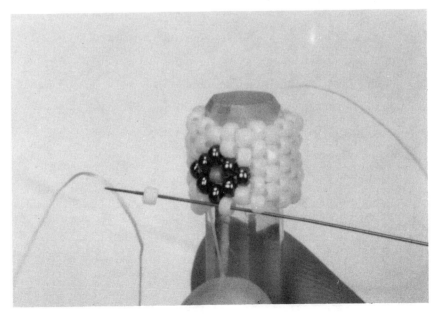

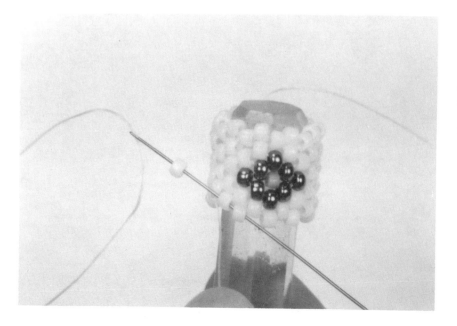

Step 28

Add 1 white seed bead, skip a bead. and sew through the first white seed bead in the eighth row and the first white seed bead in the ninth row. The ninth row is now complete.

Step 29

To add loops at the top, weave through the bead work by sewing through 1 or 2 beads at a time to the right in the bottom two rows of the bead work. Review step 28. It will be the same stitch, except you will not be adding seed beads. Sew to the right until you are about half way around the bead work. As you sew around, gradually work your way up towards the top left of the diamond pattern, one bead at a time.

NOTE: Always try to make sure that the thread and seed beads are going in the same direction. This method will hide the stitches and tighten the bead work at the same time.

Step 30

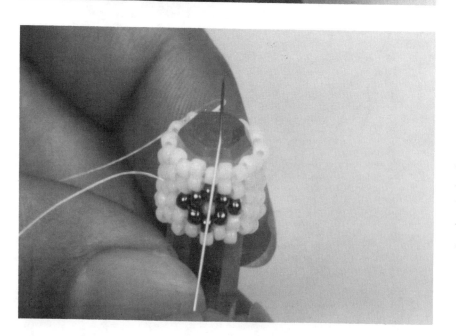

With the needle, find the center top of the diamond pattern. This will help to see exactly where you need to come out at the top of the crystal. From the top center, count 3 white seed beads over to the left. Only count the seed beads that protrude up, every other bead. You will be starting the loop, 3 protruding beads to the left from the top center of the diamond pattern.

Step 31

If you have gone to far to the right, you can reverse your needle and sew up through 2 more beads to the left. Always try and sew a few beads before the point you want to come through, and always try to stop and count exactly where that will be.

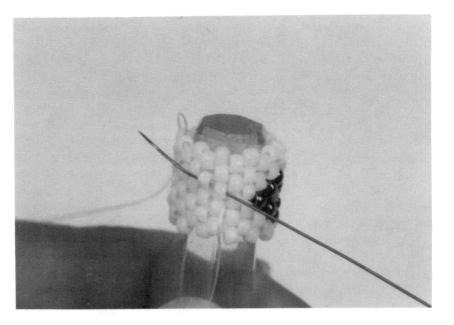

Step 32

Next, reverse the needle and sew or weave up through the seed bead right above the seed bead you just came out of and the protruding seed bead at the top of the crystal.

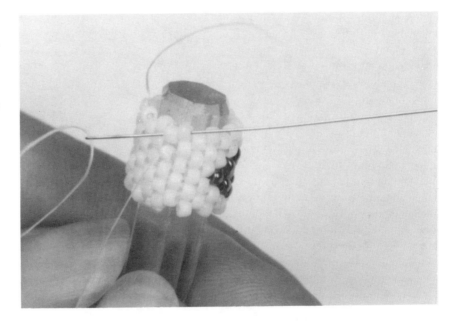

Step 33

Now that you are at the top of the crystal and you have come out the third protruding bead to the left, from the top center of the diamond pattern add 20 white seed beads and count 3 protruding seed beads over from the top center of the diamond pattern to the right. Next sew through the third protruding seed bead to the right and pull the thread lightly to form the loop at the top of the crystal.

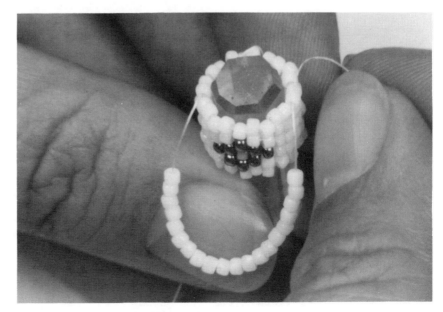

Step 34

Now reverse the needle and sew back through the same bead you have just come out of.

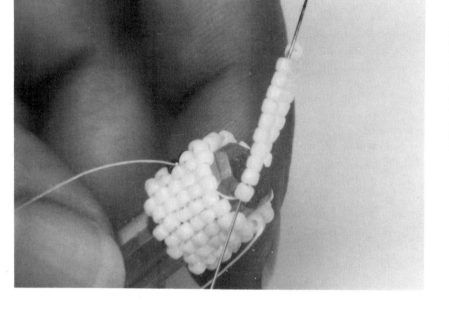

Step 35

Sew back up through the 20 white seed beads. Once you are through the 20 beads, sew back through the opposite side of the third protruding white seed bead to the top left of the diamond pattern. This is the first protruding seed bead you have begun the loop from.

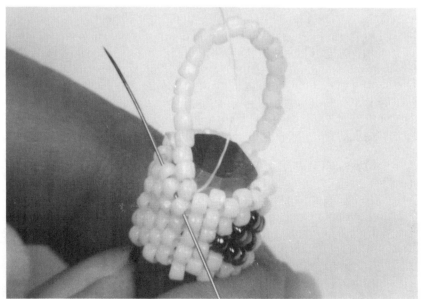

Step 36

To add the second loop, reverse the needle and sew or weave back through three white seed beads starting from the white seed bead that is directly under the third protruding white seed bead you just came out of. You are now through the next protruding seed bead to the left, directly behind the third protruding seed bead you have just came out of.

Step 37

Add 20 white seed beads and sew through the protruding white seed bead that is directly behind the back left side of the first loop you have added, the fourth protruding white seed bead from the top center of the diamond pattern. Count to the left.

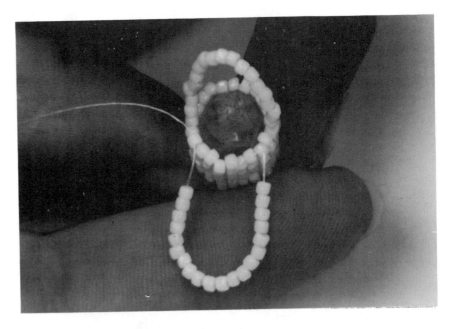

Step 38

Now... sew back through the 20 white seed beads and pull lightly on the thread to tighten the loop into place.

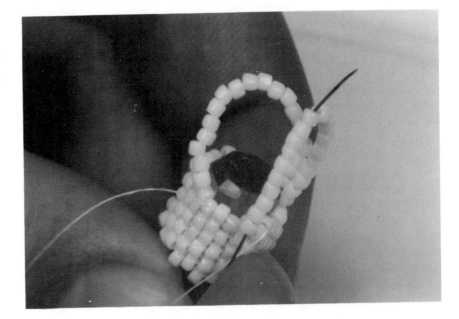

Step 39

Once you are through the 20 beads reverse the needle and sew through the fourth protruding white seed bead to the left of the center top of the diamond pattern, and through the non-protruding white seed bead directly behind the same fourth protruding white seed bead.

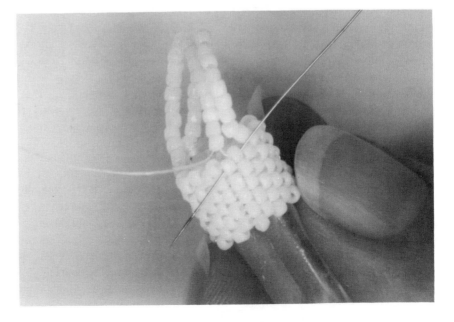

Belle Starr, *the famous outlaw, is my great, great aunt. She rode with Jesse James & the Cole Younger gang.*

My husband Glen, named our **Shooting Starr Gallery** after her.
You won't find any guns in this store...
Her memory and the inscription on her gravestone will always be in my heart.

Shed not for her the bitter tear
Nor give the heart to vain regret
'Tis but the casket that lies here
The Gem that filled it sparkles yet.....

Any questions or more information on Books, Beads and Supplies, Please feel free to contact me directly at:

The Shooting Starr Gallery
Post Office Box 2719
Camp Verde, Arizona 86322

All the Best,
Sadie Starr

Step 40

Next, sew through three more white seed beads, sewing at an angle heading to the left towards the bottom of the bead work.

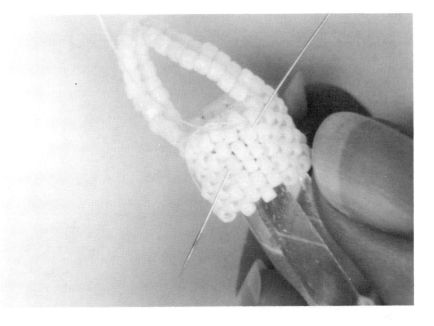

Step 41

Sew through as many as four white seed beads. Again, sewing at an angle to the left, you will now be at the bottom of the bead work.

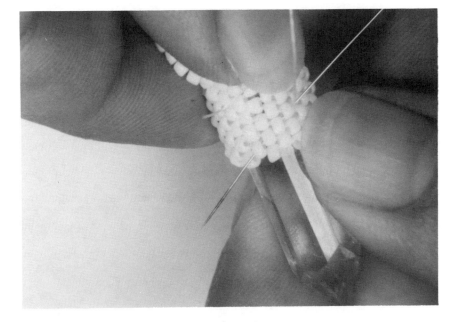

Step 43

To Change Direction, reverse your needle and sew back through the seed bead you have just come out of, and the next white seed bead to the right in the bottom row of the bead work. Any time you change direction, it is always best to do this step in the back of your bead work at the bottom.

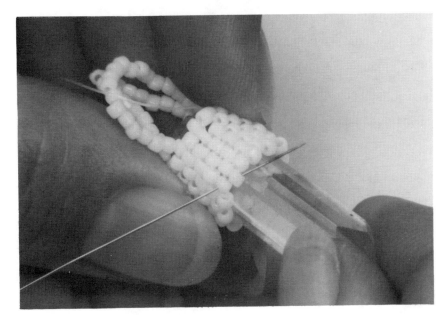

Again, repeat the previous step by sewing through 2 more white seed beads in the bottom 2 rows towards the right.

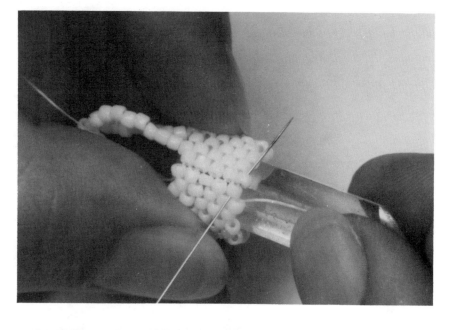

Step 44

You need to decide now, what beaded crystal you plan to make. If you plan to make this crystal without drops, advance to the FINISHING STEPS, which will be in the steps ahead.

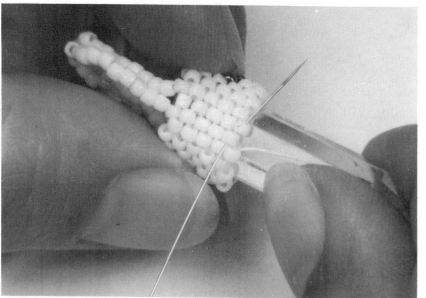

Step 45

To add drops, sew through 2 more white seed beads in the bottom 2 rows to the right. You should have approximately 32 inches or more of thread left to be able to add the drops.

Step 46

Working your way around, sew through two more white seed beads. This step is similar to previous steps, counting back from the diamond pattern, except you are at the bottom of the crystal instead of the top. Always plan to add fringe or drops by counting from the center bead in the bottom of the diamond pattern.

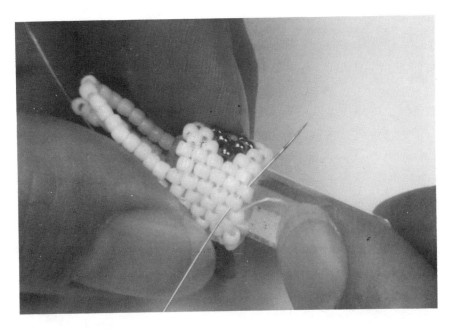

Step 47

To find the exact place to begin the drops use the point of the needle, and find the center protruding white seed bead at the bottom of the diamond pattern. The protruding bead may not always be directly in the center. Count back from the closest white protruding seed bead from the center in the bottom of the diamond pattern. Count 3 white protruding seed beads to the left from the center

Step 48

The first row of beads in the first drop will be..

5 white seed beads
1 bronze seed bead
1 turquoise seed bead
1 bronze seed bead
1 4mm clear Austrian crystal
1 bronze seed bead
5 white seed beads
1 bronze seed bead
1 6 X 10 clear glass drop

1 bronze seed bead
5 white seed beads
1 bronze seed bead
1 4mm clear Austrian crystal
1 bronze seed bead
1 turquoise seed bead
1 bronze seed bead
5 white seed beads

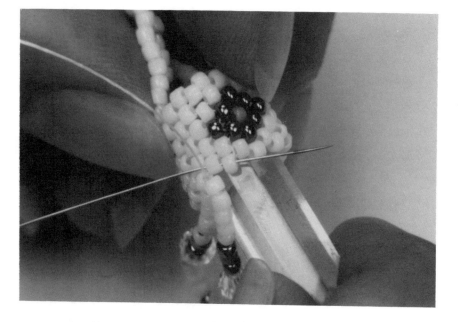

Step 49

After the first row is added, sew back through the white protruding seed bead you have just come out of. Sew through this bead through the opposite side and pull the thread to put the loop in place.

Step 50

Once the loop is pulled together, sew through the next 2 white seed beads to the right in the bottom 2 rows of the beadwork

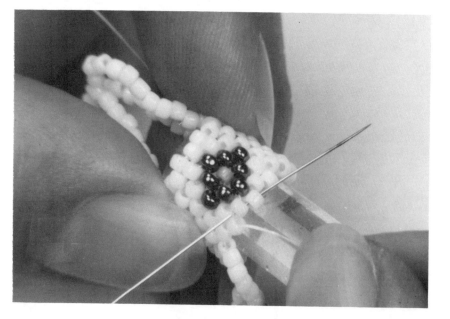

Step 51

Now, sew through the next 2 white seed beads to the right in the bottom 2 rows of the beadwork.

Step 52

With the needle, count 3 protruding white seed beads to the right from the center of the diamond pattern in the bottom row of the beadwork.

Step 53

Again sew through the next 2 white seed beads to the right in the bottom two rows of the beadwork, until you have sewn through the third protruding white seed bead to the right from the center diamond pattern.

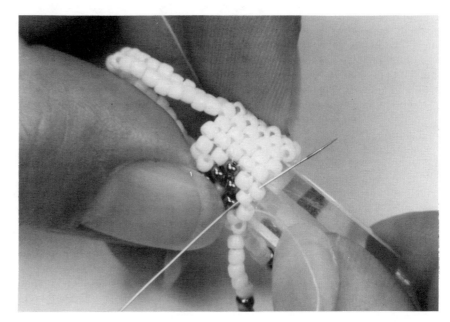

Step 54

The second row will be the same pattern as the first row. After the second row is added, sew back through the white protruding seed bead you just came out of before adding on the second row. Sew through this bead through the opposite side and pull the thread to put the second loop into place.

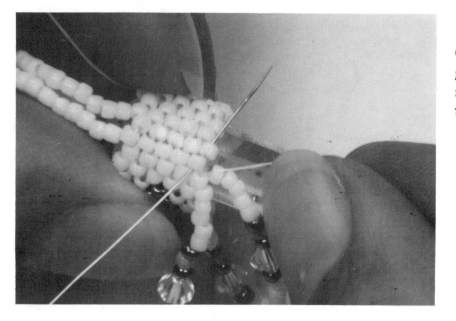

Once the second loop is pulled together, sew through the next 2 white seed beads to the right in the bottom two rows of the beadwork.

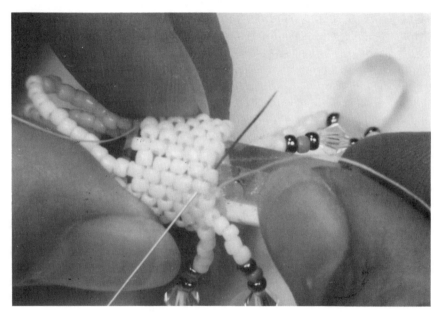

Again, sew through the next 2 white seed beads to the right in the bottom two rows of the beadwork.

Step 57

Here are two examples of how you may attach the third loop. Count the protruding white seed beads in the bottom row of the beadwork that are between the two previous loops you have just added. Divide this count to find the center back for this crystal. We will attach the third row to two white protruding seed beads. See example on the right.

Step 58

Sew through 2 more white seed beads in the bottom two rows to the right. Now add the third row:

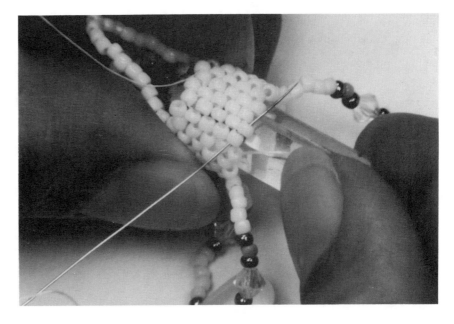

Step 59

10 white seed beads
1 bronze seed bead
1 turquoise seed bead
1 bronze seed bead
1 4mm clear Austrian crystal
1 bronze seed bead
5 white seed beads
1 bronze seed bead
1 6 X 10 clear glass drop
1 bronze seed bead
5 white seed beads
1 bronze seed bead
1 4mm clear Austrian crystal
1 bronze seed bead
1 turquoise seed bead
1 bronze seed bead
10 white seed beads
Sew through the next protruding white seed bead to the right.

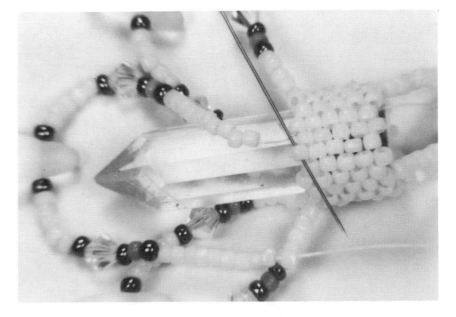

Step 60

Sew back through the third row by sewing back through the loop from right to left.

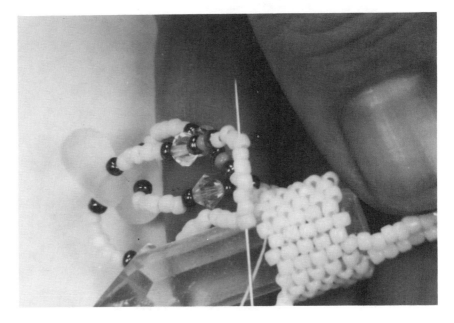

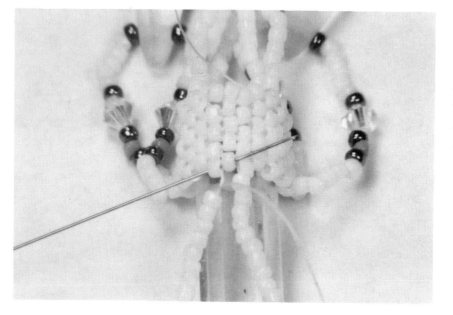

Step 61

Once you are through the third row, sew back through the opposite side of the white seed bead you came through before adding the third row and through the next non-protruding white seed bead to the right.

Step 62

Sew through the next 2 white seed beads to the right in the bottom two rows of the beadwork.

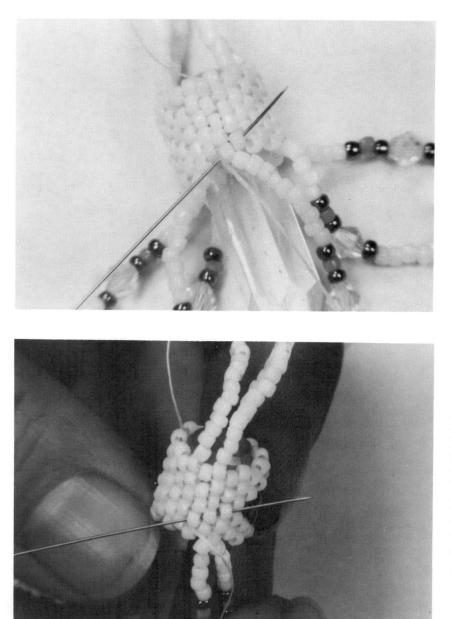

FINISHING STEPS

Sew through 2 or 3 seed beads at a time, sewing or weaving the thread all the way around the crystal 2 complete times. If you have added loops and drops to the crystal, sew back through each row of drops. You will now have 2 threads to hold the loops and secure them in place. To end the thread for this peyote project with or without loops and drops always do the next finishing step in the back of the beadwork. Use a toothpick to place a drop of Stix-All glue on approximately 2mm of thread, that is, in the middle of the next inch of thread you plan to sew through the beads. Now sew the last inch of thread through the beadwork. Pull the thread lightly as you cut it off as close to the beadwork as possible. Wipe any excess glue off the beadwork with a washcloth or towel. Carefully take the beadwork off the crystal and let the glue dry one hour.

FINISHING STEPS FOR THE TOP LOOSE THREAD

First untie the knot at the top of the crystal that you first tied when you first started this project. The knot can easily be untied by using the point of your needle to loosen it. Once the knot is untied, thread this single strand onto the needle and sew or weave the thread, sewing through 2 or 3 seed beads at a time. Sew around the crystal 1 complete time. To end this loose thread you will also place a drop of Stix-All glue in the middle of the next inch of thread you plan to sew through the beads. Pull the thread lightly as you cut it off and wipe off any excess glue. Carefully take the beadwork off the crystal and let the glue dry one hour.

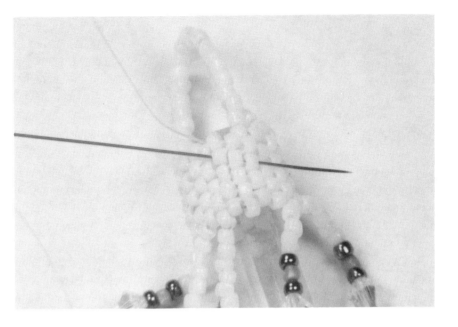

Step 2

With a toothpick, rub a thin coat of transparent glue on the inside of the beadwork. I recommend Stix-All by Elmers or 330 Epoxy. If you want to try other glues, remember you are gluing glass to glass. I do not recommend any super glues, as they can leave a frosted coating on the crystal.

Step 3

Place the crystal back into the beadwork and wipe the top of the crystal off with a towel to remove any glue that has come out and through the top. Check the crystal to make sure it is in straight. Let dry for 3 to 4 hours.

Step 4

To wire wrap the crystal, you will need approximately 4 inches of wire. Use the round nose pliers and wrap it around the pliers to make a loop with one side being 1 1/2 inches long.

NOTE: See treasure concho step for reference.

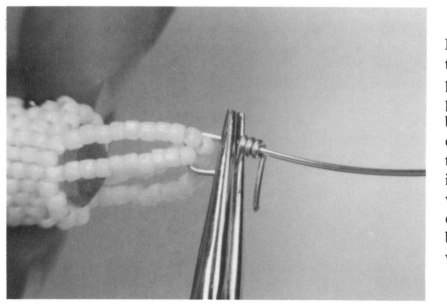

Step 5

Place the silver wire loop through the top loop of the beadwork. Hold it in place with the round nose pliers, approximately 2mm away from the seed beads. Using your finger rap the shortest wire around the longest wire at the top of the beadwork. Wrap the 1 1/2 inches of wire until you have 2 to 3 wraps. With a pair of diagonal cutters, cut the extra wire from the wrap to the back of the crystal to hide the ending wire.

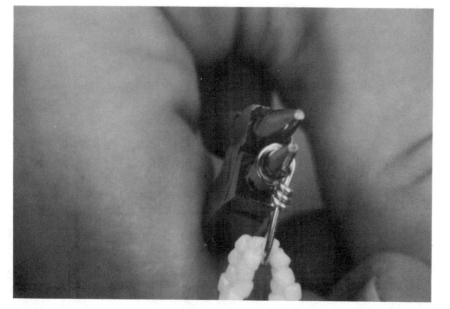

Step 6

Cut the remaining wire down to approximately 1/2 inch long and wrap it around the center of the round nose pliers until you form a loop at the top. This direction of top loop will be for the earring wire to be attached to. For a pendent you must have the top loop of wire wrap going in the opposite direction, so a silver chain may be placed through the loop, so that the pendent lays in the right direction.

COMBINING SILVER SMITHING WITH THE PEYOTE STITCH

Bear claws are not legal in every state, so ask your nearest taxidermy, if legal, use a medium size claw. With a jewelers saw and a size 3/0 blade, trim the sides of the claw to have a smooth surface to bead around. Cut a 2 inch long piece of half round 10 gauge sterling silver wire.

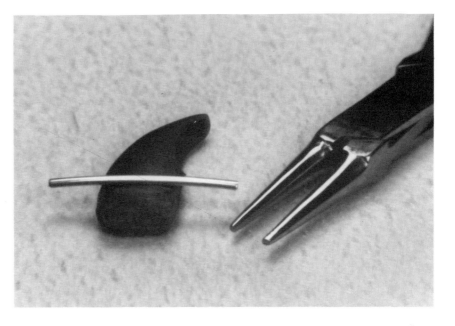

Step 2

Place the silver over the round nose pliers and bend it over in the center with the round side of the silver to the outside. Using your fingers pull the 2 ends together.

NOTE: Use leather or rubber gloves if you have tender fingers.

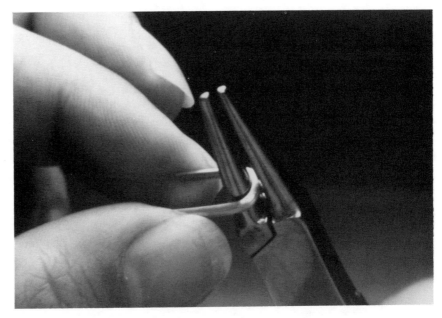

Step 3

Using a mill file, file each side of the silver that will be touching the claw. This will give a smooth look to the peyote stitch that you will be beading over. Use a clothespin to hold the claw and glue the silver band onto it with 330 epoxy. Let dry over night. Always use transparent glue on peyote projects.

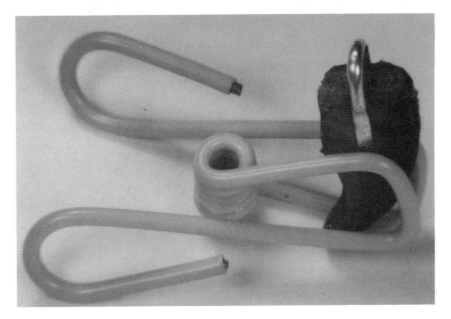

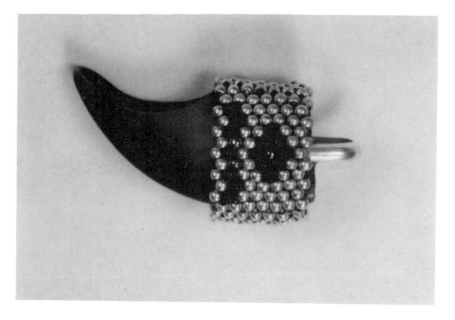

Step 4

This claw was beaded with size 14/0 antique aluminum beads from France. They are very rare and hard to find. I use them only for special one of a kind pieces. Once the bead work is done, to glue the beadwork onto the bear claw refer back to the peyote stitch pendent and earring. The steps will be the same.

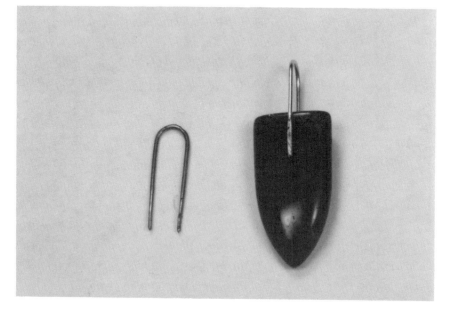

Step 5

You can also use other stone shapes, such as this Moss Agate tongue. Here we have bent over a gold plated head pin for the band at the top. Always file down the part that will touch the stone or piece so the beadwork over it will lay smooth.

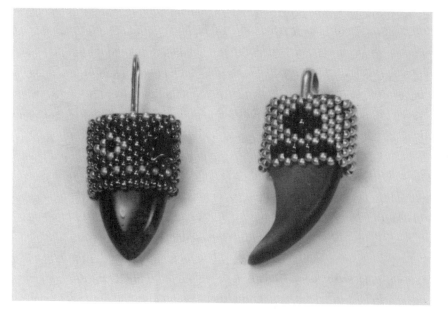

Step 6

Here are two different examples for pendants or treasures to hang from beaded bags, or other ornamental purposes. When beading any project I try always to use gold or silver colored beads for accent as it will enhance the beadwork and look like jewelry, which I feel gives them greater value and makes the pieces more appealing.

ADDING BEADS OR CABOCHON STONES TO THE PEYOTE STITCH

We are using the back of the Bear Claw Pendant to show you another technique. Disregard the black thread at the top of the claw, it is the loose thread and should be to the back of any project. For this step do not glue the beadwork to the piece until the end of this project.

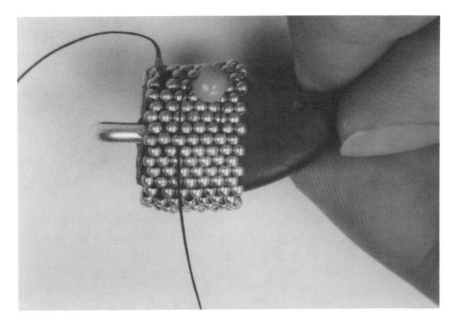

Step 2

Come out through the Peyote piece with approximately 2 feet of a single strand of the thread, which you should have left over after beading the Peyote Claw. You want to come out in the center, a few beads up from the bottom. Next, add a 4mm bead and measure 3 to 4 seed beads up to sew through one seed bead to anchor the 4mm seed bead down. Sew back through the first seed bead you first came out of and pull the thread to put the 4mm bead into place.

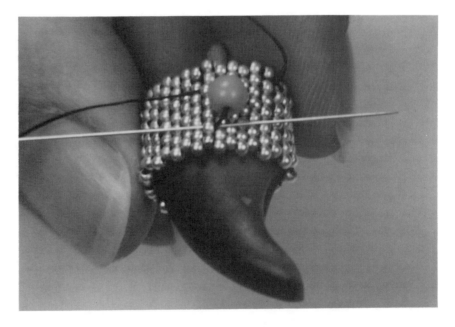

Step 3

Now add on enough seed beads to fit around the 4mm bead and sew back through the first, second and third seed bead you have just put on.

NOTE: You can also glue a cabochon stone with a flat back to the same spot you are adding the 4mm bead to. If so use 330 Epoxy and, only place the glue on the back of the cabochon, and put it onto the center of the beaded piece.

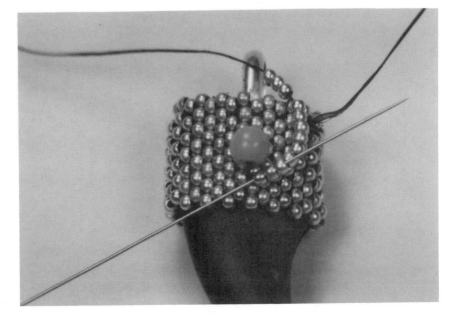

Step 4

Next, sew through 3 to 4 more seed beads until you are at the top of the Bear Claw. Now, sew through the closest seed bead in the Peyote piece to tack down the loop of the seed beads.
NOTE: Only sew through one seed bead.

Step 5

Sew back down through the loop of the seed beads till you come out 2 or 3 seed beads before you come to the bottom of the bear claw.

Step 6

Sew down through 2 seed beads in the Peyote, staying close to the loop. Now you may add a row of Peyote on to this loop of seed beads, as long as you have an even number of seed beads around the loop. Sew back up into the loop and come out of any bead to add another row of seed beads as if you are beading around a crystal. Try adding just one row of Peyote stitch around the bead or finish the claw by weaving back down through the peyote until you come to the bottom. Refer to the peyote crystal to compete this project. Then glue and let dry.
NOTE: This step can also be used on the top triangle part of a bugle bead or triangle earring.

PEYOTE STITCH AROUND A FEATHER

To do the peyote stitch around a feather, first, buy a legal feather. This is a white turkey feather that has been hand painted black on the bottom half. Trim the top of the feather with a sharp scissors keeping in mind just how much of the top you want to be beaded.

Step 2

Cut a piece of leather that will fit completely around the top part of the feather. Also, cut two, 6 inch strips of leather to place inside the piece that you will wrap around the feather. Place a thin layer of glue on one side of the leather piece. Carefully lay the top of the feather down onto the center of the glued piece. Lay the strips down on each side of the feather as close to the feather as possible and as far down as possible.

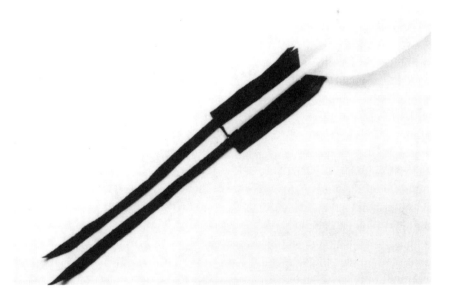

Step 3

Wrap the piece of leather around the part you will be beading and leave a small opening at the top. Let dry 2 hours. With a single strand of size B thread with a knot at one end, sew through the top from the inside out approximately 2mm from the top. Add a small amount of glue to the top, inside and the opening and press to close and hide the knot.

Step 4

Add the amount of beads needed to fit around the top of the feather. You want this first row of beads to fit very close together. Always use an even number of seed beads to start the first row such as 24,26,28,30 and so on. 25,27,29,31 will not work. Sew through the first row of seed beads twice. You are now ready to add on the second row of seed beads.

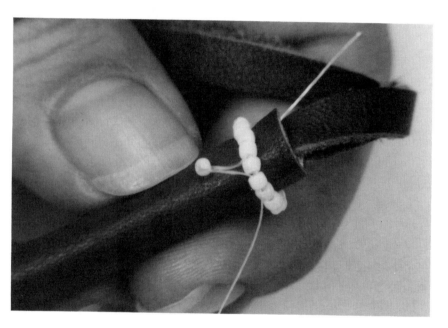

Step 5

Revue the steps of the Peyote Pendent and Earring, you will be using the same steps. Add one seed bead, skip a bead and so until you are all the way around the feather, and you come to the last seed bead in the first row, and so on....

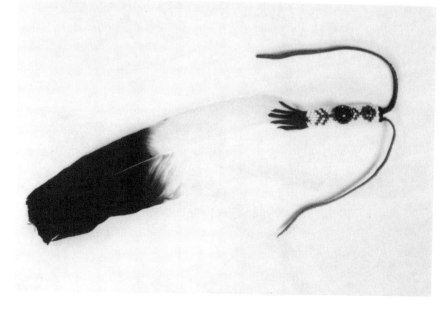

Step 6

To add beads or cabachons onto the peyote feather, revue the steps of ADDING ON BEADS AND CABACHON STONES. You can also add a small loop of seed beads at the bottom of the Peyote to hang a crystal with a jump ring. Use any small special attachments you choose. Your feather is now complete.

APPLIQUE AND PEYOTE STITCH

For this project I will show you how to combine 2 unique techniques. Use STIX-ALL glue, and glue a crystal approximately 6 X 20 mm down onto the center of a 3 X 5 inch piece of ultra swede with a 3 X 5 inch note card backing.

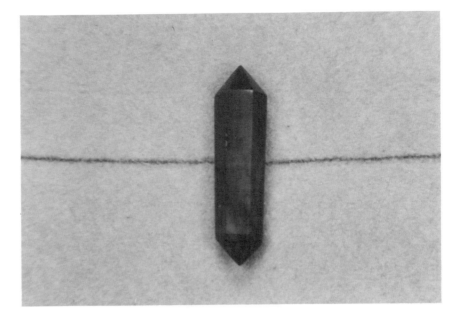

Step 2

Come from behind and sew up through the note card and Pellom from the left side of the crystal. Add on an even amount of seed beads to cover and fit around the front top part of the crystal that is not glued to the ultra swede. Sew through the right side, and pull the thread to put the first row into place. Come back up through the left side about 1 seed bead below the first row. Add 1 seed bead. Skip a bead and sew through the next seed bead in the first row.

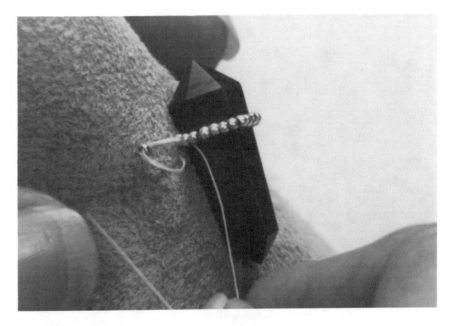

Step 3

Add 1 seed bead and skip a bead. Repeat this step till you are all the way around to the right side of the crystal. This is the same stitch as the peyote earring and pendent, except you will only bead half way around the crystal or any other object you decide to bead around

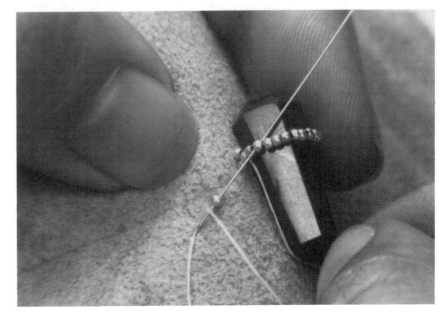

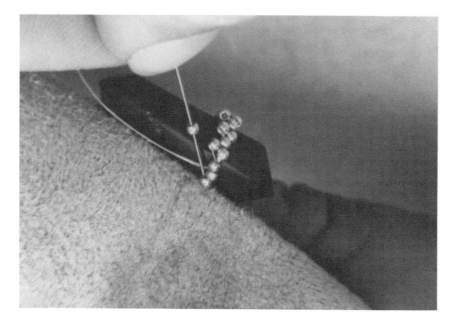

Step 4

Once you are all the way around to the right side of the crystal, the last stitch is; adding 1 seed bead, skip a bead, and sew down through the last seed bead in the first row, and down through the ultra-suede and note card. The second row is now complete.

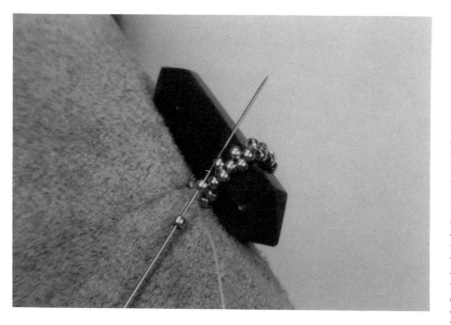

Step 5

Come from behind and sew up through the note card and ultra-suede, approximately 1 seed bead down from the last step. Add one seed bead and sew through the first protruding seed bead you come to in the second row, which is the last seed bead you have added in the second row. Repeat the same stitches by sewing the Peyote stitch only around the front half of the crystal. NOTE: This stitch can also be applied without the crystal. This is called Flat Peyote. You want all beads to lay flat down onto the Pellom. See Flat Peyote Bracelet in the color photos.

Step 6

Once the Peyote is completed. 5 mm cut glass beads have been added for the first row of beadwork around the crystal. Next, 8 to 10 seed beads are added horizontally in between each 5 mm glass bead. Each single loop of seed beads that is added will help hide where the 5 mm cut glass beads meet. Always add a single row of seed beads after adding the horizontal step. For this broach fringe I have first added the bottom fringe with the easy whip stitch. The last step is the easy outside trim stitch. Add the easy outside trim stitch all the way around, except for the bottom part of the broach where the fringe hangs.

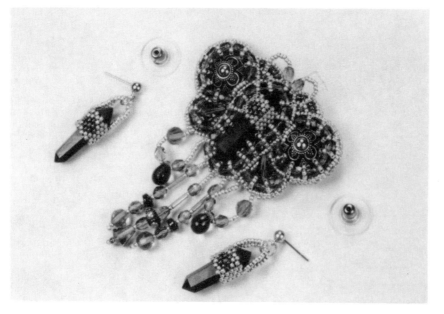

PEYOTE NECKLACE

You will need to buy at least three hanks or six - 1 oz. tubes of seed beads for a necklace. Start your peyote necklace by beading around a pencil as if it is a long crystal. This will keep the necklace even and easy for you to bead around. 12 seed beads is a recommended amount to start with.

Step 2

Use only one color of seed beads, size 11/0 for the first two yards of thread. Use the same steps to start as the Peyote Pendant, and make sure to leave 10 inches of loose thread where the necklace begins. Bead around the pencil until you have approximately 7 inches of thread left. To add on thread take the beadwork off the pencil or any other object. Take the needle off the thread and tie another single strand of thread two yards long. Tie the 2 threads together with 3 or 4 knots to secure it.

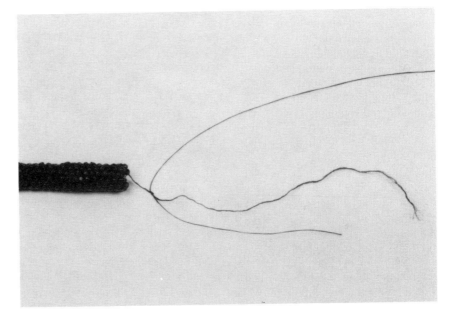

Step 3

Pull on the 2 yard strand of thread lightly to make sure the knot is tight. Next, cut the excess thread one inch away from the knot.

TECHNIQUE B OF ADDING ON THREAD

NOTE: Again always be sure to complete the last row of beads before you add on the thread. Here is another technique to add on thread to the Peyote necklace. If you plan to use transparent seed beads for the main color in the Peyote necklace or bottle, you want to sew the remaining seven inches of thread back through the necklace. Sew through two to three seed beads at a time, at a slant until you have about three inches of this thread left. Place a tiny drop of STIX-ALL glue in the center of the next inch of thread you are going to sew through. Sew through a few more beads and pull thread while you cut off the small amount of thread that is left.

Step 2

TO ADD ON MORE THREAD:
Start with a two yard single strand, sew this new thread through the beads three to four inches back from where you plan to begin the bead work again. Leave about eight to ten inches of loose thread where you first added on this two yard strand of thread. NOTE: For this technique, the loose thread should always start on the outside of the beaded necklace, as you will also be sewing this loose thread through the beads. Sew all loose threads back through the beads in the opposite direction and also glue this loose thread in place as we did in the last step.

Step 3

Sew the remaining 1 3/4 yards of thread up through the bead work until you reach the top of the bead work. Come out at the top through any protruding seed bead in the last row of beads. You are now ready to start beading again.

NOTE...

This Diamond Pattern for the Pendant and Earring can also be used for the Necklace.

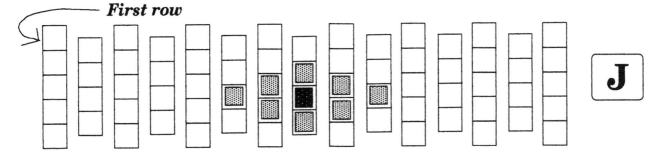

First row

J

Always use an even number of beads around the object.
Using odd numbers does not turn out right.
The second row involves beading through every other
bead for a row with half the number started with.

Notice:

*Stitching on Peyote Pendant and Earrings
creates a brick layer effect around the crystal.*

Seed beads are size 11/0

Place the needle inside the tubular part of the necklace and sew down through the center Peyote. Come out through the necklace approximately 1 1/2 inches down. Come out between any 2 seed beads.

Step 5

Sew or weave back up through the beadwork at an angle. Following the thread inside the beads until you are back to the top of the beadwork. Come out of the top through any protruding seed bead and start beading. Its time for you to design after four yards. Use the diamond design. Try something new by using Peyote graph paper to plan the front view of the necklace. You do not want this necklace to be connected at the back of your neck, so plan to start your pattern for the front of the necklace about 9 inches from where you began. This necklace should be approximately 28 - 30 inches long when it is completed. Plan the pattern part of the necklace to be 10 inches long.

Step 6

To close the necklace you will need at least one foot of thread. Measure the necklace by laying it around your neck. You want to connect the necklace on either side of the front part of the necklace. It is best not end it in the back. See the pencil to show you where to begin and end.

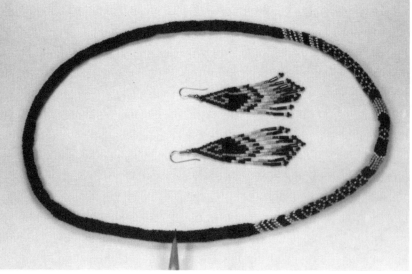

Step 7

Start by holding the necklace at one end and lettting it hang freely. This will help to untwist it before you attach the two ends. Place the two ends close together. Come out of any protruding seed bead and sew through any protruding seed bead at the opposite side of the necklace as long as the pattern lays straight, and not twisted.

Step 8

Come over through the next protruding seed bead to the opposite side of the seed bead you just came out of.

Step 9

Turn the necklace tube gradually as you weave it together. Make sure you sew through the next and opposite seed bead for each step. This is like putting and pulling a puzzle together.
NOTE: Untie the knot at the end, 10 inches of loose thread that is at the beginning of your necklace, <u>NOW.</u>

Step 10

Pull on the thread lightly as you sew all the way around the necklace. Once you are all the way around the necklace, sew back through the row above this row and the row below the first row you went through. Now sew or weave the thread back towards the back of the necklace. Sew through the seed beads using up about 1 foot of thread.

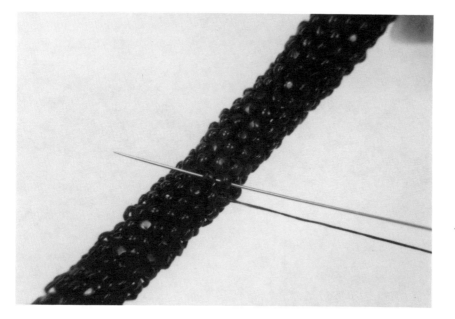

Step 11

To end this thread you will also place a drop of STIX-ALL glue in the middle of the next inch of thread you plan to sew through the beads. Pull the thread lightly as you cut it and wipe off any excess glue. Place a needle onto the end of the 10 inches of loose thread at the beginning of your necklace and weave it back through the necklace in the opposite direction of the last thread you just weaved through. Glue and cut the excess thread. The same as the previous step. Your necklace is now complete. NOTE: Be sure to wipe off the excess glue with a towel.

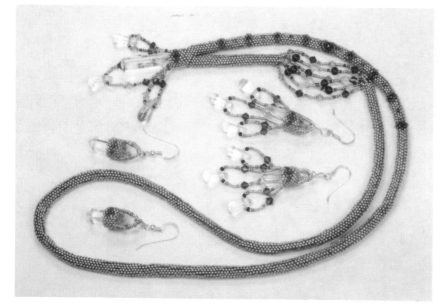

CRYSTAL - PEYOTE NECKLACE
Start this necklace approximately 3 to 4 inches above the diamond pattern. To add the loose strings of seed beads and crystals make each side of the Peyote first and then add the rows in between by attaching each end together with the same steps as adding drops of the Peyote Crystal, hanging each row to every protruding seed. For a necklace that is started with 12 seed beads you will have 6 strings. Sew all the Peyote pieces before you add the crystal point.

Step 2

Refer back to Step 9. Weave through only four protruding seed beads to begin to connect the necklace. Pull the thread to connect the piece together.

Step 3

Fold the two ends of the bead work close together. Pull the thread again to secure them in place.

Step 4

Pick the two ends of beadwork up and pull the thread a third time to make sure you have the two ends tight and close together.

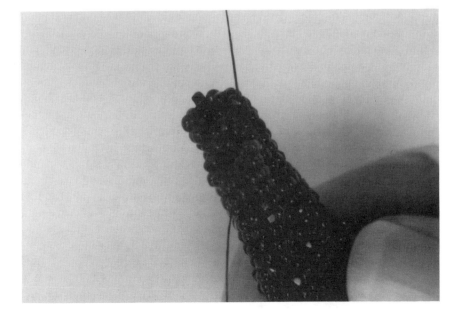

Step 5

Hold the two ends close together and add one seed bead at a time, sewing to the right. Each time you add one seed bead, skip a bead and only sew through the next protruding seed bead. Do this until you are all the way around the two ends.

NOTE: Add an extra seed bead on each side of the necklace where the ends meet, to fill in any gaps.

Step 6

End the row by using the same steps as the Peyote Pendent and necklace.

Step 7

Continue the Peyote steps until you have 1/2 inch or more of beadwork to set the crystal in. Weave back up through the necklace and glue it. End it as we have done in previous Peyote necklaces. Now you have to find a crystal to fit into this tube. Use STIX-ALL or 330 epoxy to glue the crystal in.

BOTTLES AND KEY CHAINS

This piece is beaded with size 14 Antique Aluminum beads from France, size 14 Czechoslovakian black and turquoise cut beads, size 14 Japanese bronze seed beads. There are 12 - 6mm X 10mm Czechoslovakian Antique Black Glass drops and 24 - 4mm black Austrian crystals in the fringe. The Turquoise stone is a 10mm X 12mm Natural Sleeping Beauty Cabachon. Sleeping beauty is the bluish color of the Turquoise. Cover the bottom of the bottle by gluing a round piece of leather to it. Use clear glue only. Trim the leather to fit. Refer back to the Peyote necklace for adding on thread techniques.

Step 2

Start the beading in the center of the bottle. Use the same steps as the Peyote necklace. If the bottle is a larger diameter in different areas you will need to add two seed beads at a time instead of one. To make the Peyote smaller, start the next row with one seed bead at a time. To make the Peyote even smaller, only add on one seed bead to every other protruding seed bead in each row. Glue the stone last with 330 epoxy. The beadwork should be removed from the bottle when gluing the stone. Bead around the stone after the glue has dried.

Step 3

This peyote piece can be used for a key chain, or even a lighter cover. For a lighter cover do not add fringe. To make the key chain, cut a wooden dowel, 3/4 inch X 2 1/2 inches long and trace two leather circles to cover each end. Screw an eye hook through one of the leather circles before gluing and screwing it down through the wooden dowel.

MORE TECHNIQUES ON BEADED BOTTLES

Here is another technique in beaded bottles, or lighter covers. Start by gluing a circle of thin suede or leather to the bottom of the bottle. Begin with a single strand of thread with a knot at one end. Sew the needle through the middle of the leather, approximately 1/4wide. IMPORTANT NOTE: For lighter covers do not glue the leather circle to the lighter.

Step 2

Add one seed bead, reverse the needle and sew back through the leather until you come out where the knotted thread is coming out of the leather. Sew back through the leather about 2mm in front of the knot. Pull on the thread lightly to place the seed bead close to the leather.

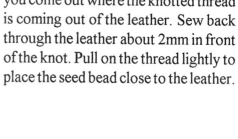

Step 3

Sew back through the same seed bead, and pull on the thread lightly to put the seed bead in place and close to the leather.

Step 4

Next add 1 seed bead, reverse the needle and sew back through the leather approximately 2mm in front of the first seed bead, until you come out where the knotted thread is coming out of the leather. Pull the thread lightly to put the seed bead in place and close to the first seed bead you have added.

Step 5

Now sew through the first and second seed bead. Pull the thread lightly to bring the 2 seed beads close together.

Step 6

Add one seed bead and reverse the needle and sew back through the leather approximately 2mm in front of the second seed bead. Come out through the leather right in front of the last seed bead that is already attached leather. Next, sew through the last two seed beads, and pull the thread lightly. Repeat the last two steps until you are all the way around the bottle. Keep the seed beads as close together as you can. Connect the row by sewing through the first seed bead, and on through the whole first row of seed beads. Your first row is complete. Now you are ready to start the Peyote stitch in the same steps as the previous Peyote Crystal earring, except the beadwork will not be removed.

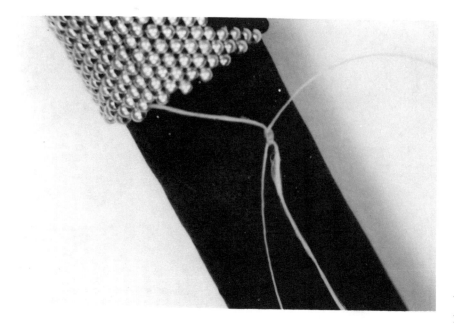

PEYOTE STITCH WAND

A crystal can be glued down into a piece of copper tubing. A silver band or leather band can be placed around the area where the crystal and the tubing meet. Contact your local jeweler to make you a silver band. This band was made by Keith Davis. To add fringe, wrap the leather around the tubing. You want the leather to lay flat. Stitch the leather using the stitch we previously used in the beaded belt buckle. Measure the leather 6 to 12 inches longer than the tubing. Only stitch down to where the tube ends. Then cut the fringe.

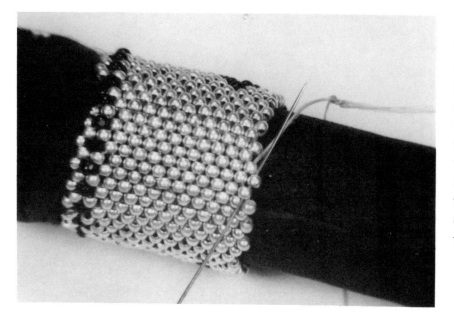

Step 2

To add on thread, tie another single strand of thread onto this loose thread and tie the two together 2 or 3 times to secure the knot. Wrap the thread one time around the tube in the same direction you are beading. Then, sew back through a few seed beads before the last step of beadwork. Once you are back through the bead where the thread is coming out, you are now ready to begin the beadwork again

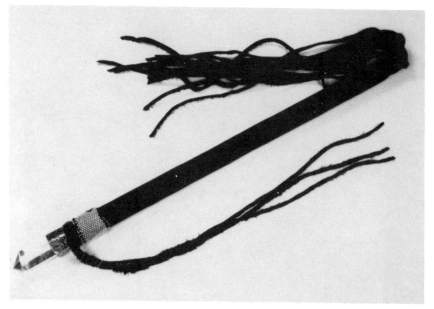

Step 3

This crystal wand is 12 inches long and will take many hours of beadwork. Wands are used for healing and meditation, or it can be just a beautiful way to adorn a special crystal. It is best to pick a crystal in very good condition, without a cracked or chipped point. Enjoy.

ADVANCED CONTOURED BEADED BOTTLES AND POTS

Here I am showing you a beaded bottle that is in progress. The needle is to mark the spot where you begin the bottle. Work your way up to the top by using the usual peyote pendent steps. When the beads begin to separate, and the threads and bottle begin to show through. Then...

Step 2

Add 2 seed beads to each step instead of the usual 1 seed bead to increase the size of each row. To decrease the size where the bottle is contoured and smaller, go back to the usual steps of adding on one seed bead at a time. You will need to check each row as it is completed to make sure all rows are flat and close together. NOTE: always end each row before changing the amount of seed beads you plan to use.

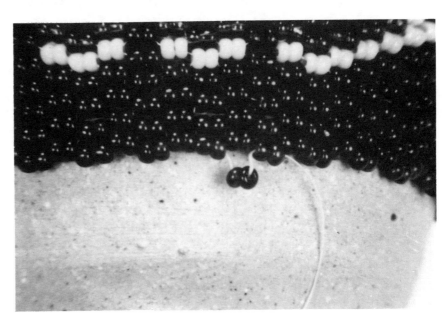

Step 3

This project can be very difficult and take many weeks to complete. Do not be in a hurry when beading a contoured bottle, it will only cause extra mistakes. Put it down for a day or two. This will give you time to observe it better and plan the next row. Use peyote graph paper to plan a pattern or make one up as you go. Have fun.

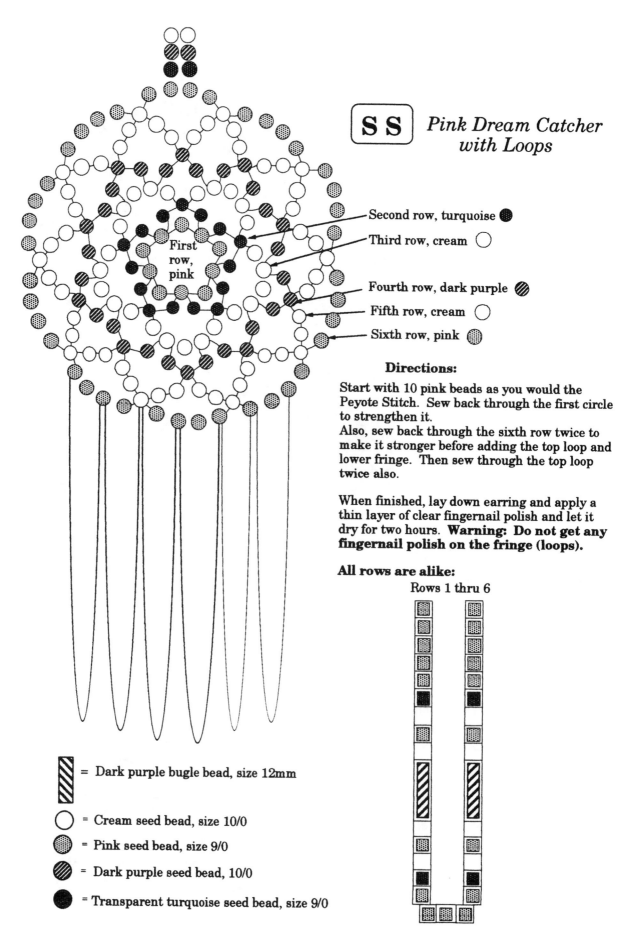

S S *Pink Dream Catcher with Loops*

Second row, turquoise ●
Third row, cream ○
Fourth row, dark purple ⊘
Fifth row, cream ○
Sixth row, pink ◍

First row, pink

Directions:

Start with 10 pink beads as you would the Peyote Stitch. Sew back through the first circle to strengthen it.

Also, sew back through the sixth row twice to make it stronger before adding the top loop and lower fringe. Then sew through the top loop twice also.

When finished, lay down earring and apply a thin layer of clear fingernail polish and let it dry for two hours. **Warning: Do not get any fingernail polish on the fringe (loops).**

All rows are alike:

Rows 1 thru 6

▨ = Dark purple bugle bead, size 12mm

○ = Cream seed bead, size 10/0

◍ = Pink seed bead, size 9/0

⊘ = Dark purple seed bead, 10/0

● = Transparent turquoise seed bead, size 9/0

DREAM CATCHER WEAVE

Start with a single strand of two yards of size B thread. The first row will have 10 pink seed beads in a circle. You want to leave 8 to 10 inches of loose thread to sew back through the woven earring when it is completed. Once the 10 pink seed beads are in a circle, sew back through the 10 seed beads twice to secure the circle in place for the first row. For the second row add three turquoise seed beads, skip a bead and sew through the next pink seed bead in the circle.

NOTE: Although this step is started as you would a Peyote stitch, you don't tie a loop knot to the first bead.

Step 2

Repeat the last step until you have 15 seed beads in the second row. To end the second row, once you add the last three turquoise seed beads in this second row, skip a bead and sew through the next pink seed bead in the first row, and through the first two turquoise seed beads in the second row. The second row is now complete. As you add each row, always start the following row of seed beads by coming out of a bead that is in the center of one of the last loops you have just added. Each row for this project is one solid color all the way around. SEE Pattern SS.

Step 3

Once the bead work is complete, place the loose thread on your needle that is in the center of the woven circle where you began, onto a needle, and sew or weave it back through the circle of beads. Sew each loose thread back through and around the top part of the woven earring with about 8-10 inches of remaining thread. Glue and cut both threads as we have done in the Peyote necklace. Lay the earring down flat and paint only the top woven circle with clear finger nail polish.

DREAM CATCHER WORK OR SPIDER WEB

Dreams have always had many meanings to the Indians. One of the old Ojibwa traditions was to have a dream catcher in their homes. They believe the night air is filled with dreams, both good and bad. The dream catcher, when hung, moves freely and catches dreams as they float by. The good dreams know the way and slip through the center hole. They slide off the soft feather so gently that many times the sleeper doesn't know he's dreaming. The bad dreams not knowing the way, get entangled in the webbing and perish with the first light of the new day. Small dream catchers were hung on cradle boards. Larger sizes were hung in lodges for all to have good dreams.

Chapter 15

- *Pricing Your Beadwork* -

The price of your work should be determined by the contents of the materials used, and the hourly wage of $5.00 to $10.00, with the exception of one of a kind pieces that may contain rare and unusual stones or beads.

The price of the pieces done in this book are as follows. (See bottom page) Gift shops and galleries sometimes, will have consignment policies, this means that you will be paid once your work is sold. Try not to put all your work in one store. It is best to have one account for each town you select to do business with. Some shops will buy your work on the spot. You can even sell them as part of an order, and put the other part on consignment. the choice is yours and could make all the difference in making a sale or landing an account.

This pricing scale is for retail only. If you are selling to stores you will need to cut the price in half.

Bugle Bead earring or Triangle earring, 5 to 7 wide........................$22.00
Bugle Bead earring or Triangle earring, 9 to 11 wide....................$30.00
Paua Stone post earring...$30.00
Paua Stone earring with 9 rows of fringe added...........................$60.00
Small Barrettes...$35 to $60.00
Large Barrettes...$60.00 to $100.00
Single Beaded Crystal Pendant.......Peyote...................$30.00 to $50.00
1 pair of Crystal Earrings........Peyote..........................$40.00 to $60.00
Small Hatbands...$150.00 to $300.00
Large Hatbands...$300.00 to $2000.00
Concho Treasure Earrings with 3 rows of fringe..........................$40.00
Concho Treasure Earrings with 5 rows of fringe..........................$60.00

Again, this will all be priced based on each piece and its contents. Also the more difficult applique pieces should be priced a bit more at least $10.00 an hour. Always take your time and be as even and neat with your work as possible.

PROTECT YOUR BEADWORK

NOTE: Please always be sure to protect your bead work when transporting it or travelling with it. Pieces such as earrings, brooches, or barrettes can be placed on a note card or heavier business card quality paper which you can get at your local printer. Cut the cards to fit into a gift box. Make holes in the card to insert findings. The cards can be placed in a white gift box with a clear plastic lid. Plastic lids are a nice display and protecion at the same time. Boxes that measure 3 1/2 inches x 5 1/2 inches are a great size for earrings. For all the hard work that you do, remember that quality is much more important than quantity. Thread will shrink if exposed for hours of high heat, so keep it cool. Sign your cards or have a logo printed on a sticker that you can attach to any card that you make. Type up a brief story about yourself to share with your customers The customer will take good care of your work if you just show them how. This will also reduce the chances of having damaged goods returned .

Chapter 16

-TREASURES
FOR
YOUR PLEASURES -

(clean out the closets)

The old necklace you have not worn in so many years, can now be used to create one of a kind, hand-crafted wearable art. Most bead stores have a good selection of beads old and new, but check local newspapers to find estate sales, swap meets, antique stores, and yard sales. Theses are great places to find broken strands. Try to be very selective when buying used or old beads, as they can be very over priced. As you become more familiar with beads from all over the world, it will be much easier to determine if you have found a good buy. $1.00 to $3.00 is a good price to pay for a used or broken strand of glass beads. If there is a bead society in your area, join it. There will be many people you will meet along the way, with advice and crazy stories of how they became hooked on beading.

Here is a list of some of the beads you can use in the treasure collection pieces:

Austrian crystals
Hand-Made Silver beads
Semi-Precious stone beads
Hand-Painted, Ceramic beads from Peru
Hand-Painted, Chinese Porcelain and Cloisonne beads
Glass beads, all shapes and sizes, from all over the world
Hand-Made Fimo clay beads
6mm X 8mm Hand-Made Venetian Chevrons (star beads)
6mm X 12mm small Hand-Carved animals. (known as fetishes)
tubular shaped shell beads (known as heishi)
6mm X 10mm Antique glass drops from Czechoslovakia
Old wooden beads, Old brass beads, Old trade beads
Hand-Stamped Sterling Silver Conchos
Sterling Silver Feathers, Sterling Silver Charms

To know that you can wear part of yesterday's history
around you neck today
is a
real
TREASURE
FOR YOUR
PLEASURE
****

happy hunting

SIMPLE HEAD PIN EARRINGS

We will start this simple project with a two inch surgical steel head pin. The first bead we put on the head pin is a 1 1/2 inch long hand painted Peruvian pottery drop bead. Add 1 bronze seed bead size 11, 1 - 5mm Czechoslovakian cut glass bead, and 1 bronze seed bead size 11.

Step 2

You must always have 1/2 inch of head pin leftover to wrap the loop at the top. If there is more than 1/2 inch of wire, cut it off with a pair of diagonal cutters, always leaving just 1/2 inch of wire. With a pair of round nose pliers, place the pliers at the very end of this 1/2 inch wire. Hold the Peruvian bead with your left hand while you roll the wire around the center of the round nose pliers.

Step 3

To stand the loop up, the end of the head pin should be directly above the last bronze seed bead you have added onto the wire. Gently take a hold of the loop with a pair of short, flat nose pliers. Hold the Peru bead with your left hand and gently press the loop to the right. A pair of needle nose pliers may also be used for this project.

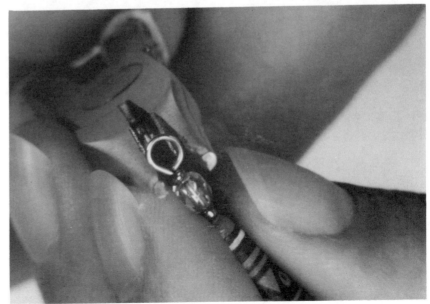

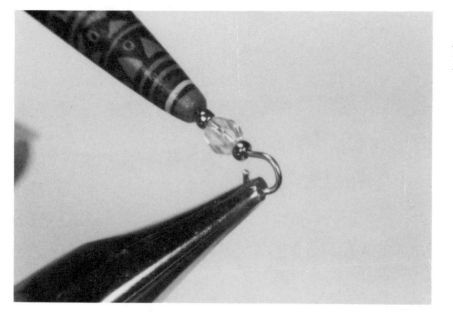

Next, open the loop by pulling out to
the right.

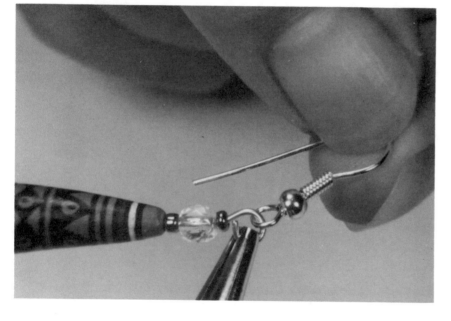

Now, place the French earwire onto the
loop and press the wire back into place.

Your earring is now complete. Make
another earring and get ready for some
real fun with the treasure conchos.

Chapter 17

- Treasure Conchos -

To make your concho earrings start by ordering the best hand made conchos you can find. There is so much work involved, and for a person that doesn't know how to make them, it's so nice to have a beautiful piece to start with.   So lets do it.......................

MATERIALS & TOOLS NEEDED:

2 - Sterling Silver Conchos with three holes in the bottom and one at the top

3 feet of Sterling Silver, 22 gauge half hard round wire

2 - Medium Sterling Silver hand-stamped feathers

1 - 24 inch strand of 2 or 3mm Black Olive Heishi,

4 - 5mm Czech Crystal Aurora Borealis

NOTE: Aurora Borealis will be called Czech Crystal A-B.

2 - 10mm hand made Fimo clay beads

2 - 4mm Austrian Plum Crystals

2 - 6mm Opaque Pink Czech Hearts

2 - 6 by 10mm Austrian Clear Crystal Drops

1 - 6mm Sterling Silver Bear

1 - 6mm Sterling Silver Bird,

2 - 4mm Clear Glass Spacers,

2 - 6mm Sterling Silver Beads,

2 - 4mm Cream or Bone Spacers,

2 - 6mm by 10mm pink Czech drops,

1 - Pair of Sterling Silver earwires,

1 - Small pair short flat-nose pliers,

1 - Small pair of diagonal cutters,

NOTE: The pliers and cutters you need to buy will be approximately 4 1/2 inches long.

WHAT IS A CONCHO?

A Concho is a sterling silver round or oval shaped disc, that is stamped with a tool to make a design in the silver. Holes are drilled to hang beads. Then, the concho is given a domed shape with a special block.   The stamped designs are painted with silver blackener so the detail of the stamped pattern will show. Next, they are buffed and polished to give them a beautiful shine. You may order many different designs of these Conchos from Shooting Starr Gallery of Gifts, although you may find very nice cast conchos from molds that are poured with sterling silver. I prefer hand-stamped conchos which were made by my talented friend Keith Davis.

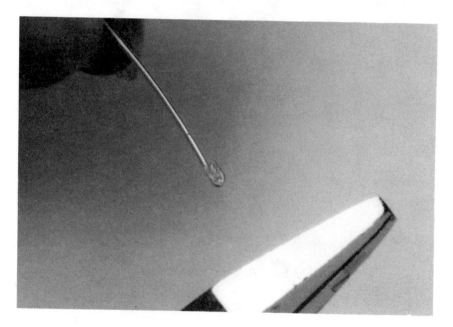

Step 1

Start the concho with approximately 5 inches of sterling silver round wire, make sure you order half hard round wire size 22 gauge. One small pair of short flat-nose pliers. One small pair of diagonal cutters. Cut a 5 inch piece of the silver wire, bend back one end of the wire approximately 3mm back, with the flat-nose pliers.

Step 2

Now press the 3mm end until it touches the 5 inch piece of wire with the small flat nose pliers. Next, press the 3mm end until it becomes flat, this will keep your beads from sliding off the end of the wire.

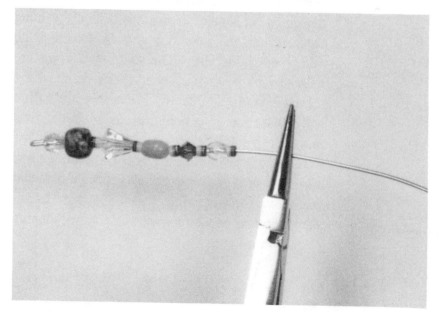

Step 3

Your center row will be:
1 - 5mm Czech crystal A-B,
1 - 10mm Fimo clay bead,
1 - Black Olive Heishi,
1 - 6 X 10 Austrian Crystal Drop
1 - Black Olive Heishi
1 - 6mm Pink Czech Heart
1 - Black Olive Heishi
1 - 4mm Plum Austrian crystal,
1 - Black Olive Heishi,
1 - 5mm Czech crystal A-B
1 - Black Olive Heishi.

Step 4

Once you have the beads on the wire, about 1/2 inch away from the last bead, bend the wire over a pair of round nose pliers, pulling each side down at a time, this will make a loop in the wire.

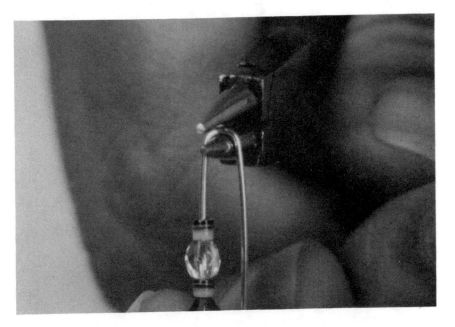

Step 5

Place the loop through the center row of the in front of the concho. Hold it in place with the round nose pliers and wrap the extra wire around the top of the row of beads you have just put on. Wrap the wire by pulling it around and gently towards you.

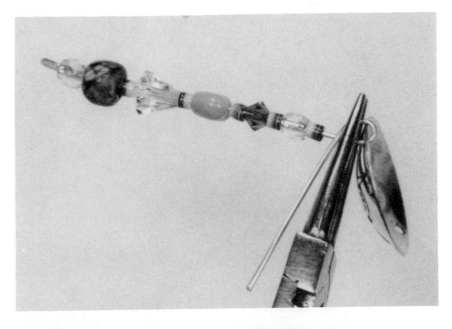

Step 6

Using your finger or the flat nose pliers, wrap the wire around the top of the center row until you have 2 or 3 rows of wrap, and you want the loop at the top to be about 3mm. It takes practice and patience.

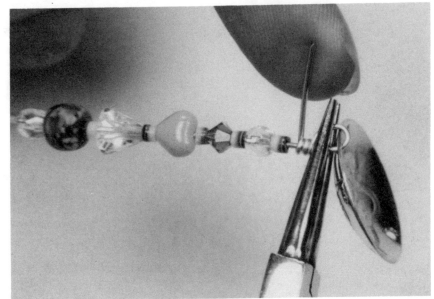

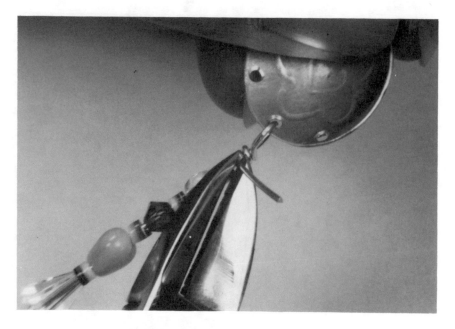

Now, with a small pair of diagonal cutters, cut the extra wire in the back of the concho so you will hide the ending wire. Your first row is now complete.

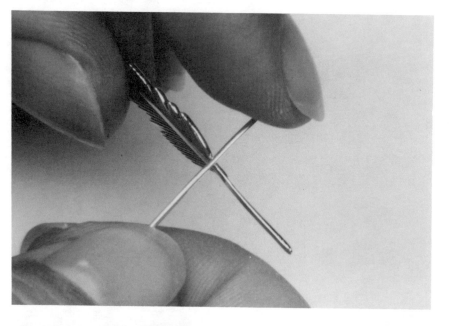

Step 8

Cut approximately a 2 inch piece of silver wire and fold about 1/2 inch over the top part of the medium size feather. You can also buy cast feathers, if so there is no need to wrap them, as they are usually pre-wrapped in the mold.

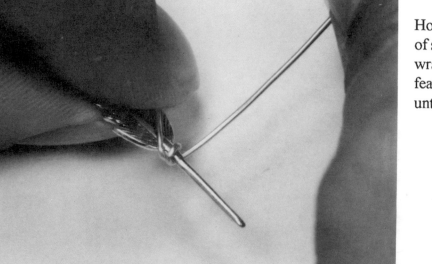

Step 9

Hold the feather and the 1/2 inch piece of silver with your left hand, while you wrap the remaining silver around the feather, always wrapping towards you, until you have 2 or 3 rows of wrap.

Step 10

Now with a small pair of diagonal cutters, cut the 2 extra wires in the back of the feather very close so you can hide the ends.

Step 11

With a small pair of round-nose pliers roll the top part of the feather down towards the back of the feather to make a loop. The loop should be about 2-3mm around.

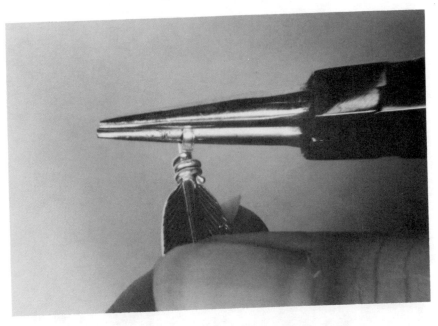

Step 12

Next, using the small pair of short flat-nose pliers hold the feather with your left hand and the pliers in your right hand, press up from the back of the loop to stand it up and give it a round shape. Your feather wrap is now complete.

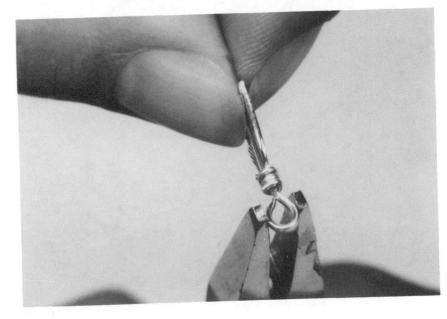

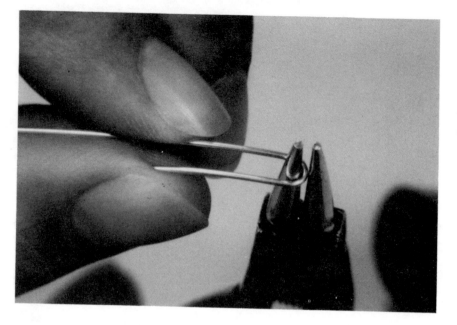

To make the loop that will attach the feather to the concho, cut a four inch piece of silver and roll about 1 inch over the round-nose pliers. Loop this end through the feather's top loop.

Step 14

Hold the one inch loop with the round-nose pliers and wrap the one inch loop around the remaining three inches of wire until you have two or three rows of wrap. You may use your finger to wrap the wire. Here we are showing you how to use a pair of short flat nose pliers. It is up to you, try both ways and find what works best for you. Cut the extra wire in the back of the feather to hide the ends.

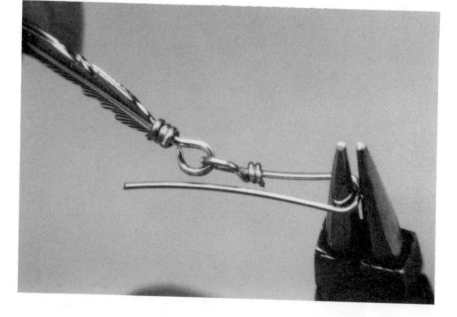

Step 15

Next, roll the remaining silver wire around the round nose pliers about 1/2 inch away from the wrap you just made. Place this loop through the front of the concho in the next hole to the left. Make sure the ends of the silver wire are always hidden in the back of the concho.

Step 16

Now, as we have shown you before, hold the loop with round nose pliers and wrap the wire around the loop above the top of the feather you have just put on, until you have two or three rows of wrap. Cut the extra wire in the back of the concho to hide the end. The feather row is now complete.

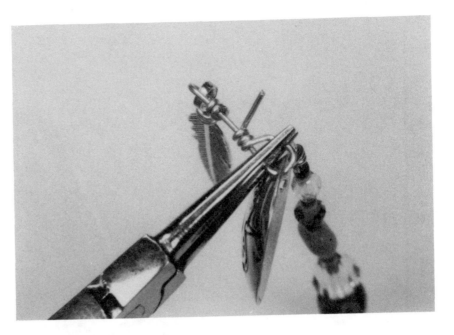

Step 17

To wrap a drop, cut a six inch piece of silver wire and place it through the drop about one inch. Hold the drop while you gently pull the silver wire up towards the top center of the drop. Pull the long opposite wire up to the top of the drop.

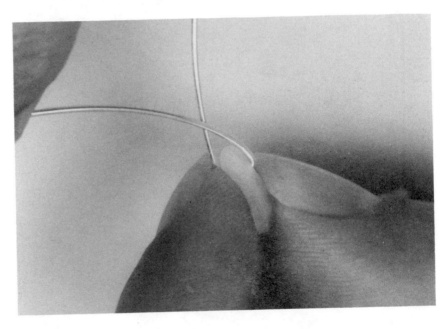

Step 18

Hold both wires at the top of the drop with the short flat-nose pliers and wrap the one inch piece of wire around the remaining 5 inches of wire until you have 2 or 3 rows of wrap. Cut the extra wire in the back of the concho to hide the end. The last row is the pink 6 by 10mm drop you have just wrapped. Now add: 1 - 4mm cream or bone spacer, 1 - 6mm Sterling Silver bead, 1 - 4mm clear glass spacer, 1 - black olive - Heishi, 1 - 6mm Sterling Silver Bear, 4 - black olive - Heishi.

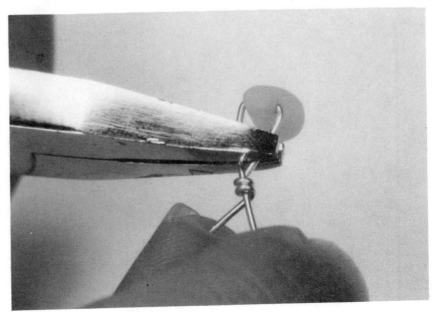

Step 19

Make a loop at the top as we have done before, about 1/2 inch away from the beads you have just put on. Place it through the front of the of the concho. Now, hold the loop in place with the round nose pliers and wrap the wire around the top of the row until you have 2 or 3 rows of wrap. Now, cut the extra wire in the back of the concho to hide the end.

Step 20

Now, place the Sterling Silver French earwire through the front of the hole in the top of the concho earring. The earring is now complete. Now, make the second concho by reversing the pattern of the two outside rows and change the silver bear to a bird.

Step 21

To attach the post to the concho, use a small piece of sand paper and gently rub it across the back-center of the concho with a circular motion. Also rub it across the post pad you will be gluing it to. This will help the two metals bond together. Place a small amount of JB Kwik by J.B. Weld Co. onto the back of the post pad. Place the pad down onto the back of the concho, let dry 2 to 3 hours.

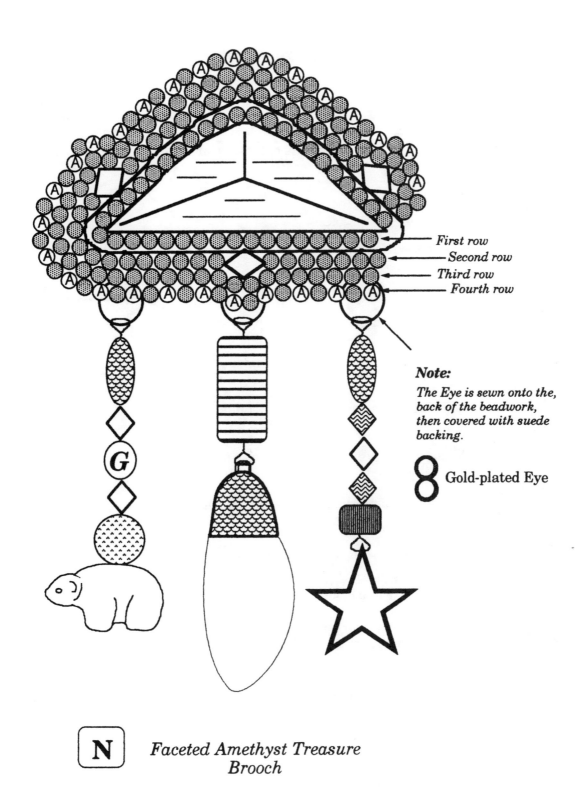

First row
Second row
Third row
Fourth row

Note:

The Eye is sewn onto the, back of the beadwork, then covered with suede backing.

8 Gold-plated Eye

N *Faceted Amethyst Treasure Brooch*

 = Faceted Amethyst

= Gold-plated head pins, 2" long
(use 3 of them, cut heads off of 2)

One-inch pin back:

= Gold-plated eyes

= Bronze seed beads, size 11/0

= Amethyst seed beads, size 11/0

= Topaz Austrian crystal, size 4mm

= Amethyst Austrian crystal, size 4mm

= Gold-plated rice bead, size 4mm x 6mm

= Czecho green faceted glass bead, size 5mm

= Purple Peru Pottery bead, size 6mm x 10mm

= Gold-plated barrel-shaped bead, 4mm

= Abalone bear fetish, size 4mm x 10mm

= Gold-plated star, approx. 12mm

= Czecho bronze bead, size 10mm

= Gold electroplated cap for crystal

= Crystal, size 8mm x 20mm

TREASURE BROOCH

Here is a unique technique to add sharp or larger objects to a beaded broach, earring, necklace, and barrette. Once the beadwork is completed, cut the excess Pellom from around the beadwork and make a paper pattern. Refer back to the pattern steps in the barrette. (Eyes-[OO] an eye ia a metal finding which is similar to 2-4mm jump rings that are attached to each other and lay side by side.) Start at the center bottom of the broach. Sew the three eyes down to the back of the beadwork, approximately 2 to 3mm apart. You only want one of the circles of the eye to protrude out from the bottom of the beadwork.

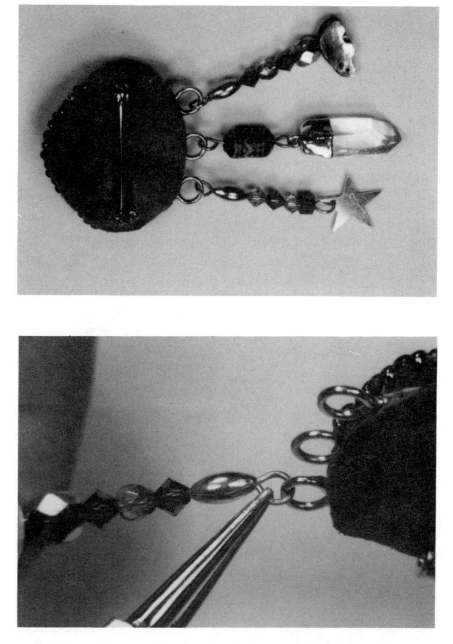

Step 2

Glue the finding pin back and backing onto the back of the beadwork. Add the fringe last. Refer back to the treasure conchos, (wire wrapping section) for the fringe part of this broach. Also, refer back to Important Notes for pin back information.

Step 3

This pyramid, triangular faceted or [cut] genuine Amethyst gemstone, is the center stone in this broach. The first row of beadwork around the stone has been built up with two rows of beadwork as the stone sets very high. When using transparent gemstones or glass use the same color of Pellom or thin felt to glue the stone down. This will help to enhance the color of the stone. The stone in this broach has been first glued onto a thin violet colored felt with 330 epoxy. The broach is now complete.

TREASURE WATCHES

Start with 0.12 diameter tiger-tail wire. Use a watch at least 1 inch wide. Take the band off the watch and place the spring bar back onto the watch. For a medium size wrist cut 6-12 inch pieces of the tiger-tail wire for a three strand watch band. Place the wire through the spring bar and fold it carefully in half so the two ends meet. Add 4mm, 5mm, and 6mm beads to both wires for the first row. You can double the wire for each row, but, make sure the beads you add at the end and close to the finding have large enough holes for 4 strands of tiger-tail to fit through.

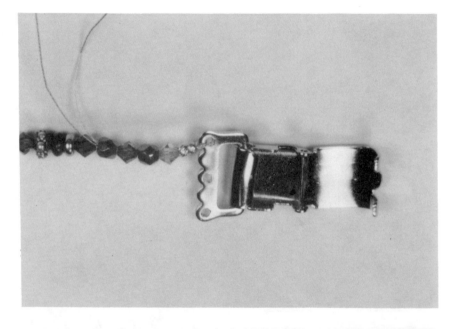

Step 2

You will need a treasure watch clasp to attach to the end of this row. Measure the watch around your wrist as you add the beads. When the watch is the correct length for you, add on two crimp beads to the ends. Insert both wires through the clasp finding and back down through the two crimp beads and at least four beads in the beaded chain.

Step 3

Pull the wire close to the finding with the flat-nose pliers. First, press down on the crimp bead that is right next to the finding. Then, press down on the second crimp bead. Cut excess wire with the diagonal cutters and the first row is now complete. Repeat all the previous steps 5 more times and you will have a 6 strand treasure watch. NOTE: Only use heavy or strong clasps that are easy to open and close.

TREASURE BRACELETS AND TREASURE ANKLE BRACELETS

The average length for a single treasure bracelet will be 8 inches, including the clasp. The average length for a single ankle bracelet is 11 inches, including the clasp.

SINGLE TREASURE NECKLACE

Single treasure necklaces are also strung on tiger-tail. This is a 28 inch single strand that can easily be slipped over your head without opening the clasp. A crystal pendant can be placed in the center. If you are adding very large, heavy pendants, double the tiger-tail to secure it. Silk cord can be used. Pearl and Bead Stringing with Henrieta is a great book to have.

DOUBLE STRAND TREASURE NECKLACE

Refer back to the Paua Stone necklace. The steps for attaching the clasp are the same. Start with a two strand clasp. Cut a 36 inch strand of tiger-tail. Add on two crimp beads. Place two inches of tiger-tail through one hole in the clasp, and back through the two crimp beads. Press the crimp beads. Add the shortest row first. Begin with a 1 3/4 inch small silver melon shaped bead, add 6 inches of size 11/0 seed beads. Add about a 16 inch bead pattern of your choice and 6 inches of size 11/0 seed beads. Next the 1 3/4 inch long melon bead and last 2 crimp beads. A good length for the first row is about 32 inches. This length will include the clasp. Attach it to the clasp for the first row, next add the second longest row. Increase this length to about 34 inches. Refer to treasure conchos to wire-wrap charms and dangles last. Lobster claws can be used to attach the charms temporarily, until you decide where you want to permanently wire-wrap them.

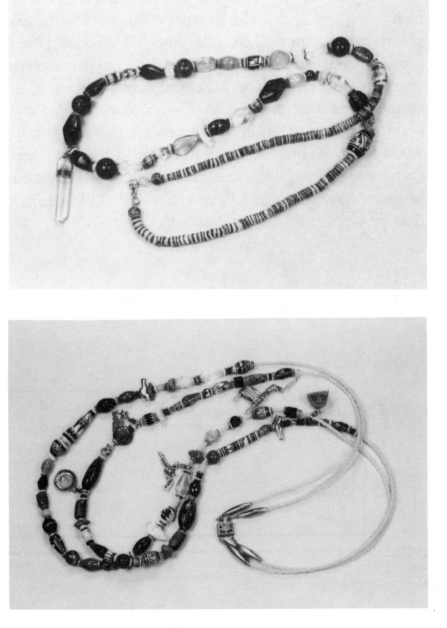

Chapter 18

-Beginning Loomwork -

This wooden Loom can be ordered from Shooting Starr Gallery or it can be made with a few simple materials, such as: wood, screws and leather.

If you want to make your own loom,begin by cutting three pieces of wood; 1 - 3 x 30 inch piece, and 2 - 3 x 3 inch pieces. Nail or screw the two small pieces, one at each end as shown in the picture. Then, glue strips of leather over the two small pieces and attach one screw at each end of the loom. Once the loom is completed, wrap size B thread around one screw to secure it in place. Make one continuous wrap, as shown in the diagram. Start the wrap in the center and work your way out with thread if you want to start with 12 seed beads wide, 13 strings of thread will be needed. However many seed beads you use, one extra string is needed in the project. Try to wrap thread about one seed bead wide. Tie off thread to the screw you end up at, to secure threads in place. Looms can be made larger for larger beaded projects. It is best to have three to four inches of thread extra on each side of the bead work. You are now ready to begin beading.

LOOM DESIGNER: *Dianne Anderson*

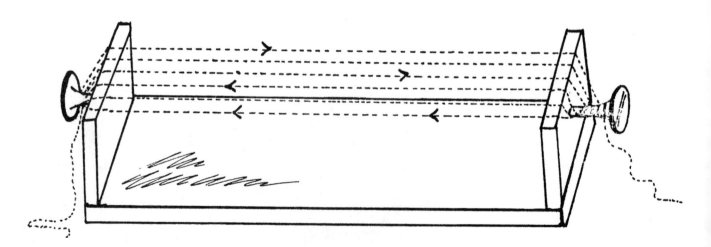

Step 2

Graph paper can be used to plan your pattern. The diamond pattern is a good and easy one to start with.

Once you have the threads wrapped in place on the loom, remember to add one extra thread for the count of the seed beads you are using. Here we are using 12 seed beads. You will need 13 threads on the loom. Start with a two yard single strand, size O thread. Thread the needle and tie the end of the thread to only one thread on the outside row, closest to you. Leave 8-10 inches of loose thread. The loose thread will be woven back through the bead work when the loom work is complete.

Step 3

Add 12 seed beads on the needle. Once the beads are on the thread, lay the 12 beads underneath the threads on the loom. NOTE: Be sure there is one thread on each outside edge of the 12 beads.

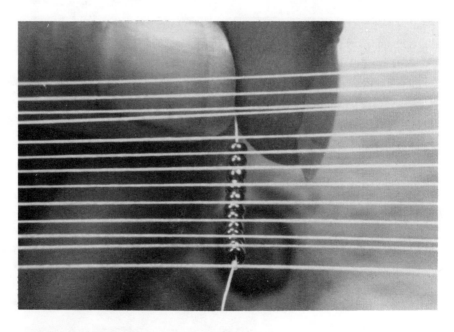

Step 4

With your left finger, press the beads up through the rows of threads. Take hold of the needle and pull the thread to place the seed beads close together and even. Next, sew down through the beads. Make sure that your needle is above all of the wrapped threads that are on the loom. Then, pull the thread to put the beads in place.

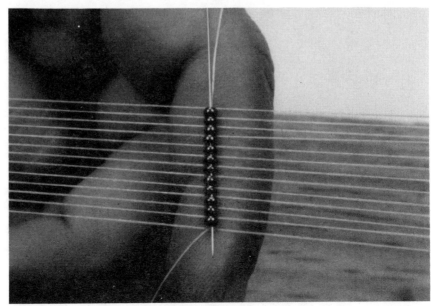

Step 5

Next, add 12 more seed beads and bring them under the threads on the loom to the right. Repeat step 4 by sewing down through the 12 seed beads. Again, make sure you always sew through the beads with your needle above all the wrapped threads on the loom. NOTE: Add on each row of 12 beads from left to right. For each row that is added to the right, make sure that the needle is <u>always</u> above and on top of all the wrapped threads that are on the loom. Sew down through the beads vertically.

Step 6

To add on thread, start with a two yard single strand, tie a knot to one of the threads that is in the center of the beaded strip, do this two or three rows back from where you plan to begin again. Leave 8 to 10 inches of loose thread to be woven back through the bead work. Thread the long part of the thread on to the needle and sew or weave back through the strip, one row at a time to the right. Each time that you sew through each row, reverse the needle. Once you are through the two or three rows, you are now ready to begin the bead work again. NOTE: Your beaded strip will be 6 to 8 inches long before you will need to add on thread.

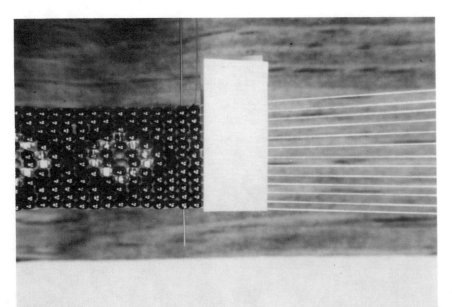

Step 7

Once the bead work is complete, all loose threads can be sewn on or woven back through the bead work. Lose thread should be knotted and hidden some where to secure them. Place cloth tape close to the bead work over separate ends of the beaded strip. Cut all thread off the loom, leaving five to eight inches of thread on each side. The thread and tape can be folded and tucked under the beaded strip. If you plan to add the strip onto fabric or leather, it is best to glue the cloth tape in place with stick all glue, or you can sew each thread down through the leather or fabric and tie two or three knots to secure each thread in place. The knots can be covered with small leather squares or triangles on the inside or outside of a bag.

My husbands and mine....
Five Beaded Hat Bands & one Belt Buckle, all created by Sadie

Necklaces and Earring Collections, from left to right: Pink Rodacrosite, Mother of Pearl Bird
inlay, Green Malachite, Chinese Turquoise, Blue Paua Stone & Fresh Water Pearls...
created by Sadie

Award winning necklace in the center is called the Green Fish. It is inlayed with Green Malachite, Serpentine and Minnesota Pipe Stone. I found the inlayed piece at a swap meet! All beadwork, created by Sadie

Peyote Pendants, Necklaces, Earrings, Bottles & Bracelet. All created by Sadie, except the beaded bottle with the Carved Dove at the top...Artist Unknown

All pieces, Necklaces, Earrings & Bolo Ties...created by Sadie

Barrettes, Buckles and Bags, all created by Sadie except the Blue Peyote Bag on the right bottom, the White, Red & Black Pin and Buckle, right bottom and the Tee Pee Rosette, center bottom. They are all traditional pieces and part of Sadies Personal Collection. The Artists are unknown.

More beaded Bags. The Earrings at the bottom right have titanium domed discs and feathers made by my husband Glen.
The Peyote Necklace(choker) was purchased in California, artist unknown.

More Barrettes, Earrings & Brooches, all created by Sadie.
The Red Rose in the center is not complete as I cannot decide what to make with it yet.

Antique bags on the right and left side and the beaded bag in the center are new and made in China. The earrings are new and created by Sadie. NOTE: All Gold earrings are porcelean molds made from antique bottoms and fired with 22 kt. gold...A Big Thanks to my Friend Kathy for making all of my wonderful porcelean molds.

Antique Beaded Bags. The bag in the center is made of antique aluminum beads from France. The small black bag under it also was made in France. The silver and black earrings on each side of the aluminum beaded bag are made from antique bottoms as was the black and gold earrings at the top right. Top left earrings are pink porcelean roses.

Top Left. Large Dream Catcher Shield, made with 4 & 5mm glass beads and 3 Macaw feathers. This beaded circle is attached to a metal hoop that is covered with white leather. Top Right: small dream catcher. Crystal wand(still in progress). Bottom Left: Large Brazilian Crystal Point protruding out through the top of a beaded bag of treasures, old and new. Bottom Center: Beaded Lighter Cover, custom made for my step father, Ron Foster. The first trip we took to Arizona we saw what we thought was a UFO, it inspired me to bead one. Beneath the red rocks and the cactus, notice the space ship in the center, drawing gemstones from the earth as it soars away.

All unique pieces created by Sadie. The three dimensional hand carved Prong-Horned Antelope head was beaded to be a Bolo Tie for a friend. The blue beaded Racu Pottery Discs above the Bolo were a gift created by one of my students Joann. After the bead work was added, I glued tiny crystal points over the top of the Racu disc, then 1/2 inch domed titanium disc, made by my husband Glen.

All beadwork created by Sadie except the large black purse, bottom center. It was on the back of the traditional beaded bag to the right, Tribe unknown. Notice the word BEAD-Z, it was done on a loom by my friend, Diane Anderson. The beaded insert on the front of the tennis shoe, is still being created by Sadie. Black Ultra-Suede was used for the beadwork attached to the Bali Baticed canvas boot. The legal eagle feather was custom beaded for a wedding gift.

The beaded painting in the center is one of many that I have done for the well known Cherokee artist Gloria Redfield Griggs. It is a joy to know her and an honor to have her work in my Gallery and my home. All beadwork done by Sadie.

All bead work done by Sadie except the beaded Bangle Bracelets, strung on fishing line and attached with crimp beads, created by Doris MacFadden. My student, Phyllis made the two pair of triangle shaped earrings, bottom center.Top Center, Corn Earrings were made by an unknown Indian artist.The Bottom Right beaded bracelet was made over a leather covered copper band. The leather is stitched together at the top front of the band and flat Peyote stitch is added. This type of beaded bracelet can also be done on a loom.

The off-white, leather dashboard cover was an idea that my son Elliot and I had for a Father's Day gift for my husband's four wheel drive truck. The flat Peyote beadwork attached to the bottom right is our blazing blue sand buggy.

This South West collection of earrings, barrettes and brooches are mostly turquoise & silver or black & silver. The tops of the earrings include: silver conchos, old buttons, new buttons and cabochons. The top center turquoise barrette has had fringe added to the bottom. One of my students, Kathy created the Man in the Maze beaded Concho, all other pieces were created by Sadie.

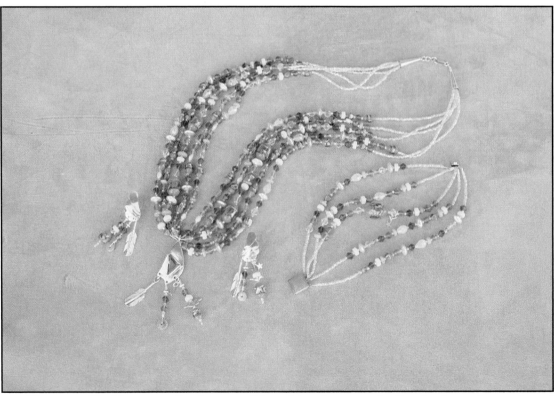

The classy Treasure Necklace, made of natural hand-made turquoise beads, faceted amythyst, Sterling Silver beads and findings. Old turquoise glass foil beads are from Czechoslovakia. The cream, opaque glass spacers are nicely faceted on the sides. This treasure collection was made for my Mother-in-Law's birthday, a lady with real class, Mom, we love you so much....

This Happy Holiday Collection is full of dressy pieces, some are in the pattern section. All pieces are created by Sadie except the Santa ornaments on the tree. They were made by a nice lady from Holland. The chili pepper barrette and earrings were made by my talented student, Jessica. The black beaded belt, at the top was made in China. Yes... the red beaded pot is still in progress...I wonder, will it ever get finished!

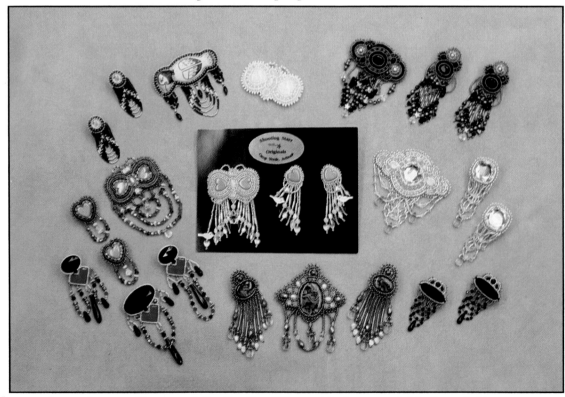

Brooches and earrings, all created by Sadie. The special carved bird and flower set at the top left is a fossilized, hand-carved collection of walrus ivory. The bird is a Puffin, found in Alaska and is in great danger of becoming extinct, the piece was custom beaded for Diane Anderson. Top Center is a turquoise butterfly brooch.

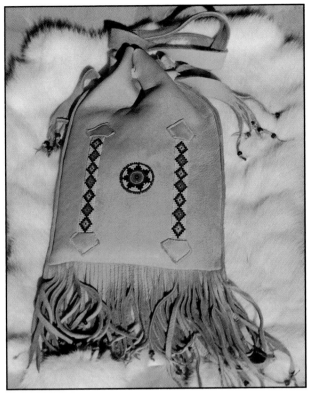

Top left, custom beaded bag with a beaded rosette in the center, created by Sadie. The two loomed, beaded strips were done by my dear friend, Dorothy Layfield. Top right, the beaded teddy bear and horse bridle were special gifts created by Sadie and given to dear friends.

Traditional beadwork. Some Indian beadwork is being copied by other countries. The eagle designs and the blue and white barrettes at the bottom are imported. The beaded lighter at the top right was created by Sadie. The other beadwork is Navajo and Shoshone.

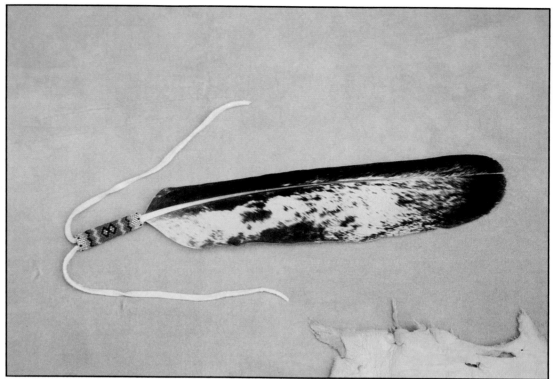

EVERLASTING FIRE

This special, real Eagle Feather belongs to the Seminole Indian Tribe. I would like to thank them for the special honor of beading it for them. Their directions were: bead only where the feather starts, use colors of the fire, red, white, blue, yellow, orange...any color you see when the fire burns. It's your mind and hands that make the feather unique. The two diamonds in the center are the two brothers.

Beaded Turkey feathers and one Blue Macaw with a crystal point coming out from underneath the feather leather strip.

Top left, the spiny oyster heart barrette and earrings made for my dearest friend Sally. She loves the color purple. The hand made sterling silver beads and button earrings used in all these pieces are hand made in Bali. This technique for the beads and buttons are known as granulation art. The antique aluminum beaded bag in the center is old, Ha, Ha. The suglite oval barrette and round beaded Balinese button and woven earrings on the right, I think I'll keep them and make a hat band to match.

Assorted Beadwork & Bags created by Sadie

Here is a great idea for barrettes that you can show off without wearing them. Button holes are made on the front pocket of the denim purse. Simply snap on or off your barrette, the choice is yours. The rattlesnake barrette and earrings were made by the talented Jerri Jeffries. Mother of pearl barrette and earrings created by Jessica.

I designed this blue denim coat. I had my talented friewnd, Dorothy Layfield do the beaded loom work. The gray halter top I made and used the same technique for the neckline fringe as the beaded white buckskin shirt that is shown on page 107. The toast color leather vest was made by the talented Diane Anderson. The Indian head necklace is imported. Both rosette earrings are Navajo.

Treasure Conchos, Earrings, all Cherokee originals by Sadie Starr. This beaded jewelery is made of hand-stamped Sterling Silver Conchos, complimented with real gemstones, antique Czekoslovakian glass drops, Sterling Silver feathers, hand-made turquoise beads and Austrian crystals, hand-painted Peruvian pottery beads made in Bali, Fimo clay beads, black olive Heishi shell. Each piece is unique and designed by Sadie. Silver Conchos hand-made by the talented Keith Davis.

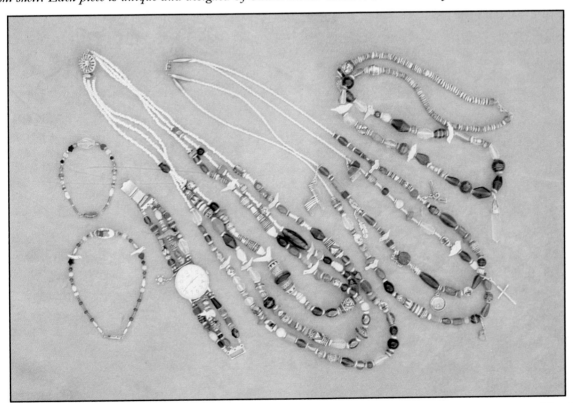

Bracelets, anklets, watch bands, one, two and three strand Treasure necklaces, created by Sadie. Small silver Treasure charms are added last by using the wire wrap technique or lobster claws and jump rings for attachment.

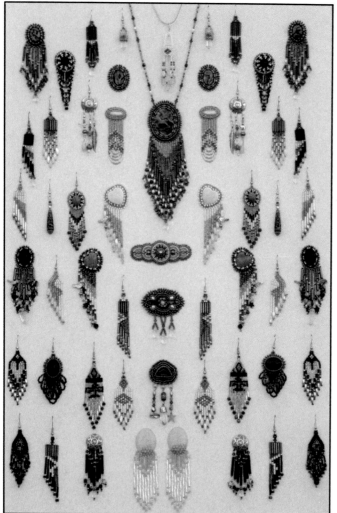

White antique glass hearts were used to bead this collection of barrette and earrings for my daughter-in-law Stephanie. She is a Seminole Indian. There are over 100 Czechoslovakian 5mm cut cyrstal Aurora Borealis beads in this barrette.

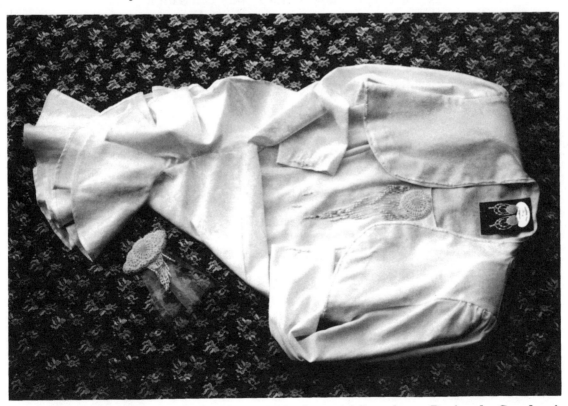

The white antique glass heart is also used in her wedding dress. Design by Stephanie, beadwork by Sadie.

INDEX FOR JEWELRY PATTERNS

NOTE: In this book, the term "Czecho bead" is used as an abbreviation for "Czechoslovakian bead."

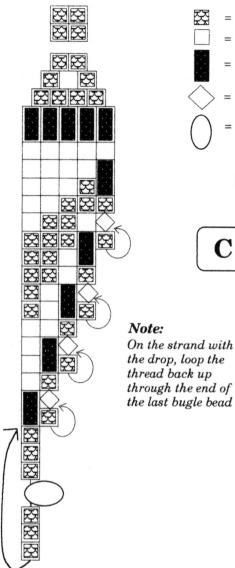

= Bronze (or gold) seed bead

= Silver seed bead

= Black bugle bead, 12mm

= Clear Crystal, 4mm

= Clear Crystal drop, 6mm x 10mm, with horizontal hole across the top of drop

Seed beads are size 11/0

C   *Black-Silver-Bronze Sideways*

Note:
On the strand with the drop, loop the thread back up through the end of the last bugle bead

Seed beads are size 11/0

Paua Stone is size 13mm x 18mm

(P) = Plum seed bead

= Light blue (or aqua satin) seed bead

◯ = Bronze seed bead

Paua Stone Earring on Post

A

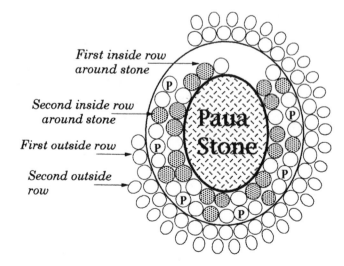

First inside row around stone

Second inside row around stone

First outside row

Second outside row

Paua Stone

Paua Stone is size 22mm x 30mm

Seed beads are size 11/0

○ = Bronze seed bead

◉ = Light blue (or aqua satin) seed bead

Ⓟ = Plum (or light purple) seed bead

Guide to rest of beads and crystals is on 2nd page of "B"

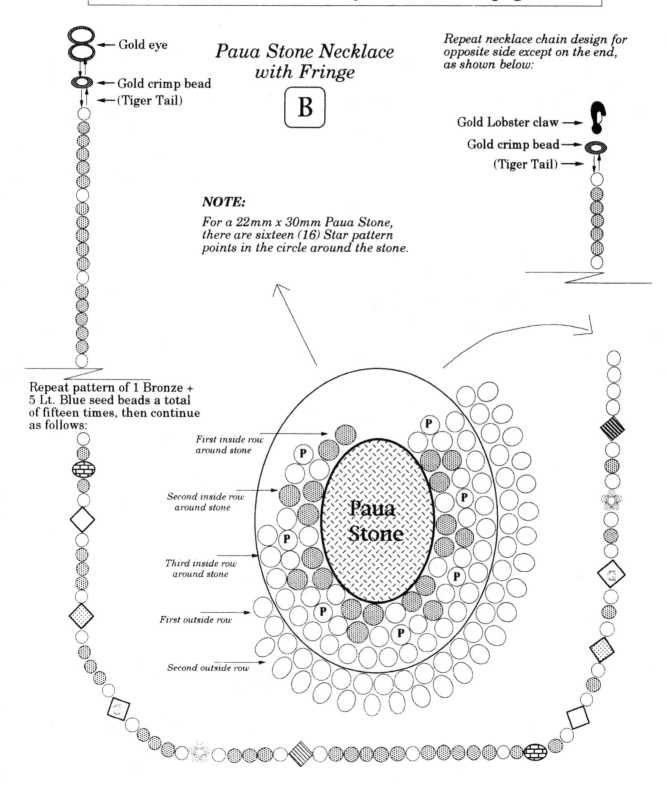

← Gold eye

← Gold crimp bead

← (Tiger Tail)

*Paua Stone Necklace
with Fringe*

B

*Repeat necklace chain design for
opposite side except on the end,
as shown below:*

Gold Lobster claw →

Gold crimp bead →

(Tiger Tail) →

NOTE:

*For a 22mm x 30mm Paua Stone,
there are sixteen (16) Star pattern
points in the circle around the stone.*

Repeat pattern of 1 Bronze +
5 Lt. Blue seed beads a total
of fifteen times, then continue
as follows:

*First inside row
around stone*

*Second inside row
around stone*

**Paua
Stone**

*Third inside row
around stone*

First outside row

Second outside row

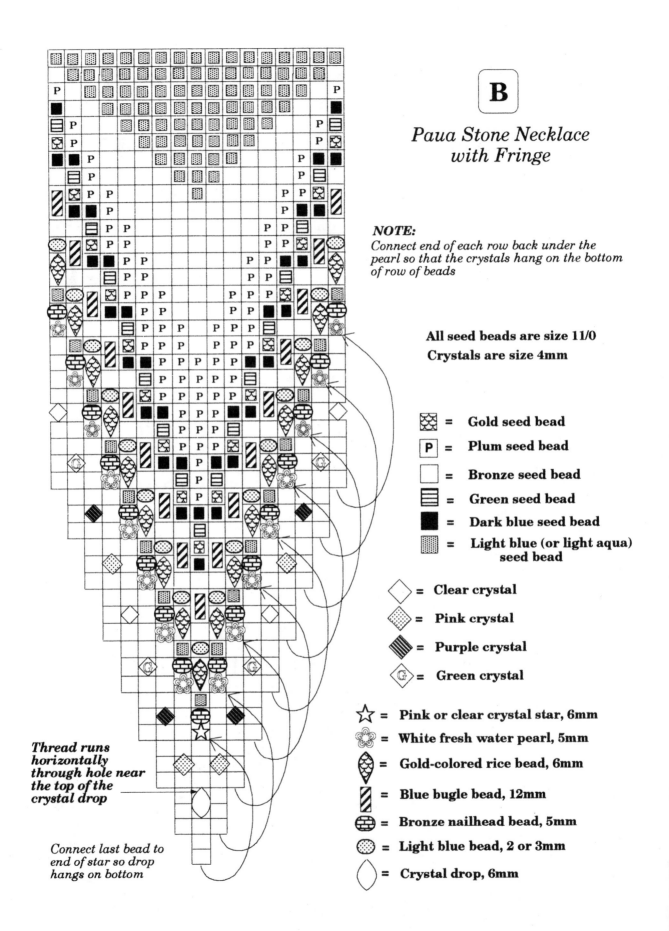

B

*Paua Stone Necklace
with Fringe*

NOTE:
*Connect end of each row back under the
pearl so that the crystals hang on the bottom
of row of beads*

All seed beads are size 11/0

Crystals are size 4mm

⬡ = **Gold seed bead**

P = **Plum seed bead**

□ = **Bronze seed bead**

▤ = **Green seed bead**

■ = **Dark blue seed bead**

▦ = **Light blue (or light aqua)
seed bead**

◇ = **Clear crystal**

◈ = **Pink crystal**

◈ = **Purple crystal**

◈ = **Green crystal**

☆ = **Pink or clear crystal star, 6mm**

❀ = **White fresh water pearl, 5mm**

⬭ = **Gold-colored rice bead, 6mm**

▯ = **Blue bugle bead, 12mm**

⬯ = **Bronze nailhead bead, 5mm**

⬤ = **Light blue bead, 2 or 3mm**

⬙ = **Crystal drop, 6mm**

*Thread runs
horizontally
through hole near
the top of the
crystal drop*

*Connect last bead to
end of star so drop
hangs on bottom*

Oval pink mussel stone is 6mm x 16mm

(P) = Pink seed bead

(✿) = Silver seed bead

*Alternate pink and
silver in two inside rows*

Second outside row
First outside row

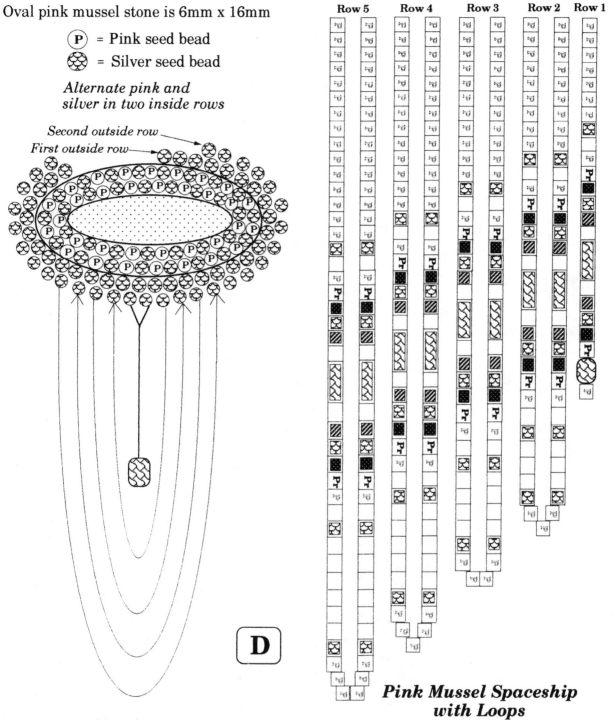

D

Seed beads are size 14/0

☐ = White seed bead

▧ = Silver seed bead

■ = Blue seed bead

Pr = Purple seed bead

▨ = Green seed bead

▫ = Pink seed bead

Row 5   Row 4   Row 3   Row 2   Row 1

Pink Mussel Spaceship
with Loops

NOTE: *The four outside fringe loops begin from
one outside silver seed bead; center row comes out
from between two outside silver seed beads.*

▨ = Silver (or aluminum) bugle bead,
6mm

⬭ = Silver end bead, 4mm

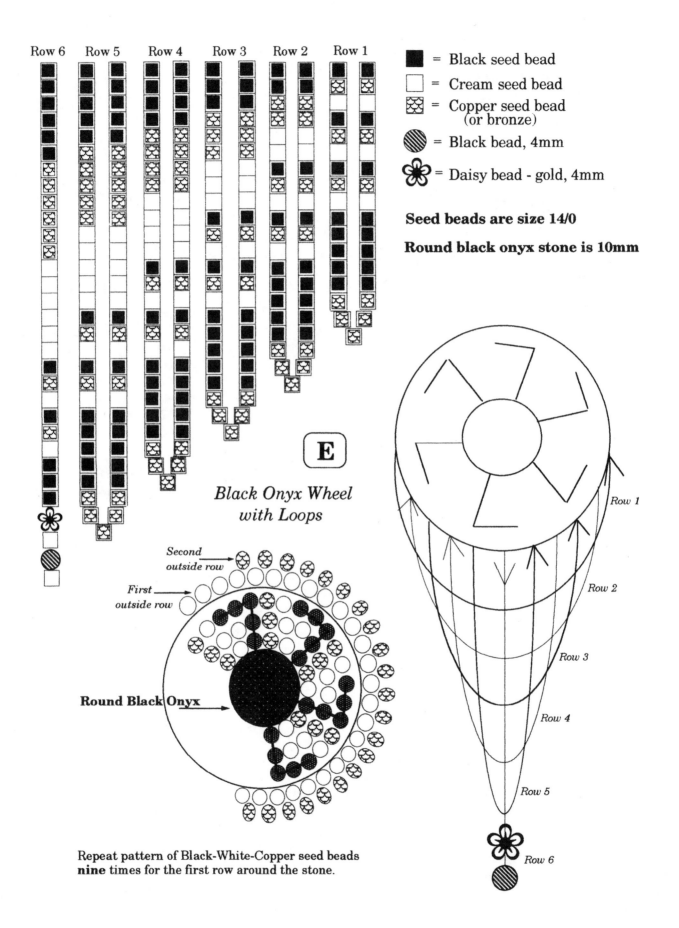

Row 6   Row 5   Row 4   Row 3   Row 2   Row 1

= Black seed bead

= Cream seed bead

= Copper seed bead
(or bronze)

= Black bead, 4mm

= Daisy bead - gold, 4mm

Seed beads are size 14/0

Round black onyx stone is 10mm

E

*Black Onyx Wheel
with Loops*

*Second
outside row*

*First
outside row*

Round Black Onyx

Row 1

Row 2

Row 3

Row 4

Row 5

Row 6

**Repeat pattern of Black-White-Copper seed beads
nine times for the first row around the stone.**

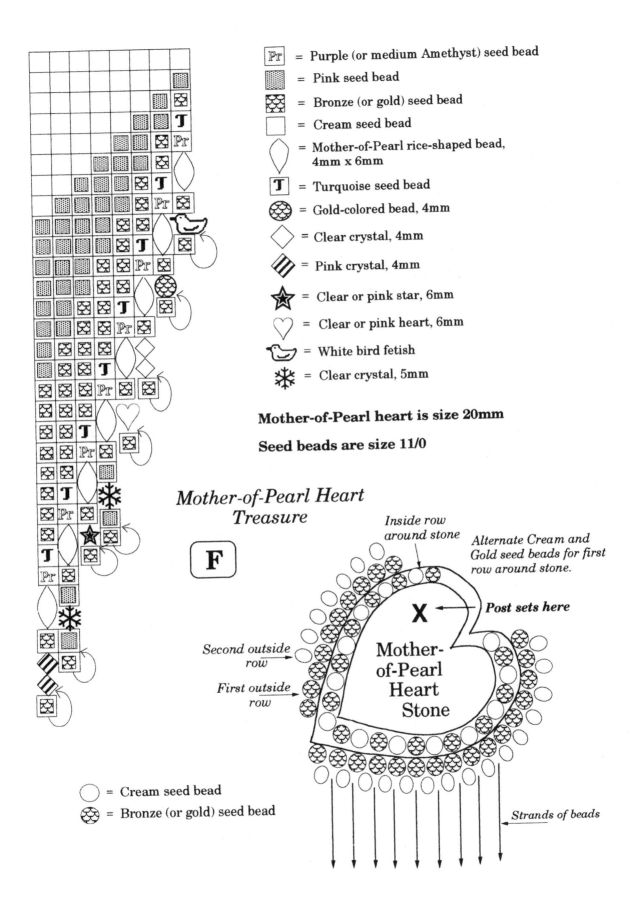

= Purple (or medium Amethyst) seed bead

= Pink seed bead

= Bronze (or gold) seed bead

= Cream seed bead

= Mother-of-Pearl rice-shaped bead, 4mm x 6mm

T = Turquoise seed bead

= Gold-colored bead, 4mm

= Clear crystal, 4mm

= Pink crystal, 4mm

= Clear or pink star, 6mm

= Clear or pink heart, 6mm

= White bird fetish

= Clear crystal, 5mm

Mother-of-Pearl heart is size 20mm

Seed beads are size 11/0

Mother-of-Pearl Heart Treasure

F

Inside row around stone

Alternate Cream and Gold seed beads for first row around stone.

X

Mother-of-Pearl Heart Stone

Post sets here

Second outside row

First outside row

Strands of beads

○ = Cream seed bead

= Bronze (or gold) seed bead

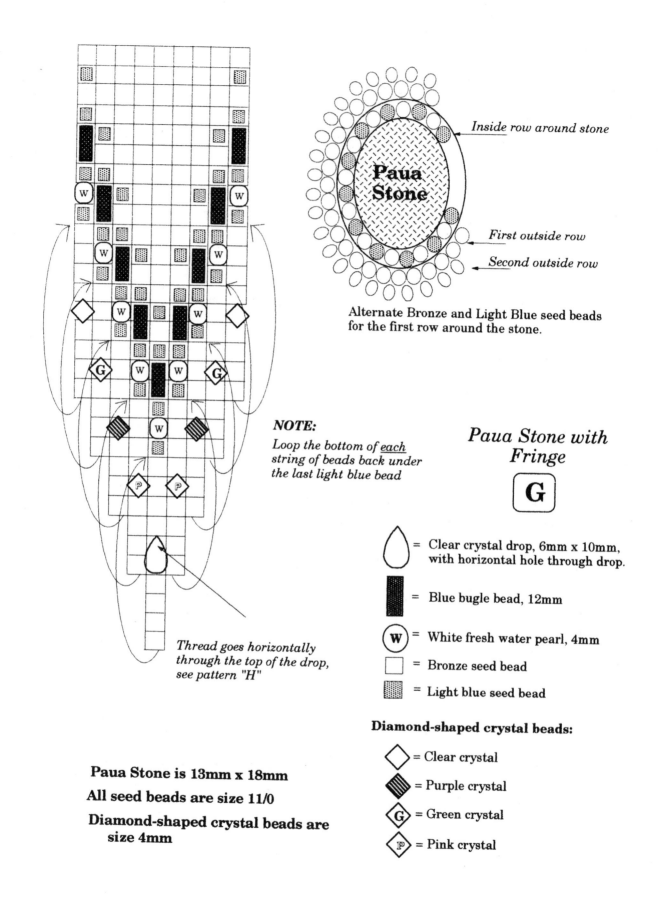

Inside row around stone

First outside row

Second outside row

Alternate Bronze and Light Blue seed beads for the first row around the stone.

NOTE:

Loop the bottom of each string of beads back under the last light blue bead

Thread goes horizontally through the top of the drop, see pattern "H"

Paua Stone with Fringe

G

= Clear crystal drop, 6mm x 10mm, with horizontal hole through drop.

= Blue bugle bead, 12mm

W = White fresh water pearl, 4mm

= Bronze seed bead

= Light blue seed bead

Diamond-shaped crystal beads:

= Clear crystal

= Purple crystal

G = Green crystal

P = Pink crystal

Paua Stone is 13mm x 18mm

All seed beads are size 11/0

Diamond-shaped crystal beads are size 4mm

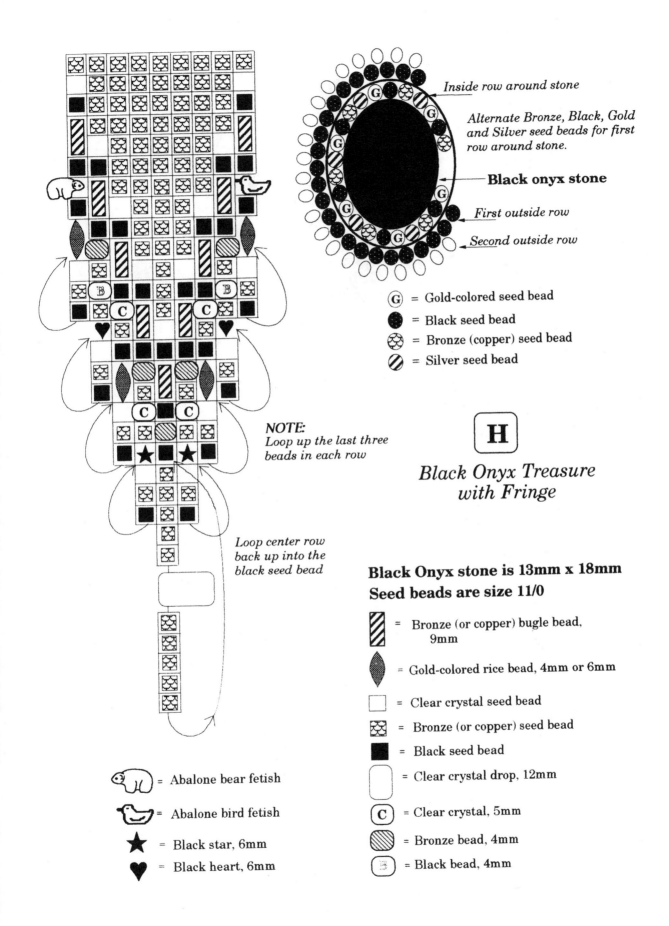

Inside row around stone

Alternate Bronze, Black, Gold and Silver seed beads for first row around stone.

Black onyx stone

First outside row

Second outside row

- G = Gold-colored seed bead
- ● = Black seed bead
- ⊗ = Bronze (copper) seed bead
- ⊘ = Silver seed bead

NOTE:
Loop up the last three beads in each row

H

Black Onyx Treasure with Fringe

Loop center row back up into the black seed bead

Black Onyx stone is 13mm x 18mm
Seed beads are size 11/0

- ⊘ = Bronze (or copper) bugle bead, 9mm
- ◆ = Gold-colored rice bead, 4mm or 6mm
- □ = Clear crystal seed bead
- ⊠ = Bronze (or copper) seed bead
- ■ = Black seed bead
- ▢ = Clear crystal drop, 12mm
- C = Clear crystal, 5mm
- ◍ = Bronze bead, 4mm
- ◉ = Black bead, 4mm

- = Abalone bear fetish
- = Abalone bird fetish
- ★ = Black star, 6mm
- ♥ = Black heart, 6mm

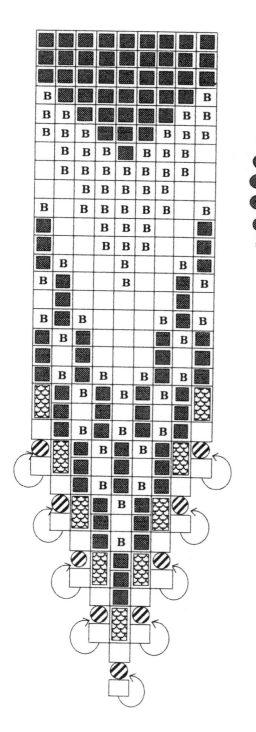

Second inside row
around stone

First inside row
around stone

Repeat pattern of 2 Brown
and 1 Cream seed bead
for first row around stone.

**Picture
Jasper
Stone**

First outside row

Second outside row

= Turquoise seed bead

○ = Cream seed bead

Ⓑ = Burgandy (or brown) seed bead

I

*Picture Jasper Stone
with Fringe*

Picture Jasper Stone is 10mm x 14mm

Seed beads are size 14/0

▨ = Turquoise seed bead

B = Brown (or Burgandy) seed bead

☐ = Cream seed bead

▦ = Bronze bugle bead, 5mm

⊘ = Green Jasper ball, 4mm

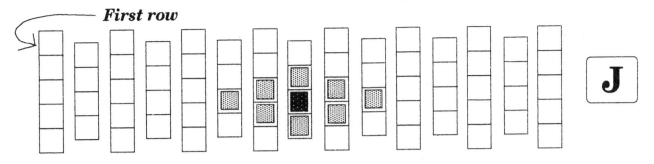

First row

J

Always use an even number of beads around the object.
Using odd numbers does not turn out right.
The second row involves beading through every other
bead for a row with half the number started with.

Notice:

*Stitching on Peyote Pendant and Earrings
creates a brick layer effect around the crystal.*

Seed beads are size 11/0

☐ = **White or Silver seed bead**

■ = **Turquoise seed bead**

▩ = **Bronze or Purple seed bead**

*Purple Earring
with Drop*

T

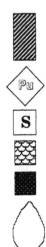 = Purple bugle bead, 12mm

⬦ᴾᵘ = Plum crystal, 4mm

Ⓢ = Silver seed bead

▩ = Bronze (or gold) seed bead

■ = Capri Blue seed bead

⬭ = Clear crystal drop, 6mm x 10mm

Seed beads are size 11/0

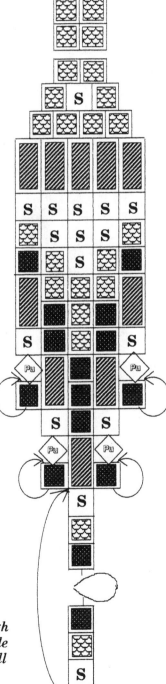

NOTE:
*Loop middle row of
beads back up through
the bottom of the bugle
bead; crystal drop will
hang in the center.*

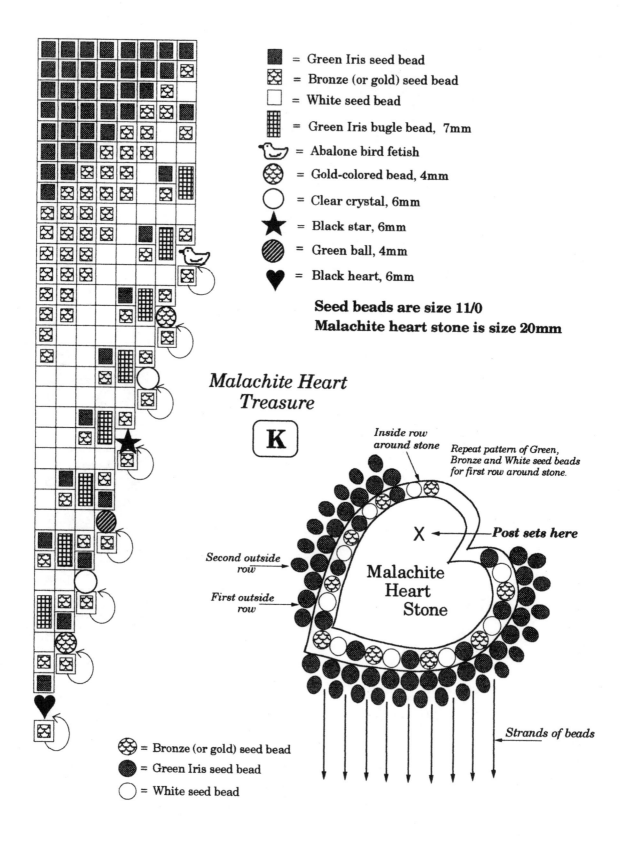

= Green Iris seed bead

= Bronze (or gold) seed bead

= White seed bead

= Green Iris bugle bead, 7mm

= Abalone bird fetish

= Gold-colored bead, 4mm

= Clear crystal, 6mm

= Black star, 6mm

= Green ball, 4mm

= Black heart, 6mm

Seed beads are size 11/0
Malachite heart stone is size 20mm

Malachite Heart Treasure

K

Inside row around stone

Repeat pattern of Green, Bronze and White seed beads for first row around stone.

X ← **Post sets here**

Second outside row

First outside row

Malachite Heart Stone

Strands of beads

= Bronze (or gold) seed bead

= Green Iris seed bead

= White seed bead

= Blue seed bead

= Silver seed bead

T = Turquoise seed bead

= White seed bead

= Aluminum (or silver) bugle bead, 6mm

= Capri Blue bugle bead, 12mm

= Mother of Pearl rice bead, 4mm x 6mm

Seed beads are size 14/0

L

Blue Earring

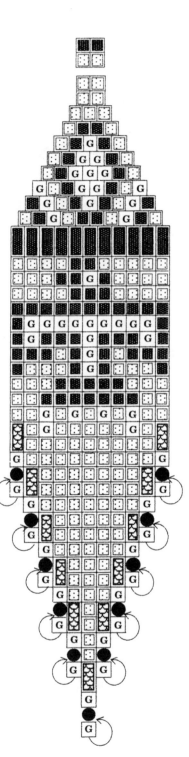

O

Eagle Earring

Seed beads are size 14/0

= Black seed bead

= Silver seed bead

G = Gold seed bead

= Black bead, 4mm

= Black bugle bead, 5mm

= Silver bugle bead, 7mm

M Spaceship Brooch with Fringe

◇ = Plum crystal, 4mm

◆ = Capri blue crystal, 4mm

= Fresh water pearls, ~ 4mm x 6mm

= Clear crystal drop, 6mm x 10mm, with horizontal hole through drop

= Marquis-shaped Paua stone, 5mm x 15mm

Ⓑ = Light blue seed bead size 11/0

● = Capri blue seed bead size 11/0

○ = Plum seed bead size 11/0

⊗ = Bronze seed bead size 11/0

Ⓒ = Round crystal, 4mm

One-inch pin back:

1st step: Sew crystal in center
2nd step: One row of plum seed beads around crystal
3rd step: Glue on Marquis-shaped Paua stones
4th step: Alternate light blue and bronze seed beads
5th step: Row of capri blue beads
6th step: Row of plum beads
7th step: Sew on the four fresh water pearls
8th step: Row of bronze beads all the way around stones and beads
9th step: Alternate capri blue and bronze beads all the way around
10th step: Cut around beadwork, add pin and glue on back
11th step: Add both outside rows of bronze beads
12th step: Add fringe as shown in the diagram.

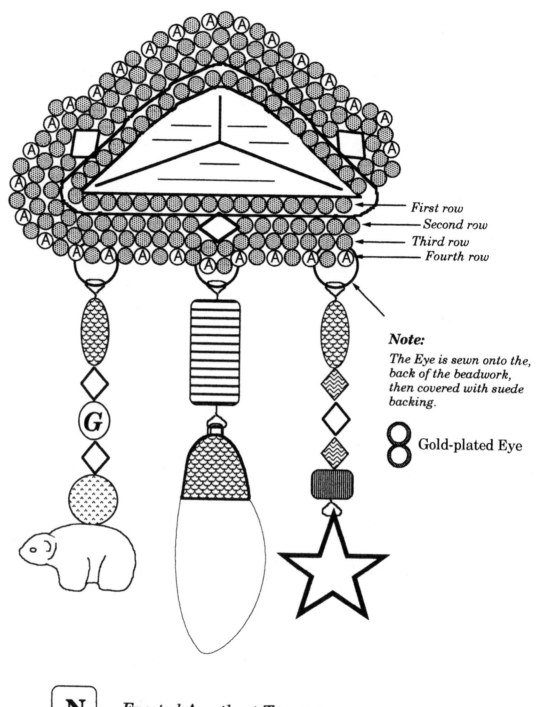

First row
Second row
Third row
Fourth row

Note:

The Eye is sewn onto the, back of the beadwork, then covered with suede backing.

8 Gold-plated Eye

N *Faceted Amethyst Treasure Brooch*

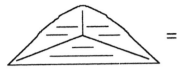 = Faceted Amethyst

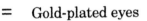 = Gold-plated head pins, 2" long
(use 3 of them, cut heads off of 2)

= Gold-plated eyes

One-inch pin back:

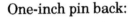

= Bronze seed beads, size 11/0

(A) = Amethyst seed beads, size 11/0

= Topaz Austrian crystal, size 4mm

= Amethyst Austrian crystal, size 4mm

= Gold-plated rice bead, size 4mm x 6mm

(G) = Czecho green faceted glass bead, size 5mm

= Purple Peru Pottery bead, size 6mm x 10mm

= Gold-plated barrel-shaped bead, 4mm

= Abalone bear fetish, size 4mm x 10mm

= Gold-plated star, approx. 12mm

= Czecho bronze bead, size 10mm

= Gold electroplated cap for crystal

= Crystal, size 8mm x 20mm

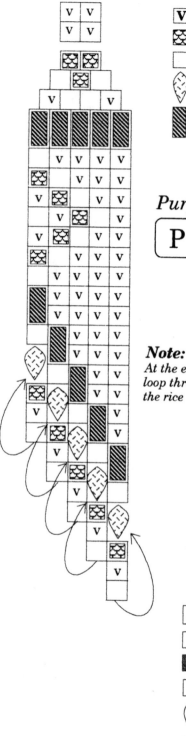

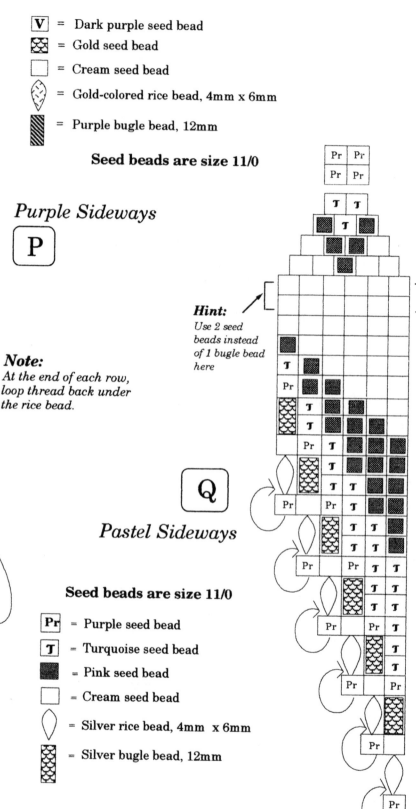

= Dark purple seed bead

= Gold seed bead

= Cream seed bead

= Gold-colored rice bead, 4mm x 6mm

= Purple bugle bead, 12mm

Seed beads are size 11/0

Purple Sideways

P

Note:
*At the end of each row,
loop thread back under
the rice bead.*

Hint:
*Use 2 seed
beads instead
of 1 bugle bead
here*

Q

Pastel Sideways

Seed beads are size 11/0

Pr = Purple seed bead

T = Turquoise seed bead

= Pink seed bead

= Cream seed bead

= Silver rice bead, 4mm x 6mm

= Silver bugle bead, 12mm

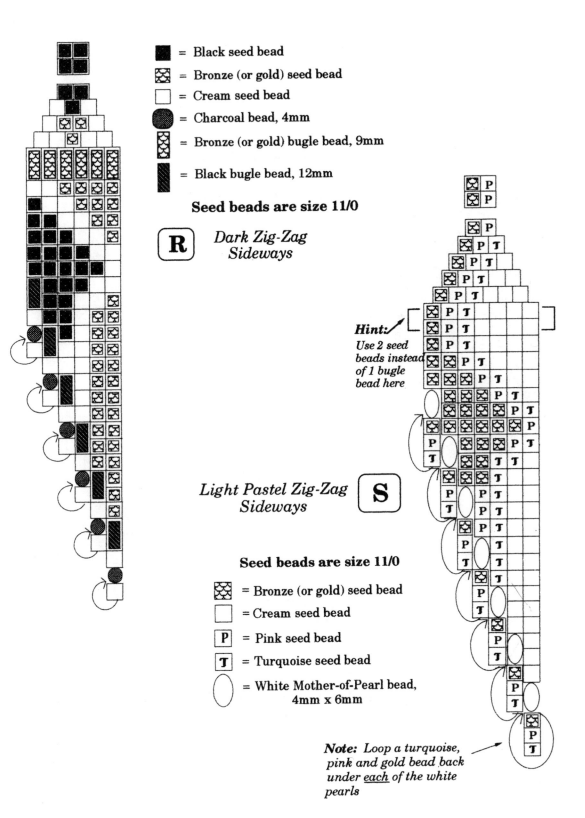

= Black seed bead

= Bronze (or gold) seed bead

= Cream seed bead

= Charcoal bead, 4mm

= Bronze (or gold) bugle bead, 9mm

= Black bugle bead, 12mm

Seed beads are size 11/0

R *Dark Zig-Zag Sideways*

Light Pastel Zig-Zag Sideways **S**

Hint: *Use 2 seed beads instead of 1 bugle bead here*

Seed beads are size 11/0

= Bronze (or gold) seed bead

= Cream seed bead

P = Pink seed bead

T = Turquoise seed bead

= White Mother-of-Pearl bead, 4mm x 6mm

Note: *Loop a turquoise, pink and gold bead back under each of the white pearls*

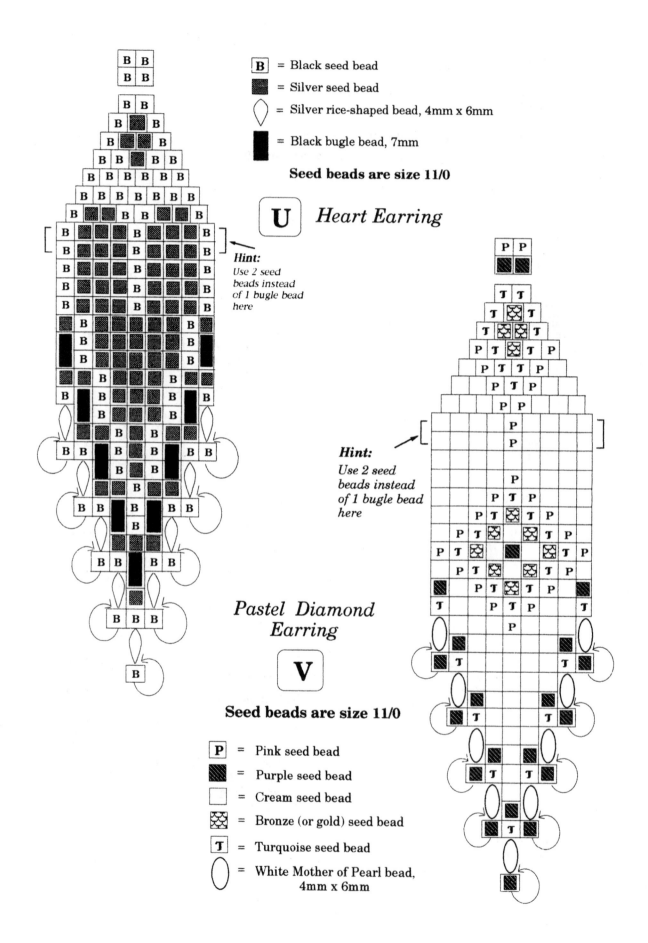

B = Black seed bead

▨ = Silver seed bead

◊ = Silver rice-shaped bead, 4mm x 6mm

▮ = Black bugle bead, 7mm

Seed beads are size 11/0

U *Heart Earring*

Hint:
Use 2 seed beads instead of 1 bugle bead here

Pastel Diamond Earring

V

Seed beads are size 11/0

Hint:
Use 2 seed beads instead of 1 bugle bead here

P = Pink seed bead

▨ = Purple seed bead

☐ = Cream seed bead

▩ = Bronze (or gold) seed bead

T = Turquoise seed bead

⬭ = White Mother of Pearl bead, 4mm x 6mm

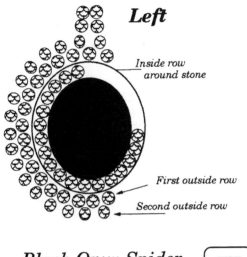

Left

Inside row
around stone

First outside row

Second outside row

Right

Black Onyx Spider with Loops

| **W** |

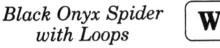

NOTE: *As you thread the rows of beads back into the next available seed bead they will automatically curl, as shown in the photo.*

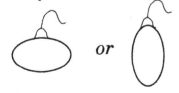

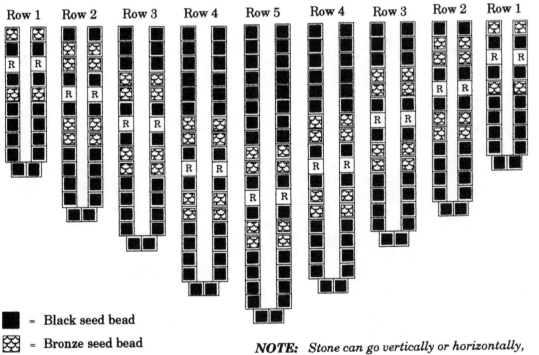

Row 1   Row 2   Row 3   Row 4   Row 5   Row 4   Row 3   Row 2   Row 1

■ = **Black seed bead**

▨ = **Bronze seed bead**

R = **Red seed bead**

Black Onyx Stone is 13mm x 18mm
Seed beads are size 11/0

NOTE: *Stone can go vertically or horizontally, the choice is yours.*

or

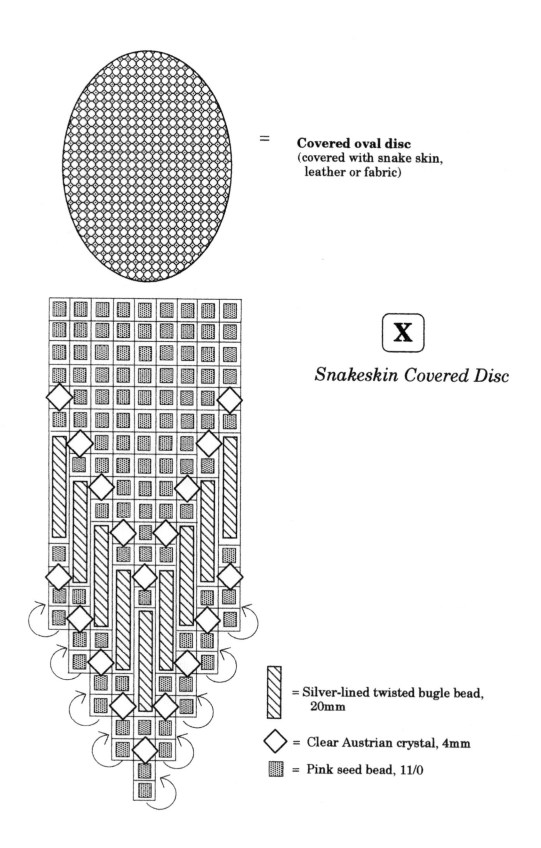

= **Covered oval disc**
(covered with snake skin,
leather or fabric)

$\boxed{\textbf{X}}$

Snakeskin Covered Disc

= Silver-lined twisted bugle bead,
20mm

= Clear Austrian crystal, 4mm

= Pink seed bead, 11/0

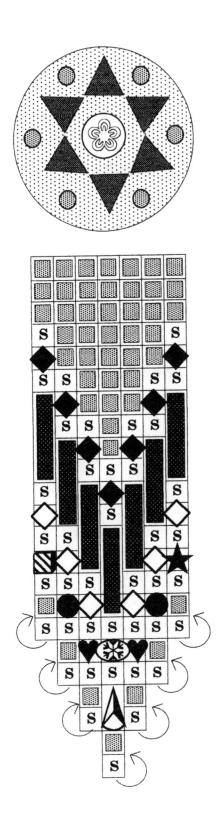

= Hand-stamped Sterling Silver concho, 3/4 inch

Silver Concho with Treasure Fringe

= Black matte seed bead, 14/0

= Silver seed bead, 14/0

= Grey Austrian crystal, 4mm

= Aurora Borealis cut glass, 5mm

= Black onyx heart, 6mm

= Hematite star, 6mm

= Czecho nailhead, 5mm

= Bali spacer bead, 6mm

= Square Hematite bead, 4mm

= Black matte bugle bead, 20mm

= Austrian crystal drop, 6mm x 10mm, with vertical hole through drop

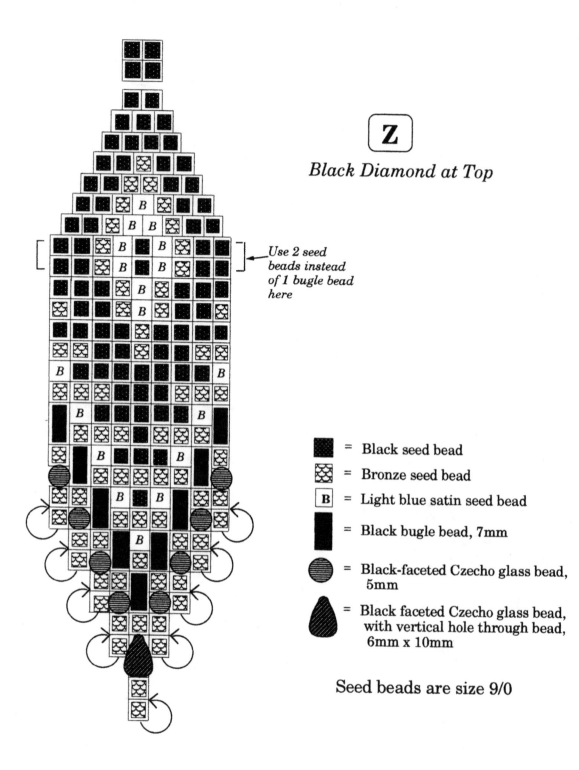

Use 2 seed
beads instead
of 1 bugle bead
here

Z

Black Diamond at Top

= Black seed bead

= Bronze seed bead

B = Light blue satin seed bead

= Black bugle bead, 7mm

= Black-faceted Czecho glass bead, 5mm

= Black faceted Czecho glass bead, with vertical hole through bead, 6mm x 10mm

Seed beads are size 9/0

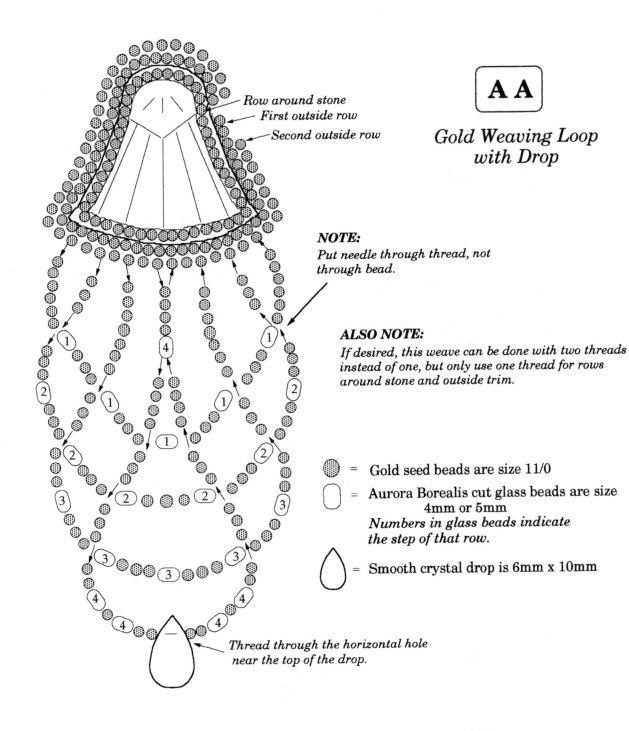

Row around stone
First outside row
Second outside row

AA

Gold Weaving Loop with Drop

NOTE:
Put needle through thread, not through bead.

ALSO NOTE:
If desired, this weave can be done with two threads instead of one, but only use one thread for rows around stone and outside trim.

= Gold seed beads are size 11/0

= Aurora Borealis cut glass beads are size 4mm or 5mm
Numbers in glass beads indicate the step of that row.

= Smooth crystal drop is 6mm x 10mm

Thread through the horizontal hole near the top of the drop.

Shapes which can be used for this pattern include the Fan Shape, Upside-Down Heart and Oval. You can have this fringe design hanging down from a brooch, barrette, stone---anything 14 beads wide.

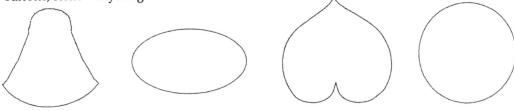

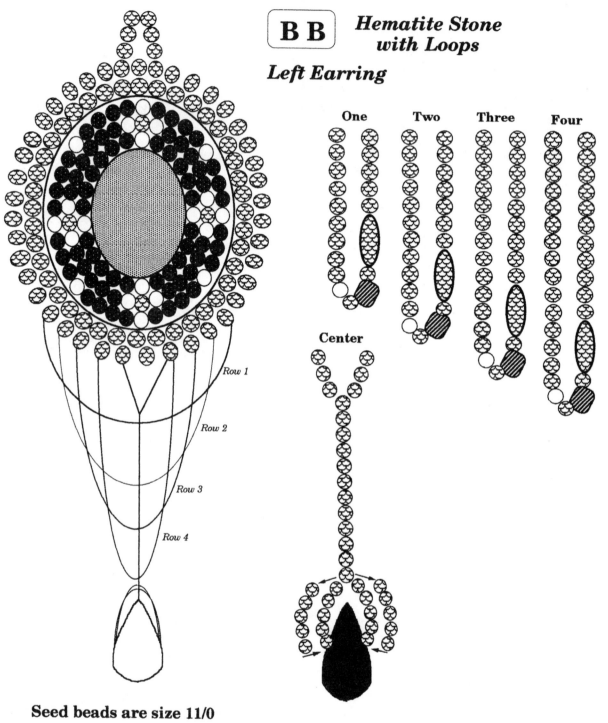

BB *Hematite Stone with Loops*

Left Earring

One Two Three Four

Center

Row 1

Row 2

Row 3

Row 4

Seed beads are size 11/0

Black crystals are size 4mm

Black glass beads are size 5mm

Gold-colored rice beads are 4mm or 5mm

Black drop is size 6mm x 10mm

Hematite Stone is 8mm x 10mm

Hematite Stone with Loops

Right Earring

Hematite Stone

Directions:

To begin, draw a straight line across pellum before gluing down stone.

Second step in row

Notes:

Add five bronze beads on each side of the drop, for a total of two rows on each side, as some drops will tend to tip with just one row of beads.

In order to add the second set of bronze seed beads, you must sew back through the row with the Black Drop a second time.

 = **Black crystal**

= **Black glass bead**

= **Black seed bead**

= **Cream seed bead**

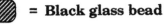 = **Bronze (or gold) seed bead**

= **Gold-colored rice bead**

 = **Black drop, 6mm x 10mm, with horizontal hole through top of drop.**

See Left Earring Pattern for bead sizes.

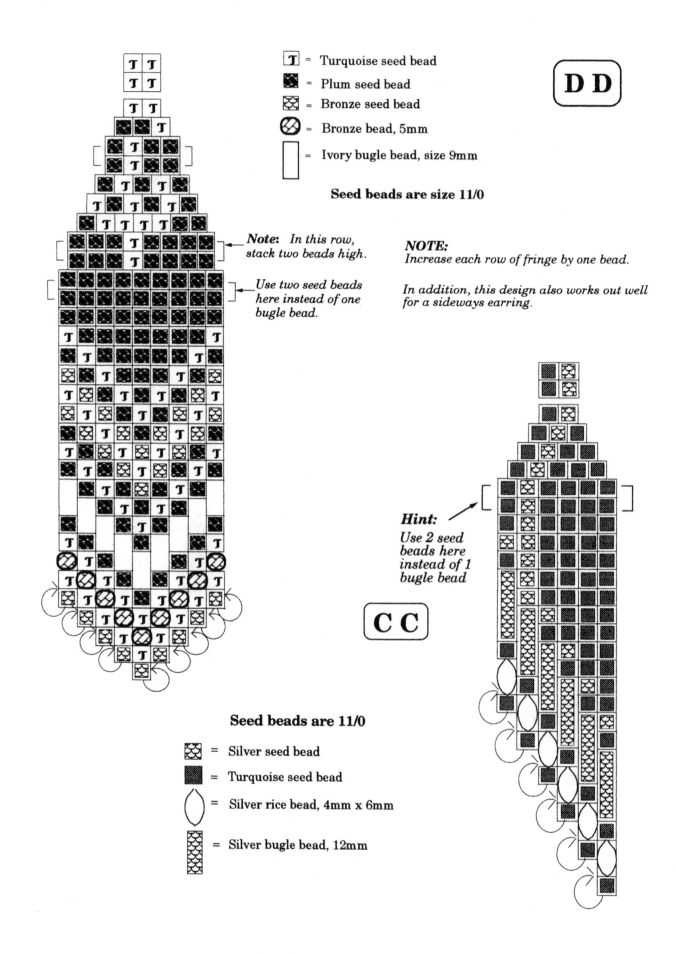

T = Turquoise seed bead

■ = Plum seed bead

▨ = Bronze seed bead

⊗ = Bronze bead, 5mm

▯ = Ivory bugle bead, size 9mm

Seed beads are size 11/0

D D

Note: *In this row, stack two beads high.*

Use two seed beads here instead of one bugle bead.

NOTE:
Increase each row of fringe by one bead.

In addition, this design also works out well for a sideways earring.

Hint:
Use 2 seed beads here instead of 1 bugle bead

C C

Seed beads are 11/0

▨ = Silver seed bead

■ = Turquoise seed bead

◇ = Silver rice bead, 4mm x 6mm

▤ = Silver bugle bead, 12mm

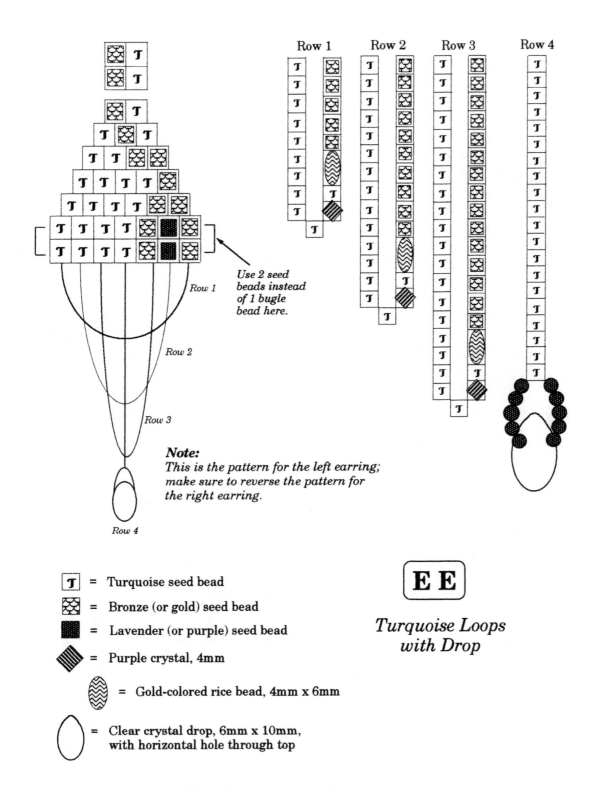

Row 1

Row 2

Row 3

Use 2 seed
beads instead
of 1 bugle
bead here.

Row 1

Row 2

Row 3

Note:
This is the pattern for the left earring;
make sure to reverse the pattern for
the right earring.

Row 4

$\boxed{T}$	=	Turquoise seed bead
	=	Bronze (or gold) seed bead
	=	Lavender (or purple) seed bead
	=	Purple crystal, 4mm
	=	Gold-colored rice bead, 4mm x 6mm
	=	Clear crystal drop, 6mm x 10mm, with horizontal hole through top

Seed beads are size 11/0

E E

Turquoise Loops
with Drop

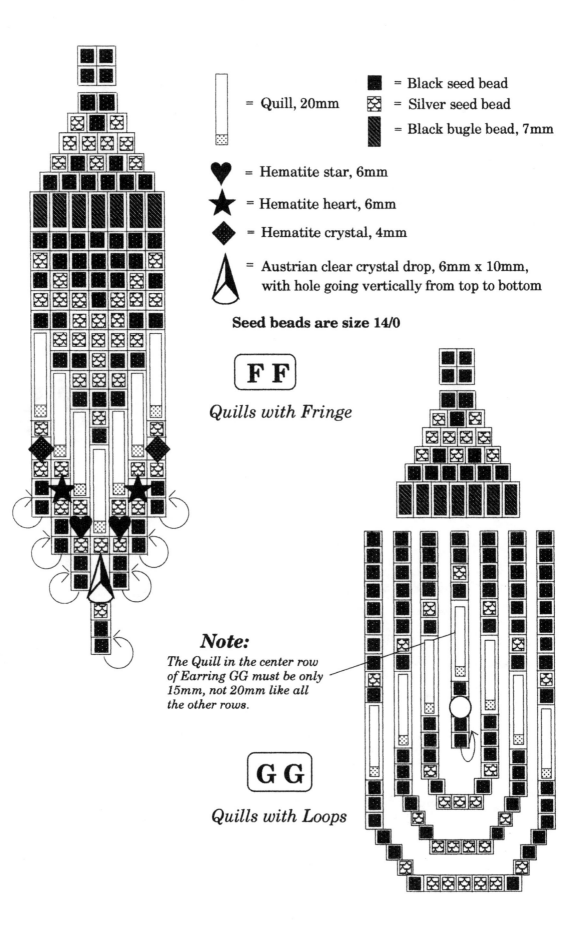

= Quill, 20mm

= Black seed bead
= Silver seed bead
= Black bugle bead, 7mm

= Hematite star, 6mm

= Hematite heart, 6mm

= Hematite crystal, 4mm

= Austrian clear crystal drop, 6mm x 10mm, with hole going vertically from top to bottom

Seed beads are size 14/0

F F

Quills with Fringe

Note:

The Quill in the center row of Earring GG must be only 15mm, not 20mm like all the other rows.

G G

Quills with Loops

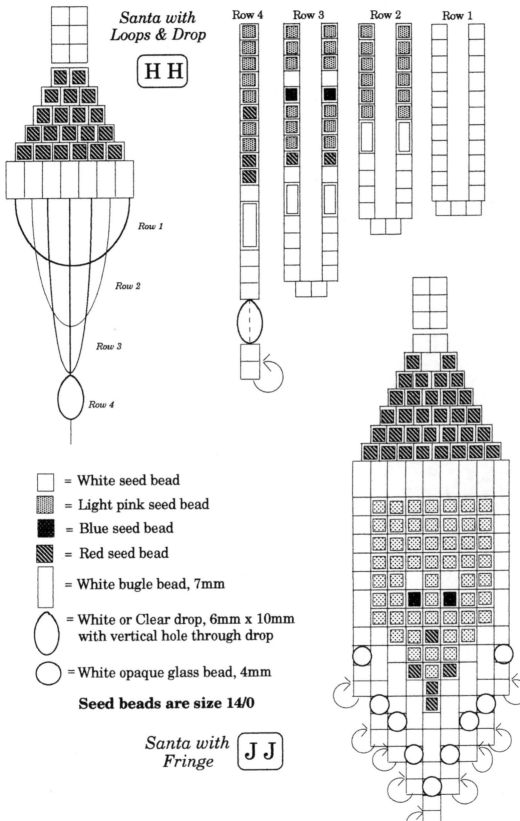

Seed beads are size 11/0

*Santa with
Loops & Drop*

H H

Row 4 Row 3 Row 2 Row 1

Row 1

Row 2

Row 3

Row 4

☐ = White seed bead

▦ = Light pink seed bead

■ = Blue seed bead

▨ = Red seed bead

▯ = White bugle bead, 7mm

⬭ = White or Clear drop, 6mm x 10mm
   with vertical hole through drop

○ = White opaque glass bead, 4mm

Seed beads are size 14/0

*Santa with
Fringe* **J J**

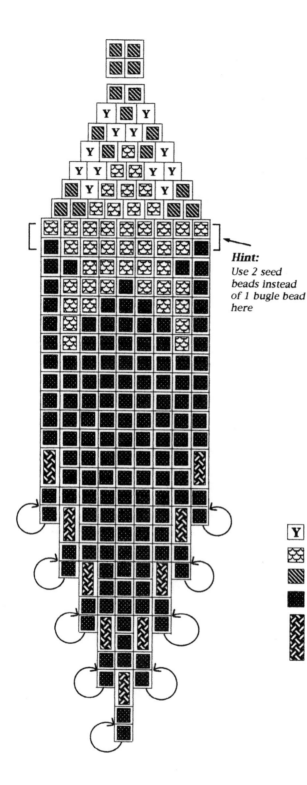

Arizona State Flag

Hint:
*Use 2 seed
beads instead
of 1 bugle bead
here*

Seed beads are size 11/0

| Y | = Yellow seed bead |

= Bronze seed bead

= Red transparent seed bead

= Cobalt Blue (or dark blue) seed bead

= Cobalt Blue (or dark blue) bugle bead, 5mm

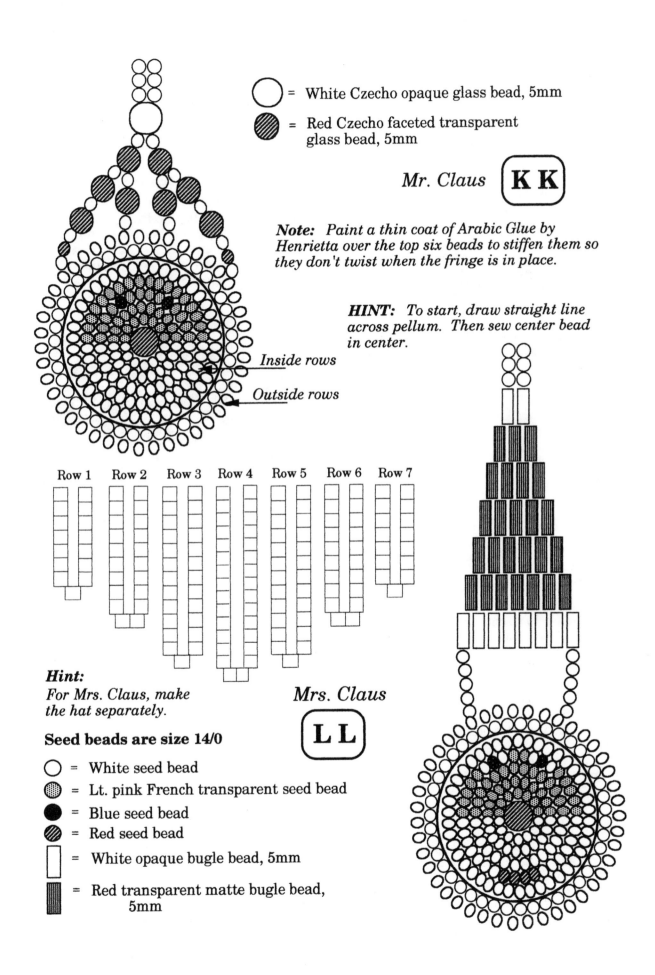

= White Czecho opaque glass bead, 5mm

= Red Czecho faceted transparent glass bead, 5mm

Mr. Claus **K K**

Note: *Paint a thin coat of Arabic Glue by Henrietta over the top six beads to stiffen them so they don't twist when the fringe is in place.*

HINT: *To start, draw straight line across pellum. Then sew center bead in center.*

Inside rows

Outside rows

Row 1 Row 2 Row 3 Row 4 Row 5 Row 6 Row 7

Hint:
For Mrs. Claus, make the hat separately.

Mrs. Claus **L L**

Seed beads are size 14/0

= White seed bead

= Lt. pink French transparent seed bead

= Blue seed bead

= Red seed bead

= White opaque bugle bead, 5mm

= Red transparent matte bugle bead, 5mm

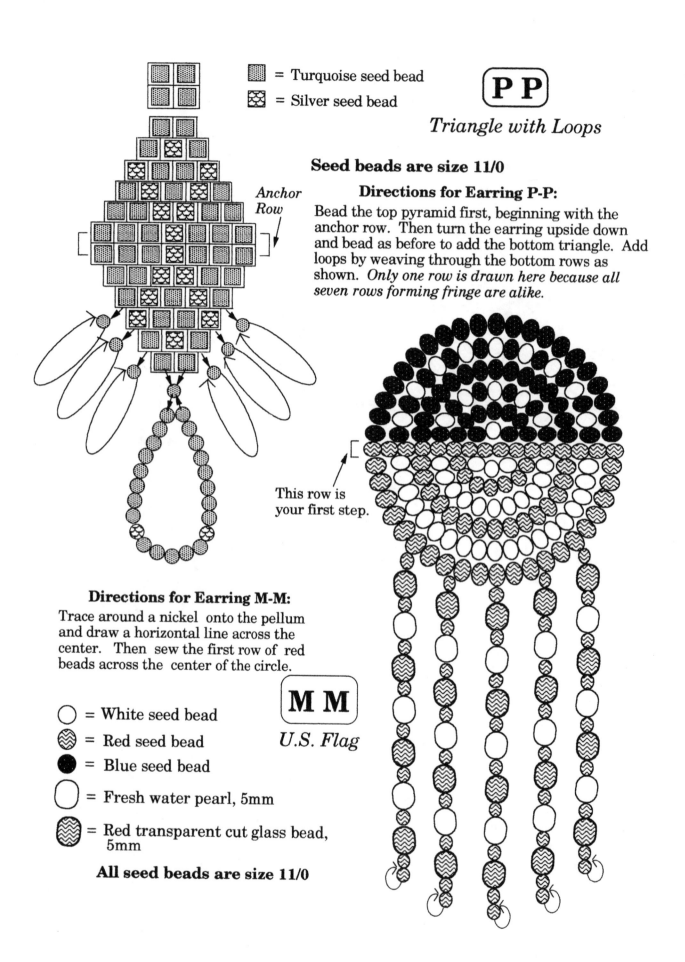

= Turquoise seed bead

= Silver seed bead

Anchor Row

P P

Triangle with Loops

Seed beads are size 11/0

Directions for Earring P-P:

Bead the top pyramid first, beginning with the anchor row. Then turn the earring upside down and bead as before to add the bottom triangle. Add loops by weaving through the bottom rows as shown. *Only one row is drawn here because all seven rows forming fringe are alike.*

This row is your first step.

Directions for Earring M-M:

Trace around a nickel onto the pellum and draw a horizontal line across the center. Then sew the first row of red beads across the center of the circle.

M M

U.S. Flag

○ = White seed bead

◉ = Red seed bead

● = Blue seed bead

○ = Fresh water pearl, 5mm

◉ = Red transparent cut glass bead, 5mm

All seed beads are size 11/0

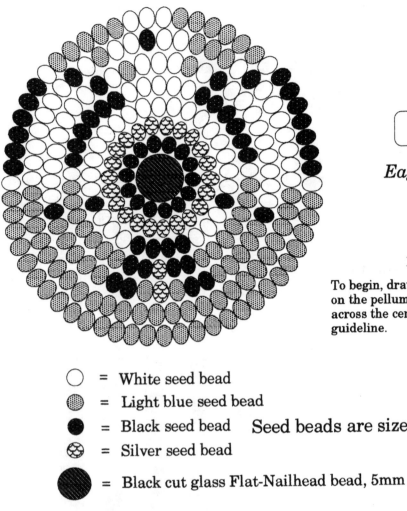

Eagle Rosette

Directions:

To begin, draw a circle around a quarter on the pellum. Draw a straight line across the center of the circle to use as a guideline.

○ = White seed bead

◉ = Light blue seed bead

● = Black seed bead   Seed beads are size 14/0

⊗ = Silver seed bead

● = Black cut glass Flat-Nailhead bead, 5mm

Turtle Rosette

Directions:

To begin, draw a circle around a nickel on the pellum. Then draw a vertical line down the center of the circle to use as a guideline.

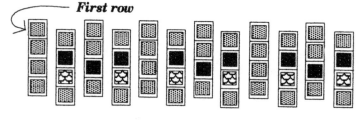

First row

Notice:
Using the Peyote stitch creates a brick layer effect.

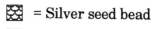

Loop at the top ←

Fringe:

Row 1 Row 2 Row 3 Row 4 Row 5 Row 6

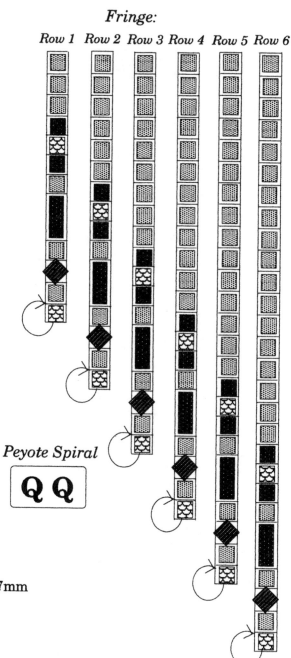

To begin, bead earring around a tubular object, starting with twelve turquoise seed beads.

To make the second row, add one turquoise bead, skip a bead, all the way around, until you end the second row.

Remember:
Always use an even number of beads around the object.
Using odd numbers does not turn out right.

NOTE:
Add the rows of fringe clockwise on the first earring. Then add the rows of fringe counter clockwise on the second earring.

Peyote Spiral

Q Q

▦ = Silver seed bead

▨ = Turquoise seed bead

■ = Black seed bead

◆ = Black Austrian crystal, 4mm

▮ = Black matte twisted bugle bead, 7mm

Seed beads are size 11/0

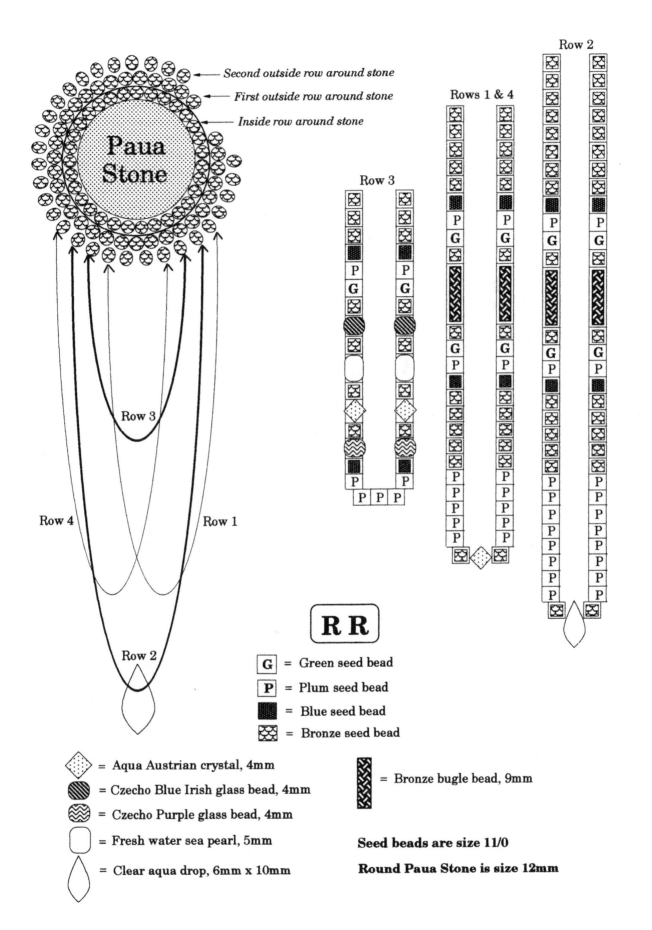

Second outside row around stone

First outside row around stone

Inside row around stone

Paua Stone

Row 3

Row 4

Row 1

Row 2

Rows 1 & 4

Row 2

R R

G	= Green seed bead
P	= Plum seed bead
■	= Blue seed bead
▦	= Bronze seed bead

◇ = Aqua Austrian crystal, 4mm

◉ = Czecho Blue Irish glass bead, 4mm

◉ = Czecho Purple glass bead, 4mm

◯ = Fresh water sea pearl, 5mm

◇ = Clear aqua drop, 6mm x 10mm

▦ = Bronze bugle bead, 9mm

Seed beads are size 11/0

Round Paua Stone is size 12mm

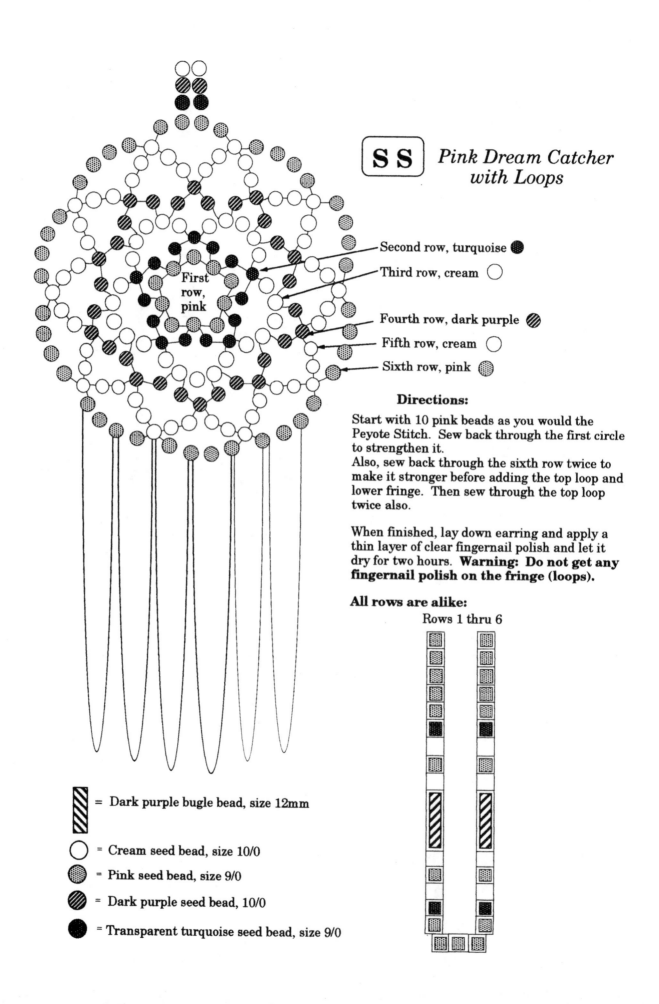

S S *Pink Dream Catcher with Loops*

Second row, turquoise ●

Third row, cream ○

Fourth row, dark purple ⬬

Fifth row, cream ○

Sixth row, pink ◉

First row, pink

Directions:

Start with 10 pink beads as you would the Peyote Stitch. Sew back through the first circle to strengthen it.

Also, sew back through the sixth row twice to make it stronger before adding the top loop and lower fringe. Then sew through the top loop twice also.

When finished, lay down earring and apply a thin layer of clear fingernail polish and let it dry for two hours. **Warning: Do not get any fingernail polish on the fringe (loops).**

All rows are alike:

Rows 1 thru 6

= Dark purple bugle bead, size 12mm

○ = Cream seed bead, size 10/0

◉ = Pink seed bead, size 9/0

⬬ = Dark purple seed bead, 10/0

● = Transparent turquoise seed bead, size 9/0

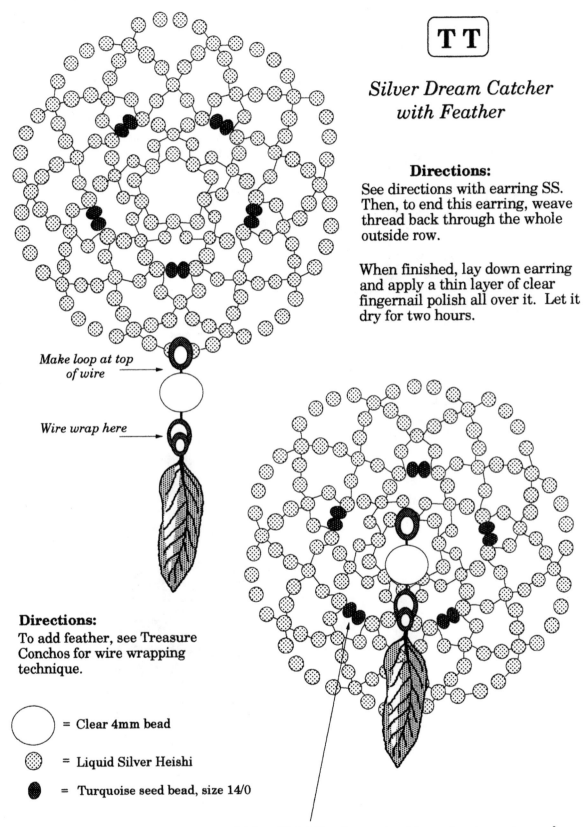

Silver Dream Catcher with Feather

Directions:
See directions with earring SS. Then, to end this earring, weave thread back through the whole outside row.

When finished, lay down earring and apply a thin layer of clear fingernail polish all over it. Let it dry for two hours.

Make loop at top of wire →

Wire wrap here →

Directions:
To add feather, see Treasure Conchos for wire wrapping technique.

◯ = Clear 4mm bead

⊙ = Liquid Silver Heishi

● = Turquoise seed bead, size 14/0

Important Note: If you plan to use Liquid Silver Heishi beads, you need to use two turquoise seed beads here to make the weave come out even. If you plan to use all glass seed beads, change this pattern from two turquoise seed beads to **one** in the third row.

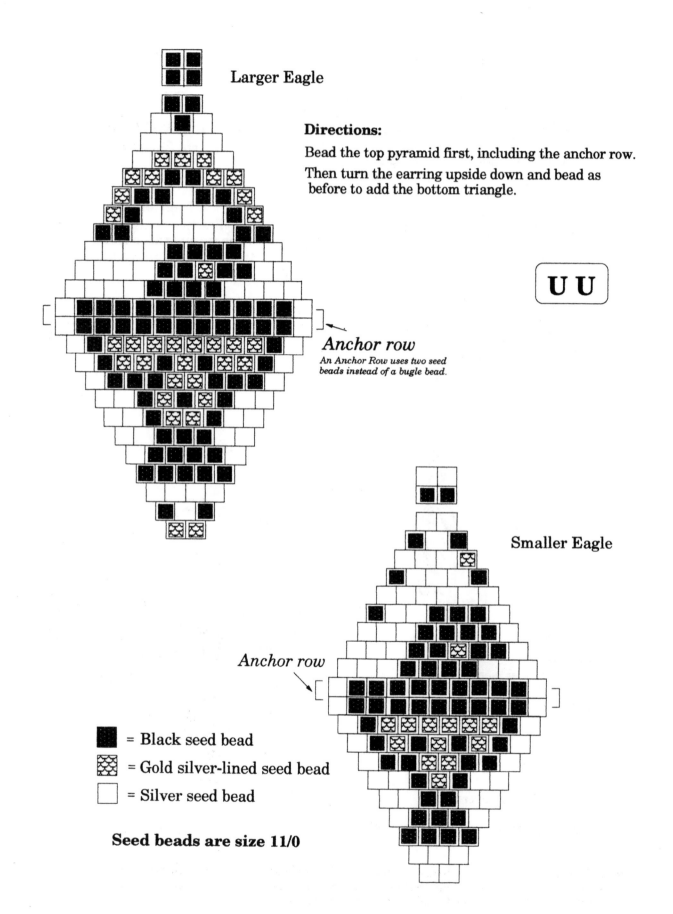

Larger Eagle

Directions:

Bead the top pyramid first, including the anchor row.

Then turn the earring upside down and bead as before to add the bottom triangle.

U U

Anchor row
An Anchor Row uses two seed beads instead of a bugle bead.

Smaller Eagle

Anchor row

■ = Black seed bead

▨ = Gold silver-lined seed bead

☐ = Silver seed bead

Seed beads are size 11/0

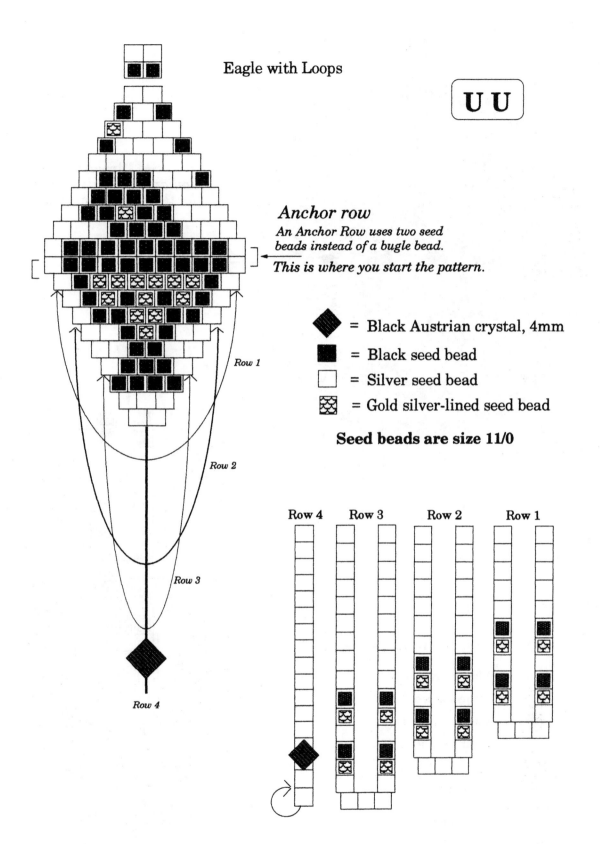

Eagle with Loops

U U

Anchor row
*An Anchor Row uses two seed
beads instead of a bugle bead.*

This is where you start the pattern.

◆ = Black Austrian crystal, 4mm

■ = Black seed bead

□ = Silver seed bead

▨ = Gold silver-lined seed bead

Seed beads are size 11/0

Row 1

Row 2

Row 3

Row 4

Row 4   Row 3   Row 2   Row 1

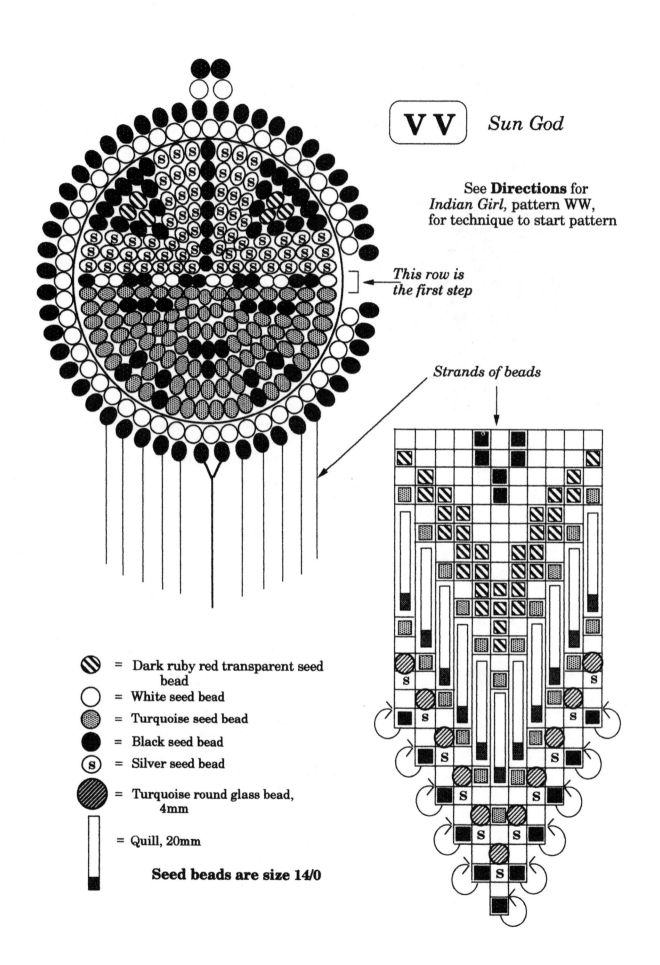

V V *Sun God*

See **Directions** for
Indian Girl, pattern WW,
for technique to start pattern

*This row is
the first step*

Strands of beads

⬤⃫ = Dark ruby red transparent seed
bead

◯ = White seed bead

◉ = Turquoise seed bead

● = Black seed bead

ⓢ = Silver seed bead

⬤⃫ = Turquoise round glass bead,
4mm

▯ = Quill, 20mm

Seed beads are size 14/0

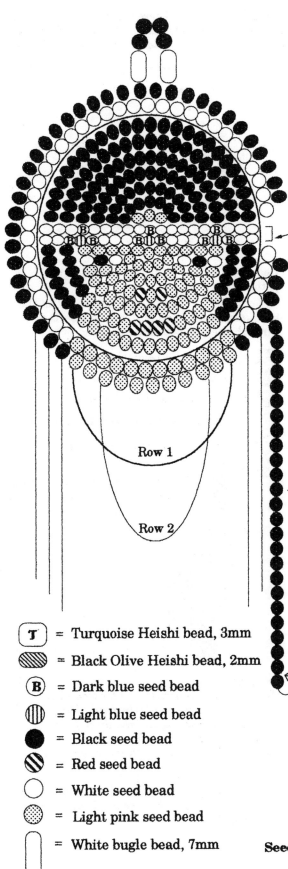

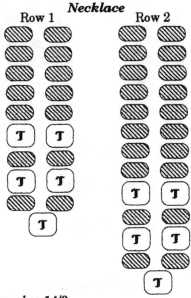

W W *Indian Girl*

*This row is
the first step*

Directions:

Draw a circle around a nickel first. Then draw a horizontal line straight across for the hat band (follow directions for pattern MM). Next make rows for black hair above the hat band. Then add the face.

Add outside trim and fringe.

Make the three rows of black seed beads the same length for the braids. Braid the rows and tie the strands together with thread.

Then make the necklace rows and drape the shorter strand in front of the longer one.

Row 1

Row 2

25 Black seed beads in each strand

Necklace
Row 1   Row 2

J = Turquoise Heishi bead, 3mm

= Black Olive Heishi bead, 2mm

B = Dark blue seed bead

= Light blue seed bead

= Black seed bead

= Red seed bead

= White seed bead

= Light pink seed bead

= White bugle bead, 7mm

Seed beads are size 14/0

XX | *End-of-Trail Disc with Loops*

NOTE: *Quiz for the day: Where is the Indian which is supposed to be on the mount below? Maybe he didn't like the horse or maybe the horse didn't like him--and bucked him off.*

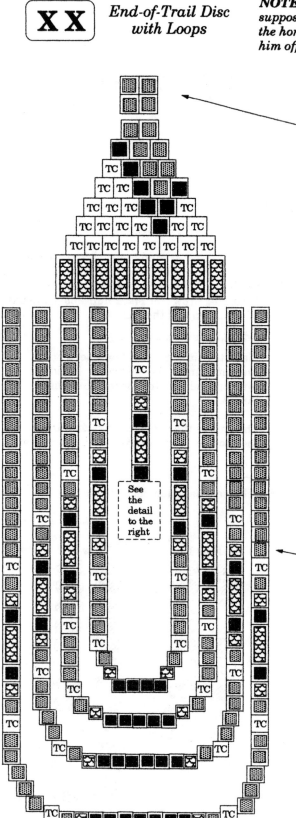

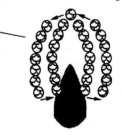

Decorated with a Peruvian hand-painted pottery disc

Glue post with flat pad with 330 epoxy on the back of the disc, then post can be inserted through the top loop of the earring.

⊠ = Bronze seed bead, size 14/0 or 11/0

■ = Black seed bead, size 14/0 or 11/0

▨ = Light blue seed bead, size 11/0

TC = Opaque Tera Cota seed bead, size 11/0

▨ = Bronze bugle bead, size 7mm

⬤ = Black drop, 6mm x 10mm, with vertical hole through top of drop

Detail for inside loop:

NOTE:

Refer to earring pattern BB for technique. Add seven bronze beads (instead of five as in BB) on each side of the drop, for a total of two rows on each side, as some drops will tend to tip with just one row of beads.

The reason for using more seed beads on each side of this drop is that the beads used here are smaller.

☐ = Green transparent seed bead

▨ = Bronze seed bead

▨ = Red Czecho faceted transparent glass bead, 5mm

ⓒ = Clear Czecho faceted transparent glass bead, 5mm

▨ = Green Czecho faceted transparent glass bead, 5mm

▨ = Bronze twisted bugle bead, 12mm

Seed beads are size 11/0

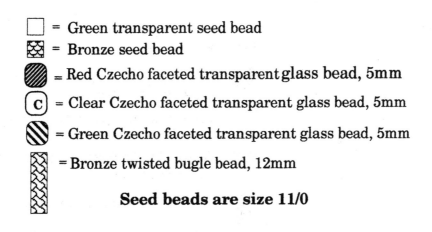

Austrian Crystal
Star, approximately
10mm in size

Use 330 epoxy glue to
afix star to a 3mm post.
Post should have small
cup shape to hold star.

Insert Star Post through
top loop. **Note:** Do not
glue Star Post to the top
loop.

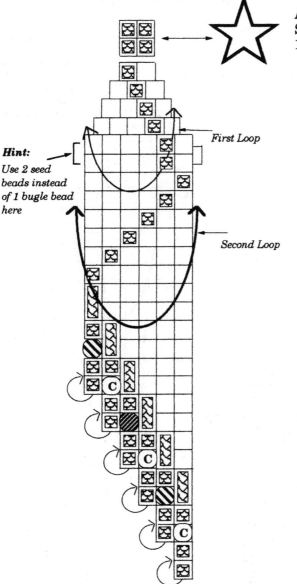

First Loop

Hint:

*Use 2 seed
beads instead
of 1 bugle bead
here*

Second Loop

First Loop　　*Second Loop*

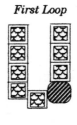　

ⓨⓨ

*Christmas Tree
with Loops &
Fringe*

Center Double Row

Third Loop

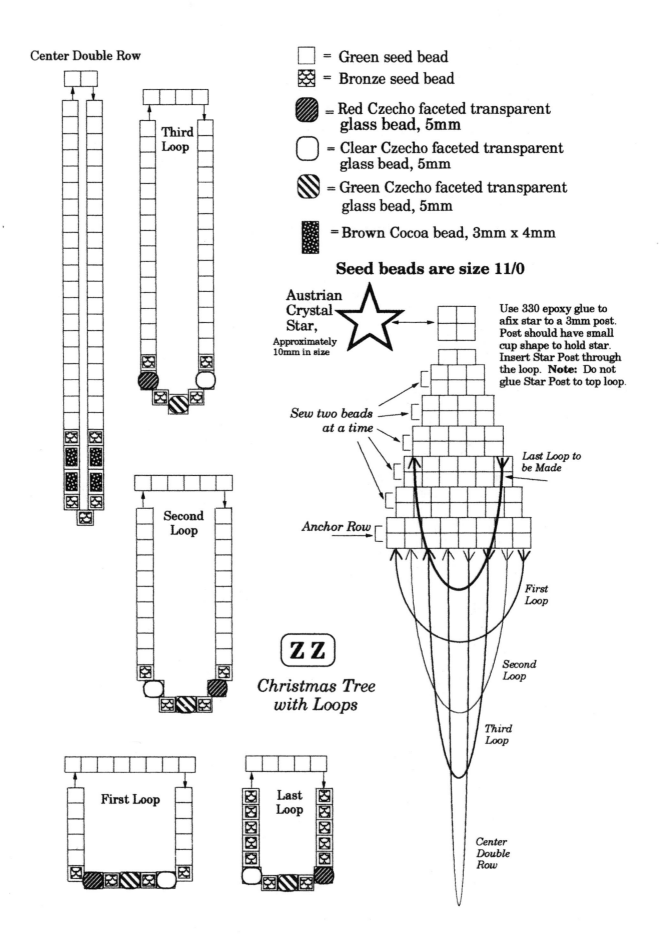

□ = Green seed bead

▦ = Bronze seed bead

◩ = Red Czecho faceted transparent glass bead, 5mm

○ = Clear Czecho faceted transparent glass bead, 5mm

◨ = Green Czecho faceted transparent glass bead, 5mm

▨ = Brown Cocoa bead, 3mm x 4mm

Seed beads are size 11/0

Austrian Crystal Star, *Approximately 10mm in size*

Use 330 epoxy glue to afix star to a 3mm post. Post should have small cup shape to hold star. Insert Star Post through the loop. **Note:** Do not glue Star Post to top loop.

Sew two beads at a time

Last Loop to be Made

Anchor Row

Second Loop

Z Z

Christmas Tree with Loops

First Loop

Second Loop

Third Loop

First Loop

Last Loop

Center Double Row

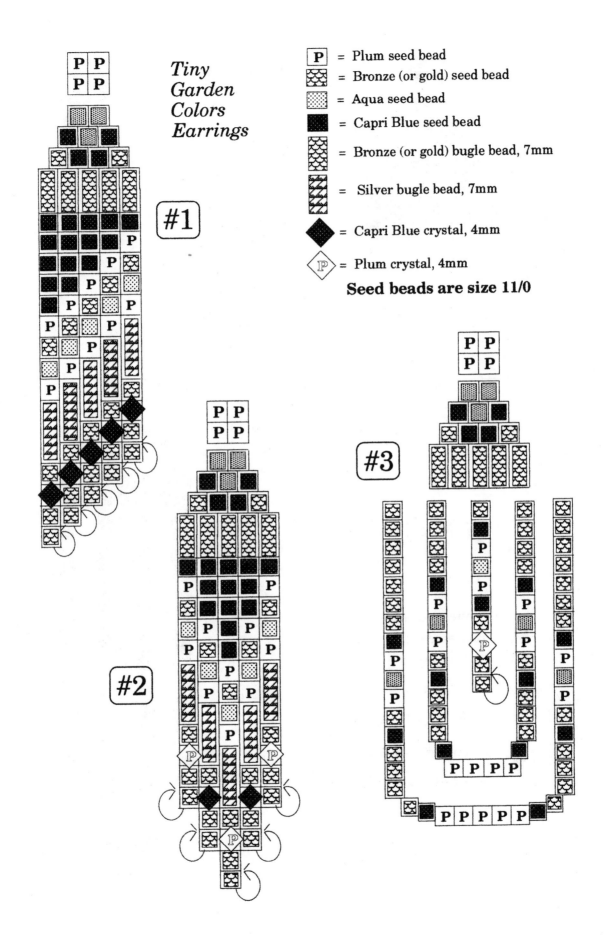

Tiny Garden Colors Earrings

#1

#2

#3

= Plum seed bead

= Bronze (or gold) seed bead

= Aqua seed bead

= Capri Blue seed bead

= Bronze (or gold) bugle bead, 7mm

= Silver bugle bead, 7mm

= Capri Blue crystal, 4mm

= Plum crystal, 4mm

Seed beads are size 11/0

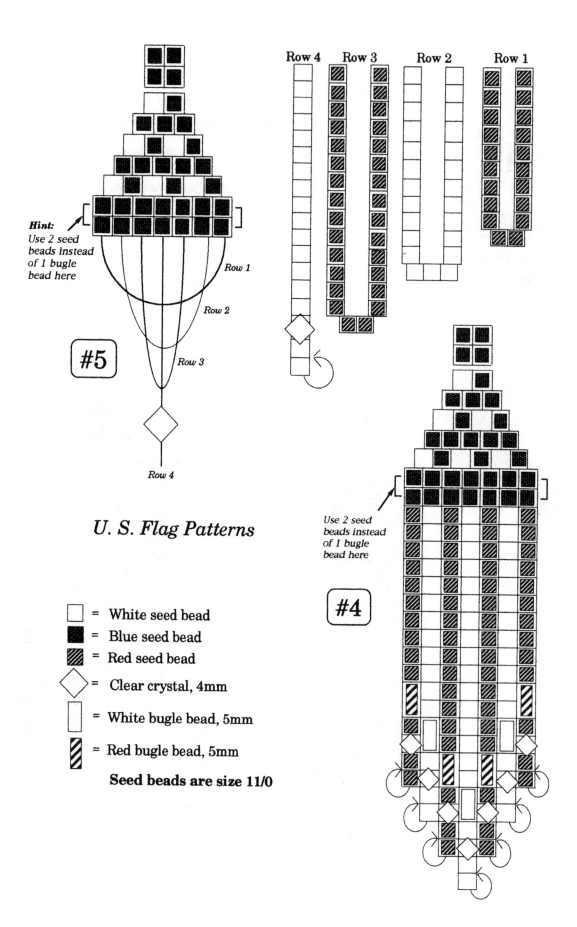

Hint:
Use 2 seed beads instead of 1 bugle bead here

Row 4   Row 3   Row 2   Row 1

Row 1

Row 2

#5

Row 3

Row 4

U. S. Flag Patterns

Use 2 seed beads instead of 1 bugle bead here

#4

□ = White seed bead

■ = Blue seed bead

▨ = Red seed bead

◇ = Clear crystal, 4mm

▯ = White bugle bead, 5mm

▨ = Red bugle bead, 5mm

Seed beads are size 11/0

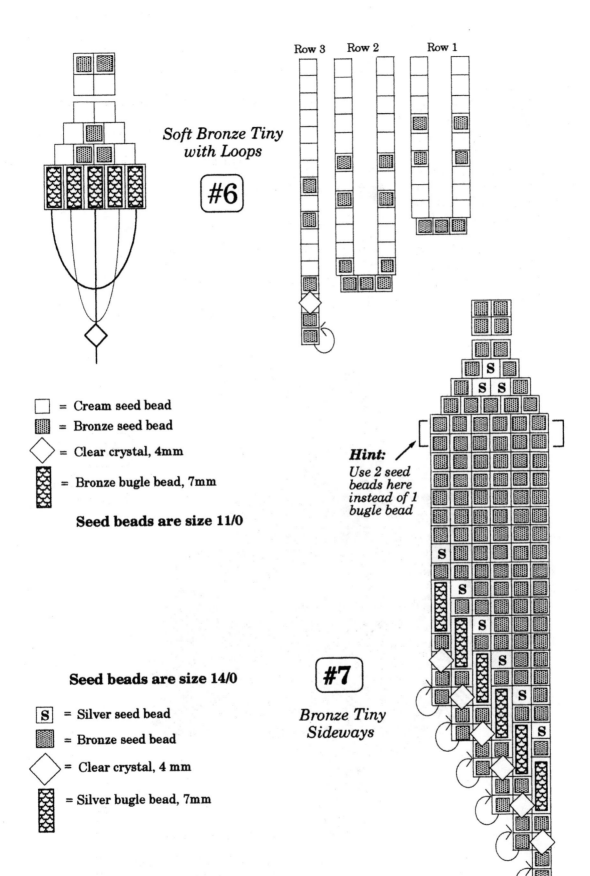

Soft Bronze Tiny
with Loops

#6

Row 3   Row 2   Row 1

= Cream seed bead

= Bronze seed bead

= Clear crystal, 4mm

= Bronze bugle bead, 7mm

Seed beads are size 11/0

Hint:

*Use 2 seed
beads here
instead of 1
bugle bead*

#7

*Bronze Tiny
Sideways*

Seed beads are size 14/0

S = Silver seed bead

= Bronze seed bead

= Clear crystal, 4 mm

= Silver bugle bead, 7mm

Directions:

Glue down the Star with 330 epoxy glue, then sew down the rest of the beads.

Start at the top with the Star and then work your way down, sewing on the center crystals first, then going around each of them with the seed beads. Note, this may not always result in the same count of seed beads.

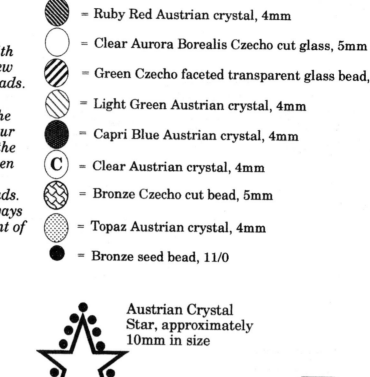

= Ruby Red Austrian crystal, 4mm

= Clear Aurora Borealis Czecho cut glass, 5mm

= Green Czecho faceted transparent glass bead, 5mm

= Light Green Austrian crystal, 4mm

= Capri Blue Austrian crystal, 4mm

C = Clear Austrian crystal, 4mm

= Bronze Czecho cut bead, 5mm

= Topaz Austrian crystal, 4mm

= Bronze seed bead, 11/0

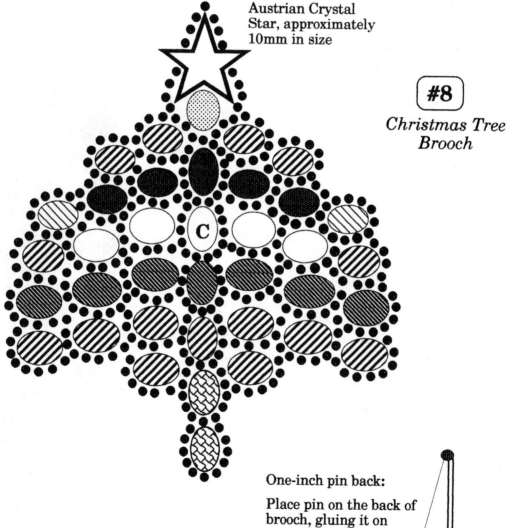

Austrian Crystal Star, approximately 10mm in size

#8

Christmas Tree Brooch

One-inch pin back:

Place pin on the back of brooch, gluing it on vertically.

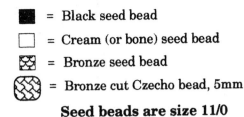

= Black seed bead

= Cream (or bone) seed bead

= Bronze seed bead

= Bronze cut Czecho bead, 5mm

Seed beads are size 11/0

The Gecko Indian Symbol means good luck and good health in life and for eternity

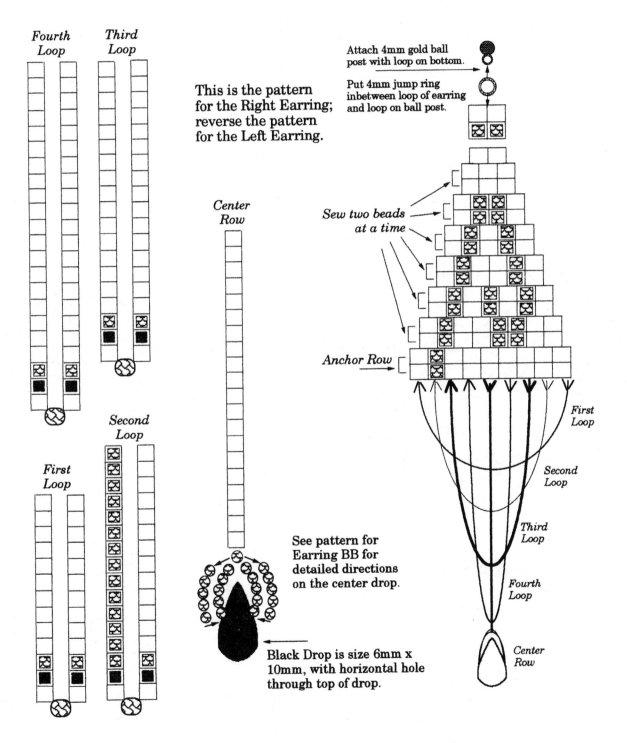

Fourth Loop

Third Loop

This is the pattern for the Right Earring; reverse the pattern for the Left Earring.

Center Row

Second Loop

First Loop

See pattern for Earring BB for detailed directions on the center drop.

Black Drop is size 6mm x 10mm, with horizontal hole through top of drop.

Attach 4mm gold ball post with loop on bottom.

Put 4mm jump ring inbetween loop of earring and loop on ball post.

Sew two beads at a time

Anchor Row

First Loop

Second Loop

Third Loop

Fourth Loop

Center Row

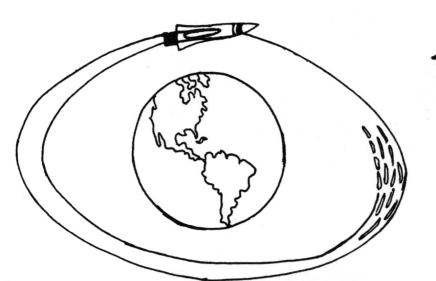